PRAISE FOR HENRY
AMERICA AT WAR

"This is the book Americans need to read now. No one is better than Henry Giroux at analyzing the truly dangerous threats to our society. He punctures our delusions and offers us a compelling and enlightened vision of a better way. *America at War with Itself* is the best book of the year."

—**Bob Herbert**, Distinguished Senior Fellow at Demos and former columnist for the *New York Times*

"In *America at War with Itself*, Henry Giroux again proves himself one of North America's most clear-sighted radical philosophers of education, culture and politics: radical because he discards the chaff of liberal critique and cuts to the root of the ills that are withering democracy. Giroux also connects the dots of reckless greed, corporate impunity, poverty, mass incarceration, racism and the co-opting of education to crush critical thinking and promote a culture that denigrates and even criminalizes civil society and the public good. His latest work is the antidote to an alarming tide of toxic authoritarianism that threatens to engulf America. The book could not be more timely."

—**Olivia Ward**, *Toronto Star*

"The current U.S. descent into authoritarianism did not just happen. As Henry Giroux brilliantly shows, it was the result of public pedagogical work in a number of institutions that were part of a long-standing assault on public goods, the social contract, and democracy itself. Giroux powerfully skewers oppressive forces with the hallmark clarity and rigor that has made him one of the most important cultural critics and public intellectuals in North America. His sharp insights provide readers with the intellectual tools to challenge the tangle of fundamentalisms that characterize the political system, economy, and culture in the current conjuncture. *America at War with Itself* makes the case for real ideological and structural change at a time when the need and stakes could not be greater. Everyone who cares about the survival and revival of democracy needs to read this book."

—**Kenneth Saltman**, author of
The Failure of Corporate School Reform

America at War with Itself

HENRY A. GIROUX

Foreword by Robin D. G. Kelley

Open Media Series | City Lights Books

Open Media Series Editor: Greg Ruggiero

Early versions of Chapter 6 and 8 appeared in
Social Identities and *Monthly Review*.

Library of Congress Cataloging-in-Publication Data

Names: Giroux, Henry A., author.
Title: America at war with itself / Henry A. Giroux ; foreword by Robin D.G. Kelley.
Description: San Francisco : City Lights Publishers, 2016. | Series: City lights open media
Identifiers: LCCN 2016020215 | ISBN 9780872867321 (paperback) | ISBN 9780872867338 (e-ISBN)
Subjects: LCSH: Toleration—United States. | Social control—United States. | Discrimination—United States. | Police brutality—United States. | Violence—United States. | BISAC: POLITICAL SCIENCE / Political Ideologies / Fascism & Totalitarianism. | POLITICAL SCIENCE / Political Freedom & Security / Terrorism. | POLITICAL SCIENCE / Political Ideologies / Democracy. | POLITICAL SCIENCE / Political Freedom & Security / General.
Classification: LCC HM1271 .G548 2016 | DDC 303.3/3—dc23
LC record available at https://lccn.loc.gov/2016020215

City Lights books are published at the City Lights Bookstore
261 Columbus Avenue, San Francisco, CA 94133
www.citylights.com

MIX
Paper from responsible sources
FSC® C011935

For Susan, Linda, and Dawn

"Memory is the enemy of totalitarianism"
—Albert Camus

CONTENTS

ACKNOWLEDGMENTS

Susan Searls Giroux has provided invaluable advice as I was thinking through various sections of this book. My administrative assistant, Maya Sabados, patiently read every page of this book and offered numerous insights and editorial suggestions. I want to thank Leila Gaind, my research assistant and student, for her initial edit of the manuscript. Colleagues are rare these days, but I do want to thank David Clark and Brad Evans for their reading of some of these chapters. Finally, I would like to thank Greg Ruggiero for accepting the manuscript and doing a terrific and meticulous job in editing the book. He has been invaluable to me as an editor and for the many conversations we have had about the book. He is a rarity among editors.

FOREWORD

WE HOLD THE FUTURE

"I love the poorly educated."
—Donald J. Trump

Once again, Henry A. Giroux slices through the thick fog of spectacle, mindless punditry, mountains of polling data, the smokescreen of corporate media—all the bullshit—and cuts to the point. These are indeed dark times, but they are dark not merely because we are living in an era of vast inequality, mass incarceration, and crass materialism, or that we face an increasingly precarious future. They are dark because most Americans are living under a cloak of ignorance, a cultivated and imposed state of civic illiteracy that has opened the gates for what Giroux correctly sees as an authoritarian turn in the United States. These are dark times because the very fate of democracy is at stake—a democracy fragile from its birth, always battered on the shoals of racism, patriarchy, and class rule. The rise of Donald J. Trump is a sign of the times.

Before you start nodding your head, Giroux does not argue that Trump is the cancer and his removal from the body politic is the answer. Trump is merely the symptom; he is the barometer of our current political, cultural, and social climate. He defies the analyses of the so-called liberal pundits who either sound the alarm, insisting that Trump is dangerous and needs to be stopped, or dismiss him as the latest clown in the two-ring circus we call American politics. What we are facing is not a crisis of Republican implosion or political deform; this is not your MSNBC smug defense of the Democratic Party's sanity in the face of Republican insanity. Giroux harbors no such illusions: "The spirit of authoritarianism cuts across both political parties." But as Giroux also notes, these same pundits sounding the alarm to "Stop Trump" do not insist that racism has to stop, foreign and domestic wars have to stop, the crimes of finance capital have to stop, policies that render most Americans—especially those of darker hue—precarious or disposable, have to stop.

Giroux is not interested in Trump the clown, Trump the narcissist, Trump the racist, or even Trump the con artist. Instead, he turns his critical sights on the society that produced and legitimized him. From his rabid and rapidly growing right-wing following to the channel surfers seeking a good chuckle to the liberal elite quick to dismiss The Donald with smug indifference, our country and its democracy is in steep decline. After all, this is the same society that holds 2.5 million in cages, most of whom are black and brown and poor; whose military budget is larger than that of China, Saudi Arabia, Russia, the U.K., India, and Japan combined; where the killing of unarmed Black people by police, security guards, or vigilantes has become almost a daily occurrence; where the toxic mix of privatization, free-market ideology, and a "punitive state" has turned our schools into high-stakes testing grounds and human warehouses in which the administration of discipline has shifted from teachers and principals to the criminal justice system; where the War on Drugs, with "zero tolerance" policing, turns some neighborhoods into open-air prisons, strips vulnerable residents of equal protection, habeas corpus, freedom of movement, even protection from torture; and where, in states such as Michigan, local governance has been replaced by so-called Emergency Financial Managers whose primary objective is to privatize public resources and basic needs (e.g., water). And the band plays on . . . or, as Giroux so aptly puts it, we move "from a culture of questioning to a culture of shouting."

America at War With Itself demolishes the pedestrian (and dangerous) argument that Trump appeals to legitimate working-class populism driven by class anger. The claim that Trump followers are simply working-class whites expressing class resentment ignores both the historical link between whiteness, citizenship, and humanity, and also the American dream of wealth accumulation built on private property. Trump's people are not Levelers! (Nor are they universally "working-class"—their annual median income clocks in at about $72,000.) They strongly believe in private property and the right to bear arms to protect that property. They don't just ignore Trump's wealth; they are enamored with it. They embrace the dream that if only America can be restored to its mythic greatness—which is to say, to return to its status as "a white MAN's country" (as if it is not now)—they, too, can become a Trump. But their racism, reinforced by civic illiteracy, has convinced them that it is the descendants of unfree labor or the colonized, or those who are currently unfree, who are blocking their ascent to the world of Trump and the billionare Koch brothers.

Giroux understands just how racist resentment feeds authoritarianism, and how this dialectic is nourished by reactionary pedagogies. While many of us are fully familiar with neoliberal policies that have redistributed wealth upward, ripped away any real safety net for the poor, and promoted capital flight, outsourcing, and free trade policies that destroy the environment and reduce much of the world's labor force to semi-slavery, we are less familiar with policies and practices that cultivate popular ignorance, that reduce the body politic to civic illiterates, and that privatize what ought to be an open and vibrant public sphere. With his inimitable insight, intellectual dexterity, and political acuity, Giroux exposes these policies and their consequences.

These are indeed dark times; the storm clouds of fascism linger overhead. But Giroux is the intellectual descendant of Antonio Gramsci, a visionary thinker who lived by his own dictum that revolutionaries should possess "pessimism of the intellect and optimism of the will." Whereas the forces of neoliberalism hypocritically scream, "Stop Trump," Giroux calls on us to wage "an anti-fascist struggle that is not simply about remaking economic structures, but also about refashioning identities, values, and social relations as part of a democratic project that reconfigures what it means to desire a better and more democratic future." He sees this future in the struggles against state-sanctioned racial violence, in the queer and transgender movement, in the immigrant rights movements, in the ongoing struggles against U.S. militarism, and in the pitched battles over the future of our schools. Critical pedagogy and insurrection go hand in hand. And in those hands, our hands, we hold the future.

—Robin D. G. Kelley
May 12, 2016

I.

Political Geographies of the New Authoritarianism

ONE

INTRODUCTION: THE SAND STORM

"And the shadow of fear again has darkly lengthened across the world."
—President Dwight David Eisenhower

In white America's collective psyche, and in its traditional narratives of historical memory, authoritarianism is always viewed as existing elsewhere. Seen as an alien and demagogic political system, it is primarily understood as a mode of governance associated with the dictatorships in Latin America in the 1970s and, of course, in its most vile extremes, with Adolf Hitler's Nazi Germany and Benito Mussolini's fascist Italy in the 1930s and 1940s. Both societies glorified war, soldiers, nationalism, militarism, fallen warriors, racial cleansing, and a dogmatic allegiance to the homeland.[1] These were states in which society became armed, security became the *raison d'être* of both the citizen and state, and fear became a pretext for giving up one's liberty. Education and the media were the indoctrination tools of authoritarianism, merging fascist and religious symbols with the language of God, family, and country. These cultural systems were used as weapons to achieve servility and conformity among the populace, something many are seeing re-emerge in our current political moment.[2]

In its earlier forms, the language of authoritarianism relied upon the discourse of command and courted mass hysteria, one that produced totalizing world views, punished dissent, disseminated hate-filled propaganda steeped in the vocabulary of ultra-nationalism and racial purity, and emptied language of any substance, reducing it to a ritualized performance.[3] This script is well known to the American public; it has been fully commercialized and marketed in the form of countless products: from films, television series, video games, and works of fiction, to museums and other cultural apparatuses. As a result, the public has been conditioned to perceive totalitarian modes of governance as dead relics from a bygone era rather than as part of a historical narrative with living legacies at play in the present.

Hannah Arendt and Sheldon Wolin, the great theorists of totalitarianism, believed that the fluctuating elements of fascism are still with us and that they would crystalize in different forms.[4] Far from being a thing of the past, they both believed, totalitarianism "heralds . . . a possible model for the future."[5] Wolin, in particular, was keenly aware that the corporatization of the state and civil society, the destruction of public goods and commons, the commercial control of the media, and the rise of an economic survival-of-the-fittest ethos posed a serious threat to American democracy. According to Arendt, the culture of traditionalism, the dismantling of civil and political rights, the ongoing militarization of society, the "religionization of politics,"[6] the attack on labor, the obsession with national security, the perpetration of human rights abuses, the emergence of a police state, entrenched racism, and the attempts by demagogues to undermine education as a foundation for producing critical citizenry were all at work in American society. For Arendt, these anti-democratic elements in U.S. society constituted what she called the "sand storm"—a metaphor for totalitarianism.[7]

Historical conjunctures produce different forms of authoritarianism, though they all share an intolerance for democracy, dissent, diversity, and human rights.[8] It is too easy to believe in a simplistic binary logic that strictly categorizes a country as either authoritarian *or* democratic and leaves no room for entertaining the possibility of a competing mixture of both forces. American politics today suggests different forms of authoritarianism. The possibility of white America becoming a fascist nation has a long legacy in American fiction that includes Sinclair Lewis's *It Can't Happen Here* and Philip Roth's *The Plot Against America*. For Native Americans who were exterminated, descendants of Africans who were dehumanized, trafficked, and enslaved by whites, Japanese Americans subjected to concentration camps, and people of color who have been degraded by violence, coercion, and various forms of apartheid for generations, questions of freedom and fascism are quite different from those historically faced by whites, who never feared racist cops, lynch mobs, or burning crosses.

Nevertheless, following World War II, the shadow of fascism was never far from U.S. shores. It is worth remembering Huey Long's response to the question of whether America could ever become fascist: "Yes, but we will call it anti-fascist."[9] Long's reply indicates that fascism is not an ideological apparatus frozen in a particular historical period, but, as Arendt and Wolin have suggested, a complex and often shifting theoretical and political register for understanding how democracy can be subverted, if not destroyed, from within.

The notion of soft fascism was articulated in 1985 in Bertram Gross's book *Friendly Fascism*, in which he argued that if fascism came to the United States it would not embody the same characteristics associated with fascist forms of the past. There would be no Nuremberg rallies, overt doctrines of racial superiority, government-sanctioned book burnings, death camps, genocidal purges, or abrogation of the U.S. Constitution. In short, fascism would not resemble the way it has been packaged, marketed, and sold to us as commercial entertainment, nor would it take the form of a previous ideological grid simply downloaded into our political moment. Gross believed that fascism was an ongoing danger and had the ability to become relevant under new conditions, taking on familiar forms of thought that resonate with nativist traditions, experiences, and political relations. Similarly, in his *Anatomy of Fascism*, Robert O. Paxton argued that the texture of North American fascism would not mimic traditional European forms but would be rooted in the language, symbols, and culture of everyday life in America. According to Paxton:

> No swastikas in an American fascism, but Stars and Stripes (or Stars and Bars) and Christian crosses. No fascist salute, but mass recitations of the Pledge of Allegiance. These symbols contain no whiff of fascism in themselves, of course, but an American fascism would transform them into obligatory litmus tests for detecting the internal enemy.[10]

It is worth noting that Umberto Eco's discussion of "eternal fascism" also argues that any updated version of fascism would not openly assume the mantle of historical fascism; rather, new forms of authoritarianism would appropriate some of its elements, making it virtually unrecognizable from preceding forms.[11] Eco contended that fascism will, if it manifests in America, have a different guise, although it will be no less destructive to democracy. Instead of an all-powerful supreme leader, the government is now controlled by the anonymous and largely remote hands of corporate power and finance capital. More recently, in the face of what Paxton has called an "alarming willingness" on the part of some Republican Party candidates to "use fascist themes and styles," he has updated his own view of fascism as "a mass nationalist movement intended to restore a country that's been damaged or is in decline, by expansion, by violent attacks on enemies, internal as well as external enemies, and measures of authority, the replacement of democracy by an authoritarian dictatorship."[12] Rather than cancel each other out, all of these theorists offer up elements that bear traces of old and new forms of authoritarianism. However, the 2016 candidacy of Donald Trump—embraced by white supremacist groups as their "Glorious Leader"—illustrates how the two forms of authoritarianism may now be advanced in one political package.[13]

Until now, the trend has been toward economic sovereignty replacing civic sovereignty as corporate power buys access to elections, governance, law enforcement, national budget, and foreign policy. The more money influences politics, the more corrupt the political culture becomes. Under these circumstances, holding office is largely dependent on having adequate corporate patronage, while laws and policies at all levels of government are mostly fashioned by lobbyists representing big business corporations and financial institutions. As Ralph Nader says, we have entered an era of a plutocracy of maximums for the wealthy few, a democracy of minimums for everyone else.

Moreover, as the politics of Obama's healthcare reform indicate—a gift to the health insurance giants—such lobbying, as corrupt and unethical as it may be, is now carried out in the open and displayed by insurance and drug companies as a badge of honor—a kind of open testimonial to their disrespect for democratic governance and a celebration of their power.

But markets are not the only major institution under the new authoritarianism. As David Theo Goldberg has argued, the military has also assumed a central role in shaping all aspects of society.[14] Militarization is about more than the use of repressive power; whether it be through the use of the police or the armed forces, it also represents a powerful social logic that is constitutive of values, modes of rationality, and ways of thinking. According to Goldberg:

> The military . . . has assumed such a central role in modern society's sense of itself, to its sense of and insistence on its own sovereignty and security, that it not only eats up the resources and revenue commandeered by the state; it likewise determines their more general social use and set of meanings. . . . [T]he military is not just a fighting machine. It is both constitutive and instrument of social power and culture. It serves and socializes. It hands down to the society, as big brother might, its more or less perfected goods, from gunpowder to guns, computing to information management, the internet and global positioning systems (GPS), vehicles to video games and gaming platforms, fashion wear to some of the very language of critical analysis itself. In short, while militarily produced instruments might be retooled to other, broader social purposes, the military shapes pretty much the entire range of social production from commodities to culture, social goods to social theory.[15]

The commercialization and militarization of the social sphere permeates American society. Rather than forcing the country to adhere to an explicit state ideology, the general public in the United States is largely depoliticized through the influence of corporations over media, entertainment, schools, higher education, and other institutions and spaces. This is what the late Herbert Schiller called "Culture, Inc." The deadening of public values and civic consciousness is also the result of the work of self-serving financial interests, right-wing ideologues, conservative think tanks, powerful commercial media, and a market-driven public pedagogy that acts relentlessly to replace the open power of citizenship with a closed set of pre-defined consumer choices: Coke or Pepsi, Burger King or McDonalds, Republican or Democrat. This neoliberal-driven culture of consumption, commerce, financialization, and self-interest also functions to depoliticize people by encouraging market-driven ideals of unrestrained individualism and self-reliance. Under these conditions, politics becomes inner-directed, lost in a language of therapy, self-help, and self-transformation that has exploded in American culture. Thus, the self becomes cut off from any sense of common purpose and solidarity.

Military glorification pervades popular culture, entertainment, policy, and social relations. For example, the blockbuster success of the *Star Wars* films, a commercial idealization of war in space, targets the youngest and most impressionable minds. In addition, a pedagogy of historical, social, and racial amnesia is constructed and circulated through a highly popular celebrity culture, all-encompassing consumer culture, and an ongoing display of violence, all of which are reinforced through a regime of neoliberal cultural apparatuses to be found in corporate-driven news, television, radio, and mass entertainment to produce a culture of stupidity, censorship, and diversionary spectacles.

Fight culture now shapes every facet of society, as warlike values, hyper-masculinity, and an aggressive militarism seep into most major institutions in the United States, including schools, the media, and local police forces.[16] The criminal justice system has become the default institution for dealing with all social problems except those caused by Wall Street, the crimes of which are managed without arrests, trials, or prison time.[17] At the same time, low-income communities—particularly communities of color—are considered ignorable or disposable, as in Flint, Michigan, where the local white political establishment stood by while Black neighborhoods were pumped filthy water poisoned with lead.

What is clear is that it is impossible to understand the rise of authoritarianism without thinking about the consolidation of the military-surveillance state at every level. Since the end of the Cold War the United States has built "the most expensive and lethal military force in the world." The defense budget for 2015 totaled $598.5 billion and accounted for 54 percent of all federal discretionary spending. The U.S. defense budget is "larger than the combined military spending of China, Russia, the United Kingdom, Japan, France, Saudi Arabia, India, Germany, Italy and Brazil."[18] Since 2001, the United States has both intensified the range of its military power abroad and increased the ongoing militarization of American society.[19] The United States circles the globe with around 800 military bases, producing a massive worldwide landscape of military force, at an "annual cost of 156 billion."[20] Moreover, "there are U.S. troops or other military personnel in about 160 foreign countries and territories, including small numbers of Marines guarding embassies and larger deployments of 'trainers' and 'advisors' like the roughly 3,500 now working with the Iraqi army."[21]

Not only is the Pentagon in an unprecedented position of power, it thrives on a morally bankrupt vision of domestic and foreign policy steeped in a war mentality and the constant evocation of well-armed enemies, looming attacks, and perpetual fear. Military-grade weaponry and armament are now donated or sold to local police departments and are used to intimidate free speech activity protected by the First Amendment, as was seen when police snipers were deployed during street protests in Ferguson, Missouri. Around the world, the U.S. disperses its machineries of war and violence through the use of drones, secret bases that support special ops, and the increasing use of Navy Seals, CIA personnel, Army Rangers, and other clandestine operational forces in multiple countries.[22] Under such circumstances, it is not surprising, as Andrew Bacevich points out, that "war has become a normal condition [and the] use of violence has become the preferred 'instrument of statecraft.'"[23]

Adding to the scope and power of militarization, Tom Engelhardt points to a number of additional registers of the growing authoritarianism in the United States, which can be found in the mobilization of the military-industrial complex in the service of privatization, and the increasing privatization and "militarization" of the military. He writes:

> In the post-9/11 era, the military-industrial complex has been thoroughly mobilized under the ru-

> bric of "privatization" and now goes to war with the Pentagon. With its $80 billion–plus budget, the intelligence bureaucracy has simply exploded. There are so many competing agencies and outfits, surrounded by a universe of private intelligence contractors, all enswathed in a penumbra of secrecy, and they have grown so large, mainly under the Pentagon's aegis, that you could say intelligence is now a ruling way of life in Washington—and it, too, is being thoroughly militarized. Even the once-civilian CIA has undergone a process of para-militarization and now runs its own "covert" drone wars in Pakistan and elsewhere. . . . In a sense, even the military has been "militarized." In these last years, a secret army of special operations forces, 60,000 or more strong and still expanding, has grown like an incubus inside the regular armed forces. As the CIA's drones have become the president's private air force, so the special ops troops are his private army, and are now given free rein to go about the business of war in their own cocoon of secrecy in areas far removed from what are normally considered America's war zones.[24]

Militarization also feeds authoritarianism at the level of ideology. As Michael Schwalbe makes clear, militarism needs to produce willing subjects, modes of identification, and desires that support war-like values and policies. This often happens at the level of what he calls micro-militarism, in which "pro-military practices" are squeezed into small cultural spaces such as gas station receipts that include the imperative to "support the troops," as well as in sports events and on national nightly news programs such as ABC, NBC, and CBS which endlessly run segments about returning war heroes, not the body bags.[25] Sporting events are now infused with the spirit of militarism, as can be seen in fighter jets flying over football games, NASCAR races, and the Superbowl. In Boston's Fenway Park, the game begins with a giant American flag descending over the Green Monster, the huge wall that cover left field.[26] Sarah Lazare writes that the military has been paying NFL football teams to celebrate and promote the merging of patriotism, sport, and military values. She writes: "That, apparently, is what Department of Defense officials thought when they shelled out at least $5.4 million of U.S. taxpayers' money to 14 NFL teams between 2011 and 2014—to pay them to promote the military on and off the field."[27]

In order to understand how a new kind of militarism is deepening and expanding the landscapes of authoritarianism in the United States, it is crucial to understand militarism in its totality as ideology, market-driven system, politics, policy, and mode of governmentality. Norman Pollack captures these interrelated elements of militarism in the following commentary, which is worth quoting at length:

> The Cold War never ended, not even, for that matter, gone underground; rather, its permanence was set in stone through systemic pressures toward market expansion, ideological exceptionalism, and

> the militarization of advanced capitalism—a triad of American national-structural characteristics the US was loath to give up or even modify (assuming either was possible and still be—to use Obama's phrase, for other purposes—who we are). Penetration, ideology, militarism, all, when tightly integrated, bespeak strength interlaced, however, with fear—else why the constant emphasis on force, the muscularity of response (overkill), being ever vigilant? To the systemic/structural characteristics, then, must be added the psychological composite of ethnocentrism and xenophobia, in which fear of the stranger, the Other, the Enemy at the Gates (inherited from falling-domino theory) falls naturally into place with the erection of defensive walls to reinforce the all-important dichotomy of We and They in international politics (and its domestic counterpart, an ingrained permanent McCarthyism, most recently found in the campaign of mass surveillance).[28]

What is so striking about the legacy of totalitarianism is that it creates a formative culture—landscapes of disimagination machines—in which commercialized emotion replaces independent reason, excitement is associated with killing, ideology is fashioned in a discourse of certainty, and terror and fear are deliberately infused into everyday life. All the while this authoritarian formative culture works endlessly to eliminate the distinction between civilians and combatants, just as it aggressively arms, militarizes, and commercializes public spaces. Given these circumstances, the glorification of killing infuses entertainment spheres extending from Hollywood movies and video games to the militarization of professional sporting events. As Carl Boggs and Tom Pollard have pointed out, earlier films such as *Top Gun* and *United 93* are examples of the public pedagogy that underlies the commercial culture of death, militarism, hyper-masculinity, and the war-like values produced by Hollywood.[29] At the same time, while films such as Kathryn Bigelow's *Zero Dark Thirty* and Clint Eastwood's *American Sniper* glorify war and militarism, in recent years there has been the development of a working relationship between Hollywood and the Pentagon in which film directors seeking the Pentagon's approval and cooperation for filming military scenes end up participating in a Faustian bargain. As David Sirota remarks, "Getting co-operation," means being willing to make seemingly apolitical entertainment products into highly ideological vehicles for pro-war, pro-militarist propaganda."[30] It gets worse.

The spirit of militarism and the spectacle of violence not only permeate the wider culture, they also dominate domestic and foreign policy. As Robert Koehler comments, "America is armed and dangerous—and always at war, both collectively and individually."[31] The outcome of this unfolding nightmare is not only political and economic instability but the disappearance of public institutions that serve public needs, if not democratic politics itself. At the same time, the destruction of a public culture that practices and defends democratic values is intensified. Surely all this points to what

Hannah Arendt believed was the harbinger of totalitarianism—the disappearance of those independent-thinking and -speaking citizens who make democracy-centered national life, education, social spaces, politics, and nonviolent resistance possible.

Particularly troublesome are the manifestations of totalitarianism in the agenda of the political extremists who now captivate the voting base of the Republican Party, and how this projects back to the nation through corporate media. One finds in the rhetoric of Donald Trump, Ted Cruz, and their Republican associates expressions of racism, disdain for women's rights, unabashed support for the financial elite, Christian fundamentalism, a glorification of war, a nod to white supremacy, a deep-seated hostility for all things public, and a "bomb them until the sand glows" eagerness that comes across like bloodlust. Chris Christie marketed himself as a bully and believes that threatening violence is a crucial element of presidential power. This was on full display when he stated that teachers' unions "are the single most destructive force in public education in America [and deserve] a punch in the face."[32]

An intimidating violence appears to be a powerful ideological register shared by many of the Republican Party's most popular leaders. Donald Trump comes close to supporting a form of racial cleansing by threatening to expel 11 million undocumented Latin American immigrants all the while demonizing them as rapists and criminals. A similar script was played out in Germany in the 1930s and 1940s. Marco Rubio wanted to abolish women's rights over their own bodies, and went so far as to argue that he would not permit women to get an abortion even if their lives depended on it. Mike Huckabee takes this threat even further. When *Rolling Stone*'s Matt Taibbi asked Huckabee if he would send "the FBI or the National Guard to close abortion clinics," he answered: "We'll see when I'm president."[33] At one point Huckabee stated that he would deny an abortion to a 10-year-old rape victim.[34] This domination of women and the need to control and domesticate them to the crudest forms of male hegemony and control is central to all fascist regimes.

Most Republicans who get media attention, including most Americans who cast ballots for Republicans, want to send U.S. soldiers abroad to combat Islamic entities such as ISIS and Al Qaeda. Trump openly claims that he not only wants to prevent ISIS from tapping regional oil, he plans to seize the oil wells in Syria in order to appropriate their wealth. Trump's disregard for international law and human rights goes even further when he states that as a Rambo president he would go so far as "to kill the family members of ISIS terrorists," because family members "know what is going on with their relatives."[35]

Few commentators with college-level education fail to miss the authoritarianism embedded in Trump's rhetoric and policy recommendations. To make such critiques acceptable in the press, the preferred vocabulary is "demagoguery." John Dean argues that Donald Trump—and this applies to most of the Republican Party leadership—has four clear traits that distinguish him and the others as authoritarian:

"They are dominating; they oppose equality; they desire personal power; and they are amoral."[36] This echoes Theodor Adorno's classic work on the authoritarian personality.

Similarly, most mainstream media profit handsomely from the spectacle of electoral controversy and political theater. The 2016 presidential contest increasingly resembled commercial reality TV shows such as *American Idol*, where the superficial trumps substance and the audience appears to communicate with the spectacle by voting. All the while, the media often refuse to acknowledge that the potential consequences of the extremism on display reveal a dark and more threatening side of politics and the impact it will have on free and open society. Totalitarianism is a complex system that is deeply woven into American ideology, governance, law enforcement, and policy. It is present in the attack on the welfare state, the downsizing of civil liberties, the indiscriminate killing of civilians during military operations, the violation of national sovereignty of other nations, the legitimation of torture, the impunity with which financial crime is perpetrated by the wealthy, and the tolerance for lethal neglect and violence against low-income people and communities of color, from Flint to Ferguson.

An increasing number of journalists have raised the specter of totalitarianism, but they largely confine the charge to the bellicose Donald Trump. For instance, Connor Lynch points to Trump's authoritarian discourse, which he insists is "full of race baiting, xenophobia and belligerent nationalism."[37] Jeffrey Tucker goes further, arguing that Trump's popularity not only draws support from "the darkest elements of American life" but also mimics a form of neoliberalism in which economics is affirmed as a way of governing all social life.[38] For Tucker, Trump is representative of a mode of totalitarianism that "seeks total control of society and economy and demands no limits on state power."[39] Those who sound the alarm, like Norman Solomon, are too often ignored. After all, isn't Donald Trump the one who speaks what's really on his mind, the one who is not afraid to be politically incorrect in order to protect the Homeland?

What is useful about these critiques is that they acknowledge, however indirectly, that democracy is irretrievably broken, if not dead, in the United States and that forces of tyranny and authoritarianism offer no apologies for their contempt for environmental sustainability, democracy, and/or the problem of mass impoverishment, as they publicly promise to serve their corporate donors and produce less regulations and taxes for the rich. What they fail to acknowledge is that the anti-democratic forces at work in the United States are not limited to the discourse of the far right. Totalitarianism cannot survive without mass support, and it is not limited to Republicans. These systemic forces have been building for quite some time in the United States and have been recognized by our most astute writers, such as Noam Chomsky, Robin D. G. Kelley, Stanley Aronowitz, Chris Hedges, and many others. What is new is the scale at which sectors of the American population act against their own class interests and enthusiastically embrace politicians who promise to address the discontent of a segment of working-class voters who have lost jobs, suffered from falling wages, lost homes and marriages, all the while supporting right-wing extremists who have no interest in dismantling an authoritarian system benefiting a financial and corporate elite that oppresses most of its followers. Of course, the spirit of authoritarianism cuts across both political parties.

Take, for instance, the comments on CNN by the alleged liberal Wesley Clark, a former four-star general and one-time Democratic presidential candidate. Clark called for World War II–style internment camps to be revived for "disloyal Americans." He unapologetically argued for people who are most likely to embrace a radical ideology to be identified, stating that, "If these people are radicalized and they don't support the United States and they are disloyal to the United States as a matter of principle, fine. It is their right and it's our right and obligation to segregate them from the normal community for the duration of the conflict."[40] Calling for domestic internment camps for radicals is more than chilling and suggests the degree to which a poisonous nationalism mimics the legacy of the fascism that plagued Europe in the 1930s and 1940s.

As Bill Dixon has pointed out, the conditions that give rise to totalitarianism are still with us, only in different forms.[41] What is equally true is that there is nothing inevitable about the new forms of neglect, violence, and intolerance now taking hold in American society. The protean forces for creating an authoritarian state are in full play in the United States and extend far beyond the shadow of a debased and corrupt politics. A set of complex forces is insidiously eroding the very foundations of a civic and democratic culture. Some of the most glaring issues are the impunity of corporate crime; massive unemployment; a rotting infrastructure; the defunding of vital public services; the dismantling of the social safety net; expanding levels of impoverishment, especially for children; and a law enforcement system largely focused on criminalizing communities of color. At the same time, a reign of impunity is overtaking the United States as police violence claims an increasing number of Black men, women, and young people. But such a list barely scratches the surface. Institutions that were once designed to benefit the public good now wage an assault against all things that serve the common good. For instance, we have witnessed in the last forty years the restructuring of public education as either a source of profit for corporations or an updated version of control modeled after prison culture, coupled with an increasing culture of lying, cruelty, and corruption. We have also witnessed the rise of private prisons, and the rise of private security forces through which justice at home and war abroad further fall under the influence of business.

Civic literacy in the United States is also in decline, and has become the object of scorn and derision. Corporate media have abandoned even the pretense of holding power accountable and now primarily serve as second-rate entertainment venues spouting the virtues of consumerism, greed, and U.S. exceptionalism. The signs of extremism are everywhere. Instead of being educated, schoolchildren are handcuffed and punished for trivial infractions, or are simply taught how to take tests and give up on any vestige of critical thinking. Celebrity culture now works in tandem with neoliberal values to represent extreme forms of solipsism and a cultivated ignorance. Such ignorance is widespread on American television and also in the bestselling books designated by the *New York Times*. According to the *Times*, for the week of October 25, 2015, the bestselling non-fiction books included works by TV Fox News host Bill O'Reilly and the truly ignorant Republican Ben Carson. Serious non-fiction books dealing with issues outside of corporate, liberal, and conservative discourse are increasingly banished to that irrelevant outpost, the public library. A form of manufactured ignorance now constitutes the modus operandi of a society that privatizes and kills the imagination by poisoning it with falsehoods, consumer fantasies, data loops, and the need for instant gratification. This is a mode of manufactured ignorance and education that has no language for relating the self to public life, social responsibility, or the demands of citizenship.

The rise of dystopian politics and cultural mystification must be exposed and challenged on the local, national, and global planes. What is crucial is that the mechanisms, discourses, policies, and ideologies that inform authoritarianism must become part of any analysis that is willing to challenge the anti-democratic forces metastasizing within the United States today. This means, in part, focusing on the ongoing repressive systems that have been developing in American society for the last forty years. It also means drawing connections between historical forms of racial, ethnic, and economic violence that have been waged against indigenous communities, people of color, and the economically disadvantaged since the days George and Martha Washington enslaved hundreds of people while flying flags of freedom. It means finding a common ground on which various elements of an ethical society can be mobilized under the banner of multicultural democracy in order to challenge the interconnected forms of oppression, incarceration, mass violence, exploitation, and exclusion that now define the militant self-interest of corporatized American politics. It means taking seriously the educational nature of politics and recognizing that public spheres must be advanced in order to educate citizens who are informed, socially responsible, and willing to fight collectively for a future in which democracy is sustainable at all levels. This suggests an anti-fascist struggle that is not simply about remaking economic structures but also about refashioning identities, values, and social relations as part of a democratic project that reconfigures what it means to desire a better and more democratic future—a struggle we can see manifesting in the Black Lives Matter movement, the Fast Food Workers campaign, strikes called by the Chicago Teachers Union, Walmart workers, and other spontaneous responses to the impunity with which the financial and corporate elite abuse workers and reproduce oppressive practices.

Hannah Arendt was right in stating that "the aim of totalitarian education has never been to instill convictions but to destroy the capacity to form any," suggesting that totalitarianism was as much about the production of thoughtlessness as it was about the imposition of brute force, gaping inequality, corporatism, and the spectacle of violence.[42] Totalitarianism destroys everything that democracy makes possible, and in doing so thrives by stoking mass insecurity, fear, and rage, all of which are marshalled to demonize the Other—the Immigrant, the Black, the Muslim, the Intellectual, the Youth in Revolt. Yet power, however tyrannical, is never without resistance. The dark clouds of authoritarianism are not ahead, they are upon us, but that does not mean that they are here to stay. *America at War with Itself* is designed to see through the sand storm that authoritarianism is unleashing, and to point toward alternative pathways offered by critical pedagogy, insurrectional democracy, and international solidarity.

TWO

DONALD TRUMP'S AMERICA

Commercial media lit up like Vegas the day Donald Trump announced his presidential candidacy and said the following: "When Mexico sends its people, they're not sending their best. They're bringing drugs. They're bringing crime, they're rapists. And some, I assume, are good people."[1] Trump's hate-mongering was perfect fodder for driving up TV ratings. Rather than presenting Trump's comments in the context of America's long legacy of racism and state violence, the mainstream media uncritically broadcast his remarks initially as those of a fearless billionaire who has achieved such supreme success that he speaks his mind without concern for consequences. Such a process, shorn of context and historical understanding of white hegemony, highlights not only commercial media's flight from responsibility, but how corporate power itself, combined with the Terror Wars, have weakened the American population's capacity to protect democracy, civil liberties, and multicultural society from the allure of fascistic forms of power.

Not only have mainstream media replayed Trump's most outrageous statements over and over again without any serious criticism, they also fill the 24/7 news cycle with endless interviews in which Trump has defended and embellished his intolerance of immigrants, Muslims, and protestors. Treated more as an indication of Trump's no-holds-barred personality than something more problematic, Trump's remarks have been viewed by many as honest, brave, and off-the-cuff rather than symptomatic of the bigotry and bias smoldering beneath the surface of high-end presidential politics. Such commentary collapses into the realm of the personal because by privatizing racism, it ignores the history of violence, exclusion, and coercion that has plagued the land since the first white people sailed to shore.

During the 2015–2016 presidential contest, Trump pushed the political envelope further and further toward intolerance and an American-style form of proto-fascism. The media got red meat, Trump's ratings soared, and his Republican rivals struggled to keep up. Senator Ted Cruz argued that he liked Donald Trump and was glad he was bringing attention to the illegal immigration issue.[2] Rick Santorum joined Cruz in praising Trump for focusing on illegal immigration, without any serious criticism of his racist remarks.[3] Other right-wing politicians such as Lindsay Graham and Rick Perry condemned Trump's remarks, but nothing was said in the press about how they had played a key role in supporting legislation that was both vicious and racist.[4]

Liberals have denounced Trump but have said woefully little about the history of how both major parties have supported unjustified military invasions, racialized tough-on-crime campaigns, and a mass-incarceration state that has decimated communities of color nationwide. For instance, Jonathan Chait seems less concerned about a Republican Party that has promoted numerous racist policies, such as trying to disable the Voting Rights Act of 1965 and militarizing the U.S.-Mexico border zone, than he is about "conservative thought leaders [who] feel compelled to defend Trump's nativist ramblings."[5] Chait's confusion is evident in the title of his article, "Why are Conservatives Defending Donald Trump?" which should read "Should We Be Surprised that Conservatives Are Defending Donald Trump?"

The mainstream media, conservatives, and a number of liberal commentators seem to have allowed Trump's brand of racial politics to cloud their understanding of recent history. After all, it was only a few decades ago that Kirk Fordice, a right-wing Republican, ended his victorious campaign for governor—orchestrated largely as an attack on crime and welfare cheaters—with a still photograph of a Black woman and her baby.[6] Of course, this was just a few years after George W. Bush ran his notorious Willie Horton ad and a year before Dan Quayle, in the 1992 presidential campaign, used the racially coded category of welfare to attack a sitcom character, Murphy Brown. And the *Washington Post* has reported that in the early years of his political career, Rick Perry hosted "fellow lawmakers, friends and supporters at his family's secluded West Texas hunting camp, a place known by the name painted in block letters across a large, flat rock standing upright at its gated entrance. . . . 'Niggerhead.'"[7]

And, of course, the racist invectives aimed at President

Obama by a number of Republicans are legion.[8] When a gorilla escaped from a zoo in Columbia, S.C., a longtime Republican activist, Rusty DePass, described it on his Facebook page as one of Michelle Obama's ancestors. Among the signs at a gathering of conservative protesters in Washington was one that said, "The zoo has an African lion and the White House has a lyin' African."[9] These are bits and pieces from what has been an increasingly unrestrained torrent of racism that is fueled by hate-mongers on talk radio and is widely tolerated, if not abetted, by Republican Party leaders. It's disgusting, and it's dangerous. But it's the same old filthy racism that has been there all along and that has been exploited by the Republican Party since the 1960s. A figure no less than conservative Robert Kagan claims that one register of the racism that has defined the Republican Party is evident in the party's unadulterated hatred of President Obama, which he calls "a racially tinged derangement syndrome that made any charge plausible and any opposition justified."[10]

Liberal commentators such as Eugene Robinson have called Trump a "farce to be reckoned with," while Juan Cole argued that Trump failed to use more discreet racial codes because "billionaires and fabulously wealthy people in general are surrounded by yes-men."[11] While Robinson and Cole may be right, their commentary appears to miss the mark. Adding to the chorus of liberal denunciations were the public announcements by a number of corporations that they were cutting their business ties with Trump because of the offensive nature of his remarks. Commentators praised such corporations for taking the high moral ground but most conveniently forgot that these were the same corporations battling unions, polluting the environment, underpaying their workers, and exercising an economic chokehold over the commanding institutions of American life.

As Trump's campaign gained support and his commentaries became more vulgar, it became clear that he would win the Republican nomination. Commentators such as Roger Cohen, Andrew Bacevich, Mike Lofgren, and Juan Cole became increasingly alarmed over Trump's endorsement of torture, his taste for bullying protesters, and his unwillingness to denounce support from David Duke, the former Grand Wizard of the Ku Klux Klan, making it clear that he was "a magnet for authoritarian desires"[12] and could pave the way for what Mike Lofgren termed "a fascist political system."[13] Many liberals have sensed something deeply disturbing about Trump's politics but initially refused to describe it in terms of fascism or authoritarianism. *New York Times* op-ed columnist Timothy Egan argued that the media were complicit in Trump's popularity and opened a space for the racist fringe to come to the surface by supporting a celebrated candidate who reflected their views.[14] For Egan, the beast resides in the deep-seated racism of a sizable swath of the American populace, but what the beast represents in political terms he refused to name. Paul Krugman went so far as to claim that as bad as Trump was, he was a better candidate than either Cruz or Rubio, who were not just con artists but dangerous. In a shocking admission of political failure and moral irresponsibility, Krugman wrote: "As I see it, then, we should actually welcome Mr. Trump's ascent. Yes, he's a con man, but he is also effectively acting as a whistle-blower on other people's cons. That is, believe it or not, a step forward in these weird, troubled times."[15]

In response to all of this fanfare over Trump's remarks, I argue that the widespread focus given to his displays of racism, narcissism, and arrogance misses the point. The real issue that needs to be examined is what kind of society produces a Donald Trump. Why have Americans flocked to his rallies and roared in support for his bigoted epithets and militant intolerance? Given how the legacies of white colonialism, enslavement, and Jim Crow politics have influenced the nation for generations—influences that scholars like Angela Davis, Michelle Alexander, and Mumia Abu-Jamal relentlessly critique—Trump is just the latest manifestation of a social order that has always been dominated by whites and that has always been deeply racist. Trump exemplifies a no-holds-barred form of intolerance that shares the ideology of hate espoused by armed vigilante groups that bomb Planned Parenthood offices, ambush immigrants on the border, and burn mosques. How else to explain that extremists such as Christian nationalists, the Ku Klux Klan, and white militia groups are flocking to support Trump? The national approval ratings that soar following Donald Trump's most outrageous statements offer clear testimony to the degree to which forces of intolerance are seething just beneath the glittering corporate surface of a democracy in deep decline. In addition, Trump provides a more direct and arrogant frontman for a society operating increasingly as a plutocracy—a society that glorifies money, excess, and celebrity, and that denigrates kindness, community, justice, and equality.

Trump is the symbol of a new authoritarianism, which is to say, the sign of a democracy unable to protect and sustain itself. Trump represents corporate domination set free, a political and economic engine that both fuels and feeds on fear and intolerance. He is also the endpoint of a long-standing political system that is "part bread-and-circuses spectacle, part celebrity obsession, and part media money machine."[16] Trump is the symbol of a frightened society that is increasingly seduced to choose the swagger of a vigilante strongman over the processes of collective sovereignty, the gun over diplomacy, and the wall instead of the bridge. Trump's public rants and humiliating snipes make for great TV, and are, as Frank Rich once argued, "another symptom of a political virus that can't be quarantined and whose cure is as yet unknown."[17] What the American public needs is an ongoing analysis of Trump's messaging in the context of the historical legacies of white bigotry and intolerance, and an analysis of how right-wing politics have tapped such bigotry to further the self-serving interests of a small economic elite. Such an analysis would situate Trump in the context of the historical racism that has smoldered as a form low-intensity warfare in the United States since its inception, and that has arguably worsened for communities of color since the rise of neo-conservativism in the 1980s. Trump has simply discarded the euphemisms and deploys the ruse of national security to take bigotry, sexism, xenophobia, and political bullying to more aggressive levels.

Trump's rise indicates the increasing confluence of religious fundamentalists and economic extremists who insist that social, racial, economic, and environmental justice are wrong, lead to big government, and are malignant to the nation. Chris Hedges captures the authoritarian and militaristic nature of the Christian right:

> The cult of masculinity, as in all fascist movements, pervades the ideology of the Christian right. The movement uses religion to sanctify military and heroic "virtues," glorify blind obedience and order over reason and conscience, and pander to the euphoria of collective emotions. Feminism and homosexuality, believers are told, have rendered the American male physically and spiritually impotent. Jesus, for the Christian right, is a man of action, casting out demons, battling the Antichrist, attacking hypocrites and ultimately slaying nonbelievers. This cult of masculinity, with its glorification of violence, is appealing to the powerless. It stokes the anger of many Americans, mostly white and economically disadvantaged, and encourages them to lash back at those who, they are told, seek to destroy them. The paranoia about the outside world is fostered by bizarre conspiracy theories, many of which are prominent in the rhetoric of those leading the government shutdown. Believers, especially now, are called to a perpetual state of war with the "secular humanist" state. The

> march, they believe, is irreversible. Global war, even nuclear war, is the joyful harbinger of the Second Coming. And leading the avenging armies is an angry, violent Messiah who dooms billions of apostates to death.[18]

Trump is just one boisterous voice speaking for a sector of white America that feels threatened by people of color, Muslims, immigrants, and people of conscience who form communities of solidarity and resistance.[19] The end-time religious wars that many in the Republican Party embrace are not much different than those professed by ISIS and other fanatics. It is also the party of political fundamentalists who hate democracy, attack women's rights, destroy or underfund healthcare programs that benefit the poor, turn back hard-won voting rights, and believe governance is a tool of the financial elite.

Trump is simply the most visible and vocal member of a fractured party made up of frightened Americans, religious fundamentalists, and self-serving economic extremists who believe that the market should arbitrate and dominate all aspects of government and society. Trump represents a new form of social disorder—intolerant, authoritarian, and violent—that sees preventable inequality as part of the natural order of things. Guns, walls, laws, surveillance, prisons, media, and wars are there to serve the interest of the wealthy winners, and to keep the rest of the population in check. Bankers who commit theft, fraud, and acts of economic mass destruction never feel the cold steel of handcuffs tighten on their wrists. Corporate suspects never get shot down accidently in the streets, as do unarmed Blacks, by white cops who feel threatened by skin color. Trump's rise reinforces these injustices and gives anxious whites a boastful businessman and TV celebrity to rule as their strongman.

More than any other recent politician, Trump speaks to the existential fears and anger of many Americans who have every right to be distressed over their lives and their futures. These are people who live on the edge of financial ruin, people who have few resources for retirement, who are either unemployed or work in dead-end jobs. Not all in Trump's base are racist. Many of them are fed up and angry over establishment political parties whose allegiance is to the rich, not to them, and it shows in the increasing anxiety and despair of middle-aged white Americans who are dying early,[20] and who "are committing suicide with guns, drugs and alcohol at shocking levels."[21] Trump has tapped into this anger by exposing the class-specific fault lines that dominate the Republican Party while directing it into a discourse of hate, fear-mongering, xenophobia, racism, and violence. Trump has proven to be a formidable foe in revealing the elitist pretentions and class boundaries of the ruling-class wing of the Republican Party, and his appeal may rest less on ideology than on his struggle to wrest power from the GOP establishment. Frank Rich is worth repeating at length on this issue. He writes:

> What GOP elites can't escape is the sinking feeling that a majority of Republican voters are look-

> ing for a president who will repudiate them and, implicitly, their class. Trump refuses to kowtow to the Establishment—and it is precisely that defiance, as articulated in his ridicule of Romney and Jeb Bush and Megyn Kelly and Little Marco, that endears him to Republican voters and some Democrats as well. The so-called battle for the "soul" of the Republican Party is a battle over power, not ideology. Trump has convinced millions of Americans that he will take away the power from the pinheads on high and return it to people below who feel (not wrongly) that they've gotten a raw deal. It's the classic populist pitch, and it will not end well for those who invest their faith in Trump. He cares about no one but himself and would reward his own class with extravagant tax cuts like any Republican president. But the elites, who represent the problem, have lost any standing that might allow them to pretend to be part of the solution.[22]

As the language of community and the public spheres collapse, people are increasingly atomized and isolated, and believe that they have little control over their lives. Republicans have taken this sense of anger and helplessness and have used it for the last thirty years to tell their supporters that they should be angry about Blacks, immigrants, big government, Muslims, terrorists, and a host of other issues that have nothing to do with the problems they face daily. As Robert Kagan points out, "it has been Trump's good fortune to be the guy to sweep them up and become their standard-bearer. He is the Napoleon who has harvested the fruit of the revolution. [Trump is] the party's creation, its Frankenstein's monster, brought to life by the party, fed by the party and now made strong enough to destroy its maker."[23]

Trump now personifies a party that makes intolerance a priority while viewing evidence-based arguments with open disdain. This is the party that censors textbooks, imposes mindless pedagogies of memorization and test-taking on students (along with the Democratic Party), denies climate change has anything to do with human activity, supports creationism, and floods the mainstream media with a never-ending stream of civic illiteracy. Jeb Bush, considered a moderate politician, while serving as Governor of Florida, signed a bill that declared, "American history shall be viewed as factual, not as constructed. That factual history, the law states, shall be viewed as knowable, teachable, and testable."[24] For all intents and purposes, this bill did more than undermine any form of teaching that recognized history is subject to interpretation; it imposed a suffocating ideology on teachers and students by declaring that matters of debate and interpretation undermine the very process of teaching and learning. This is more than conceptual ignorance; it is an attack on reason itself, one that provides security for the apostles of state power who, as Noam Chomsky has argued, are intent on dismantling dissent in order to "protect themselves from the scrutiny of their own populations."[25]

Richard Hofstadter once warned that anti-intellectualism was a strong undercurrent of American life. Not only was he right, but he would be shocked to discover that today anti-intellectualism has gone mainstream and has been not only normalized but validated by right-wing extremists governing the Republican Party, which Trump willingly embraces. Trump's comment: "I love the poorly educated" is not a gaffe but an honest recognition of the degree to which successful political campaigns are now dependent on an uninformed public. For Trump, bullying replaces any viable notion of dialogue, and emotion vanquishes reason, understanding, and thoughtfulness. Of course, Trump's embrace of ignorance and his willingness to make stupidity a trademark of his identity points to a number of forces in American life. As Susan Jacoby has argued, these would include:

> fundamentalist forms of religion in current America . . . the abysmal level of public education . . . the widespread inability to distinguish between science and pseudoscience . . . the dumbing-down of the media and politics [and] the consequences of a culture of serious reading being replaced by a rapid-fire, short-attention-span-provoking, overstimulating, largely visual, information-spewing environment.[26]

Trump is representative of a publicity-branding machine that funds and promotes conservative institutes that produce anti-public intellectuals whose role is to snarl at the victims of social injustice, to disdain public institutions in the service of the public good, and to do everything possible to promote a culture marked by a depoliticizing moral and political vacancy. Trump is simply the manifestation of a new type of authoritarianism, one that revels in thoughtlessness and the survival-of-the-fittest ethic marketed in his former TV game show, *The Apprentice*.

Corporate media love Donald Trump. He is the perfect embodiment of the spectacle that drives up their ratings. That Trump is a white nationalist, a racist, and a spewer of hate against Muslims, Mexicans, and the Pope all adds to the shock that feeds the spectacle. Karl Grossman argues that the media is intimidated by Trump.[27] He misses the point. In the age of celebrity culture, the media love Trump and he loves them. They chase audiences and he delivers them. Trump is not a media clown, he is an expert at getting the media to promote and fund his self-marketing strategy.[28] His campaign is unique in that it is modeled after the commercial superficiality of game-show TV. Sean Illing is right in stating:

> Trump's a TV man; he understands the landscape. He knows interesting is preferable to informed or reasonable or lucid. Which is why he eschews talking points or scripts and instead riffs on stage like a stand-up. Trump's free-wheeling approach means he could say literally anything at any moment, and that's the kind of thing people want to watch.[29]

Neal Gabler goes further and argues that not only did the Republican Party with their "hate-spewing, poor-bashing, government-stopping and corporation-loving for decades" pave the way for Trump, it produced him, because it created what Gabler calls the first "pseudo-campaign."[30] A pseudo-campaign is one that supports theatrics and personalities over substance. This is a campaign model that imitates movies and embraces images rather than issues. The novelty here is that Trump was not treated as a political candidate by the media. On the contrary, he was treated almost like Paris Hilton or Kim Kardashian, a celebrity for whom it was not necessary to interrogate history, policies, and statements, except to stir the kinds of controversies that make for good TV. Gabler brings the point home by citing CBS head Les Moonves, who reveals the true motives behind CBS's coverage of the Trump-dominated campaign. He writes:

> CBS head Les Moonves gave away the game earlier this week when he admitted, "It may not be good for America . . . but it is damn good for CBS," meaning the ratings. And then he kept doubling down: "The money's rolling in and this is fun." "I've never seen anything like this, and this is going to be a very good year for us. Sorry. It's a terrible thing to say. But, bring it on, Donald. Keep going. Donald's place in this election is a good thing"—presumably for CBS stockholders. To which I can only say that the networks were granted licenses to the public airwaves, our airwaves, by promising to provide a public service. Moonves just blew that pretense all to hell.[31]

Both Illing and Gabler are only partly right. Celebrity culture confers power, but at the same time it empties politics of any viable substance.

Trump is certainly aware of the power of celebrity culture and boasted that he knew how to "work the media" to a group of Republicans who asked him in 2013 to run for Governor of New York. As Illing notes:

> To their surprise, he declined but added that they would be useful when he ran for president. "I'm going to walk away with it and win outright," Trump told the group, "I'm going to get in and all the polls are going to go crazy. I'm going to suck all the oxygen out of the room. I know how to work the media in a way that they will never take the lights off of me." Trump knew all along that his celebrity and media savvy were sufficient to support his campaign. Although they didn't believe him, Trump told the Republicans in that room in 2013 that he would dominate the race without spending much on paid advertising.[32]

Celebrity culture points to a powerful fusion of power, culture, and politics, but the ideological form it takes and the politics it now serves have to be named, however difficult the task. Trump is the logical result of decades of assaults on democracy by both the Republican and Democratic Parties, which have been skewed by the enormous economic influence of financial and corporate elites. Trump's popularity in the political arena is about more than the power of politics as entertainment or his ability to direct the narrative; it is also "the distilled essence of a much larger disturbing reality," the rise of authoritarianism in the United States and the death of democracy.[33] Trump may know how to manipulate the media, but the interests that benefit from the commercial media are the product of the darker elements of elitism, racism, bigotry, demagoguery, and authoritarianism that the Republican Party helped to create. The current crisis is not simply about the power of the corporate-entertainment complex, it is about a divide between those who believe in democracy as a protected home for diversity, equality, and social justice, and those who don't.

Donald Trump's growing embodiment of the fascistic and hateful came into sharper relief when he began making statements calling for "a total and complete shutdown of Muslims entering the United States" and began speaking about "killing Islamic terrorists with bullets dipped in the blood of pigs."[34] Trump said that such a ban is necessary "until our country's representatives can figure out what is going on." When the great businessman proposed the ban at a rally at the USS *Yorktown* in South Carolina, his plan drew loud cheers from the crowd. Many critics have responded by making clear that Trump's attempts to place a religious test on immigration and travel are unconstitutional. Others have expressed shock in the face of a proposal that violates the democratic ideals expressed in America's founding documents. Fellow Republican Jeb Bush called Trump "unhinged." While the Republican Party leadership was quick to condemn Trump's poisonous remarks about banning Muslims from entering the United States, most conceded that if he won the nomination they would support him. Put another way, they would endorse Trump even though they are ashamed of him. Chris Christie opportunistically cut to the front of that line first. What almost none of the presidential candidates or mainstream political pundits have admitted, however, is not only that Trump's comments form a discourse of hate, bigotry, and exclusion, but also that such expressions of authoritarian intolerance resonate deeply in a landscape of American culture and politics crafted by forty regressive years of conservative influence on U.S. society. One of the few politicians to respond initially to Trump's incendiary comments was former Maryland Governor Martin O'Malley (D) who stated rightly that Donald Trump is a "fascist demagogue."[35] To NBC's credit, Tom Brokaw did a segment on the nightly news contextualizing Trump's call to ban Muslims within the history of demagoguery both in the United States and in fascist Germany.[36]

Surprisingly, former Ohio Governor John Kasich released an online ad suggesting that Trump's rhetoric correlated closely with that of Nazi Germany. Kasich brought the point home with an ad that featured Tom Moe, a retired Air Force colonel. In the ad, Moe uses a famous anti-Nazi quote from Protestant pastor Martin Niemöller in one of his lectures just after World War II. Moe paraphrases the quote to criticize Trump's hateful rhetoric and its dangerous implications.

Says Moe, to an ominous sound track:

> You might not care if Donald Trump says Muslims should register with their government, because you're not one. And you might not care if Donald Trump says he's going to round up all the Hispanic immigrants, because you're not one. And you might not care if Donald Trump says it's okay to rough up black protesters, because you're not one. And you might not care if Donald Trump wants to suppress journalists, because you're not one. But think about this: If he keeps going, and he actually becomes president, he might just get around to you. And you better hope there's someone left to help you.[37]

There are few politicians willing to admit that there is a long history of Islamophobia in the Republican Party. This is evident in the glut of anti-Muslim rhetoric that characterized the Republicans' 2015–2016 presidential campaign in general. Before calling for a ban of Muslims entering the United States, Trump called for the creation of a database on Muslims—echoing a dangerous parallel when Jews in Nazi Germany were forced to wear a yellow patch in the shape of the Star of David. Ben Carson later announced that a Muslim should not be allowed to assume the office of President.[38] Jeb Bush refined this religious litmus test by insisting that only Christians and orphans fleeing from ISIS should be admitted to the United States from war-torn Syria.[39] Marco Rubio stated that he would consider not only shutting down mosques, as Trump says, but also shutting down "any place where radicals are being inspired."[40] Before he dropped out of the presidential race, Scott Walker stated that only a handful of Muslims are moderates.[41] The prominent Republican congressman Steve King echoed the deeply bigoted sentiments of many of his fellow party members by stating that the only Muslims he would allow into the United States are those "most likely to be able to contribute to our society and our economy and assimilate into the American civilization." He then proffered a demonstrable lie by concluding that "Muslims do not do that in significant numbers."[42]

In November 2015 Trump's intolerance took aim at Serge Kovaleski, a *New York Times* investigative reporter with a disability, whom Trump mocked at a rally in South Carolina. The contemptuous reference to Kovaleski's physical disability was morally odious and painful to observe, but not in the least surprising: Trump's hate-mongering clearly keeps him in the limelight, and he seems to relish engaging in it in almost every public encounter. In this loathsome instance, Trump simply expanded his invective in a new direction.

Trump's mockery of Kovaleski and his blatantly discriminatory policies against Muslims are of a piece with his portrayal of Mexican immigrants as violent rapists and drug dealers, and with his calls for the U.S. to put Syrian refugees in detention centers and create a database to better monitor and control them. These comments sound eerily close to Heinrich Himmler's call for camps to hold detainees under orders of what the Nazis euphemistically called "protective custody." To quote the *Holocaust Encyclopedia*:

> In the earliest years of the Third Reich, various central, regional, and local authorities in Germany established concentration camps to detain political opponents of the regime, including German Communists, Socialists, trade unionists, and others from left and liberal political circles. In the spring of 1933, the SS established Dachau concentration camp, which came to serve as a model for an expanding and centralized concentration camp system under SS management.

Moreover, Trump's demeaning attitude toward people with disabilities points to an earlier element of Hitler's program of genocide in which people with physical and mental disabilities were viewed as disposable because they allegedly undermined the Nazi notion of the "master race." The demonization, objectification, and pathologizing of people with disabilities was the first step in developing the Nazis' "euthanasia" program aimed at those declared unworthy of life. This lesson seems to be lost on the mainstream media, which largely viewed Trump's intolerance and aggression as simply a bit over the top, as when the presidential candidate publicly said he wanted to punch a person in the face for protesting at one of his campaign stops.[43] Trump and those who benefit from his politics of intolerance are the brownshirts of our time; their cruelty, insults, and threats unburden the public of the necessity for debating complex issues. Against the backdrop of militant confrontations, and the celebration of a market in which hyper-competitiveness becomes the rule, Trump endlessly employs the rhetoric of casino capitalism, arguing that a capitalist business model is the obvious solution to every problem faced by the United States both domestically and abroad.

What is truly alarming is how corporate media benefit from Trump's raucous excess and seem to encourage him to run his campaign like *The Jerry Springer Show*. As a candidate for President of the United States, Trump represents more than the anti-democratic practices and social intolerance of Joe McCarthy;[44] he illustrates how totalitarianism can take different forms in specific historical moments. Rather than dismissing him as "careless and undisciplined," or not a true member of the Republican Party, as Ross Douthat has written in the *New York Times*,[45] it is crucial to recognize that Trump's popularity represents what Victor Wallis has described as a dangerous "political space . . . in both the wider culture and in recent history."[46] This is evident not only in his fear-mongering and race baiting, his degrading comments about women, or his call to round up and deport 11 million immigrants, but also in the mob mentality that is produced at his rallies.[47] Trump's racism is rooted in the authoritarian effort to curate spaces designed to keep out all those who do not reflect and reinforce his image of power. As the playwright John Steppling sees it, such efforts serve as filtering devices for the ruling class.

The force with which Donald Trump flaunts his intolerance through sexism, racism, and gestures of violence is unprecedented in recent national political races. "We're going to have to do things that we never did before," promises

Trump, "and some people are going to be upset about it, but I think that now everybody is feeling that security is going to rule. . . . And so we're going to have to do certain things that were frankly unthinkable a year ago."[48] What might Trump have in mind here? What might we expect from this man if he somehow manages to assume the full suite of power at his disposal as commander-in-chief of the world's most destructive nuclear arsenal? Trump's anticipation of doing "the unthinkable" is a fundamental principle of any notion of totalitarianism, and openly prepares the U.S. population for the possibility that he will not just attack his enemies, but hunt them and destroy them with bullets that he has dipped in filth.

While Trump's demagoguery represents something new in American politics, his discourse resembles previous fascists, particularly in what has been called by Patrick Healy and Maggie Haberman, Trump's "dark power of words."[49] As they point out in a recent *New York Times* article, Trump's use of language is characterized by "divisive phrases, harsh words and violent imagery characteristic of demagogues of the past." Moreover, Trump, like many past agitators, presents himself as a prophet incapable of being wrong; he disdains any sense of nuance and uses a discourse of intolerance populated by words such as "hate," "kill," "destroy," "attack," "fight," and "smack," showcasing a strongman mentality characteristic of the style of demagogues such as Pinochet, Mussolini, Hitler, and other tyrants. Trump is an anti-intellectual who appeals to anxiety, not possibility; he prioritizes insults and emotions over facts, evidence, or analysis. In reference to journalists, he said at a rally in Grand Rapids, Michigan, on December 21, 2015: "I hate some of these people but I'd never kill them."[50] But would he violate international human rights agreements and torture them if the accusations against them could be framed as a threat to national security? Trump trades in insults and uses the punitive rhetoric of humiliation as a weapon to deflect any criticism of his ideas and policies. How else to explain the following comment that Trump made about the comedian and actress Rosie O'Donnell: "If I were running *The View*, I'd fire Rosie O'Donnell. I mean, I'd look at her right in that fat, ugly face of hers, I'd say 'Rosie, you're fired.'"[51]

At a rally in South Carolina in 2015, Trump stated that he would use not only waterboarding but also similar interrogation techniques that "are much worse," and that waterboarding is "not nearly tough enough."[52] Trump's line that "torture works," flies in the face of the 2014 Senate torture report that stated that coercive interrogation techniques do not work in securing information.[53] Trump's call to implement torture as needed burnishes his self-image as an uncompromising strongman. His discourse echoes the totalitarian regimes of Europe in the 1930s and the Latin American dictatorships of 1970s. Heather Digby Parton is right when she writes that Donald Trump "may be the first openly fascistic frontrunner for the Republican presidential nomination but the ground was prepared and the seeds of his success sowed over the course of many years. As I have pointed out earlier, we've had fascism flowing through the American political bloodstream for quite some time."[54] There is a long, smoldering history in the United States in which fear, racism, resentment, precarity, and anxiety fueled a discourse all too similar to previous authoritarian regimes. For example, Trump's hate-laced rhetoric of aggression and intolerance is unleashed to support his claims of an embarrassing national decline, and his disdain for democratic procedures and the rule of law; this rhetoric is also used to legitimate his eagerness to address problems with violence and coercion as well as his shameless appeals to group purity, all of which have been part of previous fascist and authoritarian political manifestations.[55] This is a discourse that betrays dark and treacherous secrets not simply about Trump and the Republicans, but about the shifting boundaries of what the nation is willing to countenance—and even rally around—as the new American normal: acceptance of the "unthinkable" horrors to come.

The rise of acceptable forms of right-wing fascism in the United States today demonstrates the extent to which corporate evisceration of democracy and the long-term impact of the Terror Wars have weakened American society, and we should pay close attention to promises for more wars and walls, mass expulsions, censorship, and aggressive repression of protest and dissent. Trump's brutal racism, cruelty, and Nazi-style policy recommendations are more than shocking; they are emblematic of totalitarianism's hatred of multiculturalism, its call for racial purity, its mythic celebration of nationalism, its embrace of violence, its disdain for weakness, and its anti-intellectualism. This is the discourse of terror. And yet, these elements are increasingly a part of the new American normal. The conditions that produced the torture chambers, intolerable violence, extermination camps, and the squelching of dissent are still with us. Totalitarianism is not simply a relic of the past. It lives on in new forms, and its potential to dominate is just as terrifying and dangerous today as it has ever been.[56]

Mark Summer is right in arguing that the ghost of fascism runs through American society, indicating that fascist sympathies never went away and that the threat of fascism has to be taken seriously. He writes that while fascism didn't win on the battlefield, it won ideologically.

> It won because the same fears, the same greed, the same hatred that fueled its growth in the first part of the twentieth century never went away. The symbols of fascism became anathema, but the causes . . . went deep. And gradually, slowly, one step at a time, all those vices became first tolerated, then treated as virtues, and then as the only acceptable view. . . . [For instance] our long, stumbling lurch to the right; the building force of corporate power; the relentless need for war; a police whose power of enforcement is divorced from law; a preening nationalism that rewards the full rights of citizenship only to those who fit an ever-narrower mold. . . . I'm not saying we're moving toward fascism. I'm saying we started that drift a long time ago, and now we're well across the line.[57]

Trump is not an aberration. Rather, he is the successor of a long line of fascists who shut down public debate, attempt to humiliate their opponents, endorse violence as a response to dissent, and criticize any public display of democratic principles. The United States has reached its endpoint with Trump, and his presence should be viewed as a stern warning of the possible nightmare to come. Trump is not an isolated figure in U.S. politics; he is simply the most visible and popular expression of a number of extremists in the Republican Party who now view democracy as a liability. Ben Carson, Ted Cruz, and Marco Rubio all support an ideology that reduces certain populations to "anonymous beings." Think about their prevailing attacks on immigrants, refugees, and economically disadvantaged people. Primo Levi, the great writer and survivor of Auschwitz, called this use of dehumanizing abstractions one of the core principles of Nazi barbarism. Fast forward to Trump's incitement of violence at his rallies, coupled with his overt bigotry, his call for mass surveillance, his discourse of mass hatred, his willingness to arm other nations with nuclear weapons, and his embrace of politics as an extension of war.

This is not the discourse of Kafka, but of those extremists who have become cheerleaders for totalitarianism, especially in the present make-up of the Republican Party. As my colleague David L. Clark points out in personal correspondence, the frankness of Trump's call for violence coupled with his unapologetic thirst for injustice position him as the "latest expression of a fascism that has poisoned political life throughout modernity. He is unabashedly vicious because he is both an agent and a symptom of a barren political landscape in which viciousness goes insolently unhidden."[58] Trump is a monster without a conscience, a politician with a toxic set of policies. He is the product of a form of finance capitalism and a long legacy of racism and violence in which conscience is put to sleep, democracy withers, and public values are extinguished. This is truly a time of monsters, and Trump is simply the most visible and certainly one of the most despicable.

Trump is the most detailed manifestation of a new form of authoritarianism identified by the late political theorist Sheldon Wolin. According to Wolin, all the elements are in place today for a contemporary form of authoritarianism that he calls "inverted totalitarianism." He writes:

> Thus the elements are in place: a weak legislative body, a legal system that is both compliant and repressive, a party system in which one part, whether in opposition or in the majority, is bent upon reconstituting the existing system so as to permanently favor a ruling class of the wealthy, the well-connected and the corporate, while leaving the poorer citizens with a sense of helplessness and political despair, and, at the same time, keeping the middle classes dangling between fear of unemployment and expectations of fantastic rewards once the new economy recovers. That scheme is abetted by a sycophantic and increasingly concentrated media; by the integration of

> universities with their corporate benefactors; by a propaganda machine institutionalized in well-funded think tanks and conservative foundations; by the increasingly closer cooperation between local police and national law enforcement agencies aimed at identifying terrorists, suspicious aliens, and domestic dissidents.[59]

Totalitarianism destroys everything that makes democracy, civil rights, and openness possible. It is both an ideological poison and a brutal mode of social, economic, and martial control. But Trump also reminds us of totalitarianism's seductive appeal, the allure of the strongman who promises to clean things up, kill the enemy, and deliver the nation to greatness. What is crucial to acknowledge is that the stories, legacies, and varieties of coercion that are part of totalitarianism's history must be told over and over again so that recognizing them, understanding them, and resisting them becomes more widespread. The call for greater national security in authoritarian societies is code for illicit spying, criminalizing disadvantaged populations, militarizing law enforcement, consolidating the surveillance state, and ultimately expelling or neglecting all those who do not fall into the accepted racialized caste system. The fervor that Trump has stirred up should be a wake-up call for resistance against the tyranny of totalitarianism in its new and proto-fascist forms.

Trump's excesses, buffoonery, and incendiary remarks are welcome fodder for the mainstream media spectacle in which news is replaced by entertainment, violence, and idiocy parading as serious commentary. The exclusive focus on his outlandish aspects is also a political and depoliticizing diversion engineered to misrepresent reality rather than engage with it critically. What should be addressed when reporting about Trump is not how offensive he is politically, intellectually, and morally, but how he has come to symbolize something dangerous in American society—a society increasingly haunted by the ghost of Augusto Pinochet and the legacy of other dictatorships—as it quickly moves toward becoming an unapologetic authoritarian state.

In fact, Matthew MacWilliams, a student of authoritarianism, argues that "America's inclination to authoritarian behavior" is the primary factor behind Trump's success. According to MacWilliams, Trump's supporters are "individuals with a disposition to authoritarianism and demonstrate a fear of 'the other' as well as a readiness to follow and obey strong leaders. They tend to see the world in black-and-white terms. They are by definition attitudinally inflexible and rigid. And once they have identified friend from foe, they hold tight to their conclusions."[60]

Authoritarian tendencies are deeply rooted in American history. It is important to note that Donald Trump is just a symptom of a much larger reality, one in which a large segment of the American population has been mobilized by a legacy of intolerance for "outsiders" such as Muslims and immigrants, "threats that come from abroad, such as ISIS or Russia or Iran,"[61] and disruptive social change—such as the growing prevalence of same-sex marriage and racial diversity. Amanda Taub writes:

> [Such threats] could come in the form of evolving social norms, such as the erosion of traditional gender roles or evolving standards in how to discuss sexual orientation. It could come in the form of rising diversity, whether that means demographic changes from immigration or merely changes in the colors of the faces on TV. Or it could be any changes, political or economic, that disrupt social hierarchies. What these changes have in common is that, to authoritarians, they threaten to take away the status quo as they know it—familiar, orderly, secure—and replace it with something that feels scary because it is different and destabilizing, but also sometimes because it upends their own place in society. According to the literature, authoritarians will seek, in response, a strong leader who promises to suppress the scary changes, if necessary by force, and to preserve the status quo.[62]

Rather than despair or laugh over the spectacle of Trump's media-fueled rise, a more promising beginning might be to recognize the utter intellectual, moral, and political bankruptcy of the extremists now running the U.S. government that has set the stage for Trump. This suggests the possibility of rethinking politics in the way the Black Lives Matter movement is doing: connecting different groups under a banner of solidarity for real ideological and structural change at home and internationally. I believe that

Trump's candidacy offers the possibility for a new discourse of hope, of sustained criticism and the possibility to imagine what the next decade could be like with the advent of a massive innovative social and political formation willing to unite a fragmented Left around a call for a resurgent and insurrectional democracy. The good news is that the type of hateful ideology and harsh economic policies that Trump embraces cannot support a democratic society and, if he assumed the presidency, would make visible an oppressive social system, which would prompt massive resistance on many fronts. Ruptures and contradictions happen under neoliberalism, but they must be seized as a matter of informed consciousness, as a detour through new framing mechanisms, as an investment in new concepts, ideas, and thoughts that unsettle common sense, offer new alternatives, and infuse the present with a sense of a future that is ripe with new possibilities.

THREE

THE MENACE OF AUTHORITARIANISM

In the current historical moment in the United States, the assault on social tolerance is nourished by the assault on the civic imagination. One of the most egregious examples of these attacks can be found in the political rise of Donald Trump. Trump's popular appeal speaks not just to the boldness of what he says and the shock his inflamed rhetoric provokes, but the increasingly large numbers of Americans who respond to his aggressive bigotry with the eagerness of an angry lynch mob. Marie Luise Knott is right in noting, "We live our lives with the help of the concepts we form of the world. They enable an author to make the transition from shock to observation to finally creating space for action—for writing and speaking. Just as laws guarantee a public space for political action, conceptual thought ensures the existence of the four walls within which judgment operates."[1] The concepts that now guide our understanding of American society are produced by a corporate-influenced model that brings ruin to language, community, and democracy itself.

Missing from most of the commentaries by mainstream

media regarding the current rise of Trumpism is any historical context that would offer a critical account of the ideological and political disorders plaguing U.S. society.[2] A resurrection of historical memory in this moment could provide important lessons regarding the present crisis, particularly the long tradition of white racial hegemony, exceptionalism, and the extended wars on youth, women, immigrants, people of color, and the economically disadvantaged. As Chip Berlet points out, what is missing from most media accounts are traces of history that would make clear that Trump's presence on the American political landscape is the latest expression of a long tradition of "populist radical right ideology—nativism, authoritarianism, and populism . . . not unrelated to mainstream ideologies and mass attitudes. In fact, they are best seen as a radicalization of mainstream values."[3] Berlet goes even further, arguing that "Trump is not an example of creeping totalitarianism; he is the injured and grieving white man growing hoarse with bigoted canards while riding at the forefront of a new nativist movement."[4] For Adele M. Stan, like Berlet, the real question that needs to be asked is: "What is wrong with America that this racist, misogynist, money-cheating clown should be the frontrunner for the presidential nomination of one of its two major parties?"[5] Berlet is on target when he suggests that understanding Trump in terms of fascism is not enough. But Berlet is wrong in suggesting that all that the Trump "clown wagon" represents is a more recent expression of the merger of right-wing populism and racist intolerance. History does not stand still, and as important as these demagogic elements are, they have taken on a new meaning within a different historical conjuncture and have been intensified through the registers of a creeping totalitarianism wedded to a new and virulent form of savage capitalism. Racism, bigotry, and xenophobia are certainly on Trump's side, but what is new in this mix of toxic populism is the emergence of a predatory neoliberalism that has decimated the welfare state, expanded the punishing state, generated massive inequities in wealth and power, and put into place an ethos in which everybody has to provide for themselves. America has become a society of permanent uncertainty, intense anxiety, human misery, and immense racial and economic injustice.[6] Trump offers more than what might be called a mix of *The Jerry Springer Show* and white supremacist ideology; he also offers up domestic and foreign policies that point to a unique style of neo-fascism, one that has deep roots in American history and society. What is necessary in the current political moment is an analysis in which the emergence of a new form of totalitarianism is made visible in Trump's rallies, behavior, speeches, and proposals.

One example can be found in Steve Weissman's commentary in which he draws a relationship between Trump's casual racism and the rapidly emerging neo-fascist movements across Europe that "are growing strong by hating others for their skin color, religious origin, or immigrant status."[7] Weissman's willingness to situate Trump in the company of European radical right movements such as Jean-Marie Le Pen's populist National Front, Greece's Golden Dawn political party, or Vladimir Zhirinovsky's Liberal Democratic

Party of Russia provides a glimpse of what Trump has in common with the new authoritarianism and its deeply racist, anti-immigration, and neo-Nazi tendencies.

Unfortunately, it was not until late in Trump's presidential primary campaign that journalists began to acknowledge the presence of white militias and white hate groups at Trump's rallies, and almost none have acknowledged the chanting of "white power" at some of his political gatherings, which would surely signal Trump's connections not only to historical forms of white intolerance and racial hegemony but also to the formative Nazi culture that gave rise to genocide.[8] When Trump was told that he had the support of the Ku Klux Klan—a terrorist organization—Trump hesitated in disavowing such support. Trump appears to have no issues with attracting members of white hate groups to his ranks. Nor does Trump seem to have issues with channeling the legitimate anger and outrage of his followers into expressions of hate and bigotry that have all the earmarks of a neo-fascist movement. Trump has also refused to condemn the increasing racism at many of his rallies, such as the chants of angry white men yelling, "If you're an African first, go back to Africa."[9] Another example of Trump's embrace of totalitarian politics can be found in Glenn Greenwald's analysis of the mainstream media's treatment of Trump's attack on Jorge Ramos, an influential anchor of Univision.[10] When Ramos stood up to question Trump's views on immigration, Trump not only refused to call on him, but insulted him by telling him to go back to Univision. Instead of focusing on this particular lack of civility, Greenwald takes up the way many journalists scolded Ramos because he had a point of view and was committed to a political narrative. Greenwald saw this not just as a disingenuous act on the part of establishment journalists, but as a failure on the part of the press to speak out against a counterfeit notion of objectivity that represents a flight from responsibility, if not political and civic courage. Greenwald goes further, arguing that the mainstream media and institutions at the start of Trump's campaign were too willing, in the name of objectivity and balance, to ignore Trump's toxic rhetoric and the endorsements and expressions of violence. He writes:

> Actually, many people are alarmed, but it is difficult to know that by observing media coverage, where little journalistic alarm over Trump is expressed. That's because the rules of large media outlets—venerating faux objectivity over truth along with every other civic value—prohibit the sounding of any alarms. Under this framework of corporate journalism, to denounce Trump, or even to sound alarms about the dark forces he's exploiting and unleashing, would not constitute journalism. To the contrary, such behavior is regarded as a violation of journalism. Such denunciations are scorned as opinion, activism, and bias: all the values that large media-owning corporations have posited as the antithesis of journalism in order to defang and neuter it as an adversarial force.[11]

Timothy Egan argues that it would be wrong to claim that Trump's followers are simply ignorant, or to suggest that they are only driven by economic issues. Though he underplays the diversity of Trump's supporters and the legitimacy of some of their complaints, I think he is right in suggesting that many of them know exactly what Trump represents, and in doing so embody the darkest side of Republican Party politics, which have a long history of nurturing hate, racism, and bigotry. Egan writes:

> Donald Trump's supporters know exactly what he stands for: hatred of immigrants, racial superiority, a sneering disregard of the basic civility that binds a society. Educated and poorly educated alike, men and women—they know what they're getting from him. . . . But ignorance is not the problem with Trump's people. They're sick and tired of tolerance. In Super Tuesday exit polls, Trump dominated among those who want someone to "tell it like it is." And that translates to an explicit "play to our worst fears," as Meg Whitman, the prominent Republican business leader, said. "He's saying how the people really feel," one Trump supporter from Massachusetts, Janet Aguilar, told *The Times*. "We're all afraid to say it."[12]

Robert Reich draws a number of parallels between early twentieth-century fascism and Trump's ideology, practices, and policies.[13] He argues that the fascist script is repeated in Trump's use of fear to scare and intimidate people, his "repeated attacks on Mexican immigrants and Muslims," his appeal as the patriotic strongman who can personally remedy economic ills, his vaunting of "national power and greatness," his willingness to condone or appear to legitimate violence against protesters at his rallies, and his preying on the economic distress, misery, and collective anxiety of millions of people "to scapegoat others and create a cult of personality."[14]

Mike Lofgren echoes a number of Reich's criticisms but goes further and argues that Trump represents the decision on the part of the American public to choose fascism over what he calls a "managed democracy."[15] According to Lofgren, a managed democracy has been produced in the United States by a culture of war and fear, especially since the massacre of thousands of Americans on 9/11. The effects of such a war psychosis were evident in the lies made by the Bush administration regarding nonexistent weapons of mass destruction, lies that were repeated ad nauseam to dupe Americans into an unjustified war against Iraq. It is also evident in the rise of the national insecurity surveillance state and its declared notion that everyone is a potential suspect, a notion that helps to further the internalization of the Terror Wars. Another boost to America's culture of fear, insecurity, and war was the economic crash of 2008, which furthered anxiety to levels not seen since the Great Depression. Amidst this decade-long culture of fear and war, Lofgren argues that the United States may very well become a fascist political system by 2017.[16]

Predictions about America's descent into fascism are not new and should surprise no one who is historically literate. Rick Perlstein is correct in arguing that Trump provides a service in making clear how conservative ideology works at its deepest levels, and that he exposes the hypocrisy of dressing reactionary politics in a discourse of liberation.[17] Journalists such as *Wall Street Journal* columnist Peggy Noonan predictably downplay the racist and fascist undertones of Trump's candidacy, arguing that Trump is simply a symptom of massive disillusionment among Americans who are exhibiting a profound disdain, if not hatred, for the political and economic mainstream elites.[18] Disappointingly, however, this argument is often bolstered by progressives who claim that criticism of Trump's bigotry and racism cannot fully account for his political appeal. For instance, Thomas Frank observes that Trump actually embraces a number of left-leaning positions that make him popular with less educated working-class whites.[19] He cites Trump's criticism of free trade agreements, his call for competitive bidding with the drug industry, his critique of the military-industrial-complex and its wasteful spending, and his condemnation of companies that displace U.S. workers by closing factories in the United States and opening them in much less developed countries such as Mexico in order to save on labor costs.

In this view, the working class becomes a noble representative of a legitimate populist backlash against neoliberalism, and whether or not it embraces an American form of proto-fascism seems irrelevant. Frank, however, has a long history of ignoring cultural issues, ideologies, and values that do not simply mimic the economic system. As Ellen Willis pointed out in a brilliant critique of Frank's work, he makes the mistake of imagining popular and media culture as simply "a pure reflection of the corporate class that produces it."[20] Hence, racism, ultra-nationalism, bigotry, religious fundamentalism, and other anti-democratic factors get downplayed in Frank's analysis of Trump's rise to power. This view is reductionist and ignores research indicating that a large body of Trump supporters, who back explicit authoritarian polices, rarely complain about the predatory economic policies pushed by the Republican and Democratic parties.[21] If anything, such economic pressures intensify these deep-seated authoritarian attitudes. What Trump's followers have in common is support for a number of authoritarian policies mobilized around "an outsize fear of threats, physical and social, and, more than that, a desire to meet those threats with severe government action—with policies that are authoritarian not just in style but in actuality."[22] Such policies include:

> Using military force over diplomacy against countries that threaten the United States; changing the Constitution to bar citizenship for children of illegal immigrants; imposing extra airport checks on passengers who appear to be of Middle Eastern descent in order to curb terrorism; requiring all citizens to carry a national ID card at all times to show to a police officer on request, to curb terrorism; allowing the federal government to scan

> all phone calls for calls to any number linked to terrorism.[23]

John Judis extends this progressive line of argument by comparing Trump with Bernie Sanders, claiming that they are both populists and outsiders while suggesting that Trump occupies a legitimate outsider status and raises a number criticisms regarding domestic policies for which he should be taken seriously by the American people and not simply dismissed as a racist, clown, or pompous showman. Judis writes:

> Sanders and Trump differ dramatically on many issues—from immigration to climate change—but both are critical of how wealthy donors and lobbyists dominate the political process, and both favor some form of campaign finance reform. Both decry corporations moving overseas for cheap wages and to avoid American taxes. Both reject trade treaties that favor multinational corporations over workers. And both want government more, rather than less, involved in the economy. Sanders is a left-wing populist. He wants to defend the "collapsing middle class" against the "billionaire class" that controls the economy and politics. He is not a liberal who wants to reconcile Wall Street and Main Street, or a socialist who wants the working class to abolish capitalism. Trump is a right-wing populist who wants to defend the American people

> from rapacious CEOs and from Hispanic illegal immigrants. He is not a conventional business conservative who thinks government is the problem and who blames America's ills on unions and Social Security. Both men are foes of what they describe as their party's establishment. And both campaigns are also fundamentally about rejecting the way economic policy has been talked about in American presidential politics for decades.[24]

Some liberals, such as Arthur Goldhammer, go so far as to suggest that Trump's appeal is largely an extension of the "cult of celebrity," his management of "a very rational and reasonable set of business practices," and his attention to the anger of a disregarded element of the working class.[25] He asserts without irony that Trump "is not an authoritarian but a celebrity," as if one cancels out the other. While celebrity culture confers authority in a society utterly devoted to consumerism, it also represents less a mode of false identification than a manufactured spectacle that cheapens serious and thoughtful discourse and puts into play a focus on the commercial world of fashion, style, and appearances. This has given rise to mainstream media that devalue politics, treat politicians as celebrities, refuse to give them a serious hearing, and are unwilling to raise tough questions. Precisely because it is assumed that celebrities are too dumb to answer such questions and that the public is more concerned about their personal lives than anything else, they are too often exempt from being held accountable for what they say, especially if it doesn't square comfortably with the spectacle of banality. Celebrity culture is not simply a mode of entertainment, it is a form of public pedagogy central to creating a formative culture that views thinking as a nuisance at best, or at worst, as dangerous. Treated seriously, celebrity culture provides the architectural framing for an authoritarian culture by celebrating a deadening form of self-interest, narcissism, and civic illiteracy. As Fritz Stern, the renowned historian of Germany, has argued, the dark side of celebrity culture can be understood by the fact that it gave rise to Trump and represents the merger of financial power and a culture of thoughtlessness.[26]

Roger Berkowitz, the director of the Hannah Arendt Center, takes Goldhammer's argument further and claims that Trump is a celebrity who knows how to work the "art of the deal" (a reference to the title of Trump's well-known neoliberal manifesto). That is, Trump is a celebrity with real business acumen and substance. In particular, he argues, Trump's appeal is due in part to his image as a smart and successful businessman who gets things done. Berkowitz goes into overdrive in his claim that Trump is not a Hitler, as if that means he is not a demagogue unique to the American context. Without irony, Berkowitz goes so far as to write, "It is important to recognize that Trump's focus on illegal immigrants, protectionism, the wall on the Mexican border, and the terrorist danger posed by Muslims transcends race."[27] I am assuming he means that Trump's racist ideology, policies, and rhetoric can be removed from the poisonous climate of hate that he promotes, the policies for which he argues (such as torture, which is a war crime), and the violence he breeds at his rallies. Indeed, Berkowitz implies that these policies and practices derive not from a fundamental orientation of white intolerance but from a sound understanding of free-market economics and business.

The sound business practice that Berkowitz finds admirable has a name; it is called neoliberal capitalism and it has spread an untold degree of human misery, political corruption, and inequality throughout the world. It has given us a social and political formation that promotes militarization, attacks the welfare state, aligns itself slavishly with corporate power, corrupts politics, and aggressively demeans women, Blacks, Latinos, Muslims, protesters, and immigrants.

Trump and his followers may not yet be a fascist party in the strict sense of the word, but they certainly display elements of a new style of American authoritarianism that comes close to constituting a proto-fascist movement.[28] Trump's call to raise the nation to greatness, the blaming of Mexican immigrants and Muslims for America's troubles, the vitriolic disdain for protesters, the groups of thugs that seem to delight in cheering at Trump's references to violence and gladly administer it to protesters, especially members of the Black Lives Matter movement, all echo historical elements that have shaped totalitarian regimes that have plagued the West from the Nazis of Europe to the dictators of Latin America.

Berkowitz's confusion appears to go off the cliff when defending Trump as not being a racist, particularly in his claim that the difference between Trump and Sanders is one of attitude and not policy, even going so far as to suggest they have both "pushed the limits of racial propriety."[29] This statement whitewashes Trump's overt racism and appears to suggest that both candidates share similar ideological positions toward people of color and inhabit the same racist landscape, a patently false claim that borders on the absurd. Of course, if Berkowitz had used the word racism instead of "racial propriety," the latter claim would not make sense. If elected president—which is no longer an unlikely scenario given his sweep of the Republican primaries—Trump has pledged to ban Muslims from entering the U.S., expel 11 million undocumented Mexican immigrants, and kill terrorists *and* their families, and he has threatened to use state-sponsored torture, among other egregious policy practices. Clearly, such policies constitute more than simply a matter of different attitudes between Trump and Bernie Sanders. The false equivalency at work in such a comparison is a bit too casual and covers up the fact that Trump attempts to breed intolerance out of misfortune, while Sanders goes to the political, economic, and social roots of the problems that cause it. Sanders has always been a strong supporter of civil rights and a fierce critic of racism. On the other hand, Trump promotes an intense culture of anxiety that cannot be overlooked by focusing on his business résumé or, for that matter, his criticism of some of the Republican Party's more regressive domestic and foreign policy endeavors. On the contrary, Trump's appeal to white fear, aggression, and violence appears to seduce and silence people, especially those who have been politically victimized, and seems to render them more vulnerable to his image as the white bossman.[30]

Berkowitz's argument is more than apologetic, it is a species of post-racial discourse that became commonplace during the Obama years. It is also disingenuous and nonsensical. It is hard to make up such apologetic reasoning at a time in which racist invective and actions are more visible than ever: Authoritarian brutality against people of color is being exposed to a degree without precedent, racist comments against Obama proliferate without apology, and hate groups target people of color, immigrants, Muslims, and Planned Parenthood with repeated acts of violence. We also live at a time when a dangerous resurgence of racism, Islamophobia, and anti-immigration sentiments is on the rise. Against the reality of a society immersed—if not saturated—in racial violence, Berkowitz's post-racial and market-drenched discourse mimics a form of right-wing ideology too afraid to name itself, and too unwilling to address Trump's authoritarian and myopic drive for power.

David Theo Goldberg is right in arguing that this line of argument is a form of "postraciality [that] heightens the mode of racial dismissal. . . . [It] renders opaque the structures making possible and silently perpetuating racially ordered power and privilege."[31] Trump's followers cannot be defined simply by an anger that is associated with oppressive economic institutions, policies, and structures. They are also the spawn of anti-democratic politics deeply educative in the production of identities, desires, and values that embrace the long legacy of racialized human trafficking, enslavement, and hatred of immigrants. They inhabit modes of agency and identification that mimic the irresponsible values of casino capitalism, including a one-sided celebration of financial self-interest, hatred of government, and embrace of the ethos of privatization, harsh competition, and a survival-of-the-fittest ethos. The authoritarian tendencies of Trump's followers cannot be explained through economic analysis alone. Denying the importance of social politics, corporate-driven pedagogies, and the educative nature of a culture in the hands of the financial elite greatly ignores modes of domination that go far beyond economic discontents and are produced and legitimized daily in mainstream cultural venues.[32] Domination is not only structural; it also lies on the side of beliefs, persuasion, rhetoric, and the pedagogical dimensions of politics. What Trump has tapped into is not simply economic resentment but decades of a formative culture that is antagonistic to diversity and democracy.

Unfortunately, what these positions often downplay is the toxic intolerance that mimics an updated neo-fascist rhetoric "designed to demonize an entire class of people by reducing them to objects fit only for elimination."[33] What is disturbing about accounts that celebrate, however cautiously, Trump's more liberal tendencies is that, "they give racist contempt the impeccable alibi of ethical and secular legitimacy."[34] Rather than being insightful, this type of restricted discourse runs the risk of performing a cleansing operation, ridding the Republican Party, and Trump and his followers, of some of their most vile legacies. It also overlooks a moment in which political authoritarianism is clearly on the rise, and points to a time when the very fate of humanity and the planet are at risk. As Don and Kurtis Lee observe:

> If Donald Trump were president, he would [end abortion rights, repeal Obamacare], put U.S. ground troops in Iraq to fight Islamic extremists, rescind President Obama's executive orders that protect millions of immigrants from deportation, eliminate American citizenship for U.S.-born children whose parents are in the country illegally and "police" but not necessarily revoke the nuclear pact with Iran. Trump wants to deport all immigrants in the U.S. illegally—an estimated 11 million people—but says he wouldn't break up families because their families would be deported too. "We're going to keep the families together . . . but they have to go," he said in a wide-ranging interview on NBC's *Meet the Press.* "We have to make a whole new set of standards. And when people come in, they have to come in legally." Deportees who qualify could return, he said. Trump would end Obama's Deferred Action for Childhood Arrivals program, which allows young people brought to the country illegally as children to work and attend college without facing deportation.[35]

An important example of Trump's demagogic ideology is also evident in Matt Taibbi's commentary on the ways Trump's bigoted discourse can lead to violence and how

Trump reacted when it did. According to Taibbi, when two brothers from South Boston urinated on, and then used a metal pipe to severely beat, a Latino man, "one of the brothers reportedly told police that 'Donald Trump was right, all of these illegals need to be deported.' When reporters confronted Trump, he hadn't yet heard about the incident. At first, he said, 'That would be a shame.' But right after, he went on: 'I will say, the people that are following me are very passionate. They love this country. They want this country to be great again. But they are very passionate. I will say that.'"[36] Trump later modified his response, one that appeared to both condone and legitimate the violence done in his name, but the fact remains that he is not just disseminating hate, but contributing to conditions that increase hate-crimes and bloodshed. In what can only be interpreted as an openly racist justification for acts that are reminiscent of similar attacks against Jews and Gypsies in Nazi Germany, Trump's initial response reflects the degree to which white right-wing intolerance has become an acceptable register of American politics.

When an activist named Mercutio Southall Jr. started shouting "Black Lives Matter!" at a Trump rally in Birmingham, Alabama, on November 21, 2015, Trump supporters punched and choked him. When asked to comment on the assault, Trump said: "Maybe he should have been roughed up."[37] What has often been overlooked is that Trump supporters have a history of attacking those protesting Trump's policies. For instance, Dara Lind observes of the Southall Jr. attack:

> This isn't an isolated incident. Trump supporters have gotten physical with protesters at several other events throughout his candidacy. A protester was dragged out of a Trump rally in Miami. A Trump supporter ripped up a protester's sign. A Trump bodyguard was filmed sucker-punching a protester outside Trump Tower in early September. And at a rally in DC, photographers captured a Trump supporter pulling a protester's hair.[38]

The lynch-mob mentality conjured at Trump events was made visible at a rally in Fayetteville, North Carolina, in March 2016, when Rakeem Jones, a 26-year-old Black protester, was attacked by John McGraw, a Trump supporter. In a video that captured the incident, violence drew cheers from the crowd as the police threw the victim to the ground and handcuffed him as if he had been the assailant. "The police jumped on me like I was the one swinging," Jones said. "My eye still hurts. It's just shocking. The shock of it all is starting to set in. It's like this dude really hit me, and they let him get away with it. I was basically in police custody and got hit."[39] McGraw later boasted during an interview with *Inside Edition*:

> "You bet I liked it," McGraw said when asked if he liked the event, "clocking the hell out of that big mouth." McGraw was then asked why he punched Jones.
>
> "Well, number one, we don't know if he's

> ISIS," McGraw said, "We don't know who he is, but we know he's not acting like an American and cussing me . . . and sticking his face in my head. If he wants it laid out, I laid it out."
>
> He added: "Yes, he deserved it. The next time we see him, we might have to kill him."[40]

Such actions find support in Trump's comments when he states he "would like to punch" someone or when he labels people as "bad Americans." These comments make clear that at the core, Trump's politics and appeal are "built around aggression and . . . violence."[41] A not too subtle hint of Trump's incitement of violence can be seen in his claim that he was looking into paying for McGraw's legal fees. In defense of such actions, Trump told *Meet the Press* that McGraw "obviously loves his country," and that he might "have gotten carried away."[42]

Trump's rise coincides with the fall of democracy in the United States and a consolidation of "supranational forces that evade any democratic control."[43] Citizen sovereignty has given way to economic rule programmed to further the private self-interest of the ultra-wealthy. A new historical conjuncture has emerged in which longstanding social institutions are being discredited, underfunded, and dismantled—"subjected to processes of . . . deregulation, fragmentation and privatization."[44]

In such circumstances, traditional ideologies and discourses fail to comprehend what might be called a historic break, one in which totalitarian ideologies, rhetoric, and imagery become normalized. Loneliness, anxiety, uncertainty, fear, and anger provide the conditions for authoritarian movements to "convince the public that acts long considered profoundly immoral have suddenly become morally obligatory."[45] We live in a moment of political climate change in which democratic public spheres are disappearing before our eyes, and it has become easier to target certain groups by dehumanizing them and subjecting them to violence, while at the same time not holding the perpetrators accountable in the future. In this new totalitarian discourse, Trump turns language into a weapon, ideology into an act of hate, racism, and destruction. The process of dehumanizing Black protesters, Latino immigrants, Muslims, and others is informed by a dark history of political intolerance and ethnic cleansing. The connection between Trump's legitimation of violence at his rallies, his defaming of diverse groups, his call for mass deportations, and his targeting of immigrants and Muslims has too close a relationship with other totalitarian regimes that moved quickly from demonization to annihilation. Trump has become the modern version of Mr. Kurtz in Conrad's *Heart of Darkness*. As Arendt describes them: "These men were 'hollow to the core,' 'reckless without hardihood, greedy without audacity and cruel without courage. . . . The only talent that could possibly burgeon in their hollow souls was the gift of fascination which makes a 'splendid leader of an extreme party.'"[46]

As America's social fabric unravels, individuals are socially uprooted, lose their sense of community and compassion, and are thrust into a world "that destroys politics, methodically eliminating speaking and acting human beings and attacking the very humanity of first a selected group and then all groups."[47] As the political sphere is diminished, authoritarianism gains ground, exploiting working-class resentments and fears while ushering in the tyranny of intolerant elite control. This is most evident in Trump's campaign rhetoric of anxiety, hatred, war-mongering, bigotry, and racism, which is designed to appeal to the white male economic underclass, a strategy that has a long tradition in the outer fringes of both major parties, but particularly in the Republican Party. As Eugene Robinson has pointed out: "Trump has given voice to the ugliness and anger that the party spent years encouraging and exploiting. He let the cat out of the bag, and it's hungry."[48] The cat he has let out of the bag is the possibility of a unique form of authoritarianism in America. The debate over whether Trump directly emulates Nazi Germany misses the point. The real issue is how the United States might descend into proto-fascism through its emergence under distinct social formations unique to the times in which we live. As mentioned in Chapter 2, this is, of course, a theme elaborated in great detail by Sheldon Wolin, who claims that if authoritarianism comes to the fore in the United States, it will be a form of inverted totalitarianism;[49] that is, a manifestation of proto-fascism that will profess to be the opposite of what it actually is, a militant break from democracy—one that marshals fundamentalist movements to support the economic self-interest of the ultra-rich.

What is clear is that a widespread avoidance of the past has become not only a sign of the appalling lack of historical consciousness in contemporary American culture, but a deliberate political weapon used by the powerful to keep people passive and ignorant of the truth, if not reduced to a discourse drawn from the empty realm of commercial entertainment products. This is a discourse in which images of an intimidating master and commander come to dominate in what Hannah Arendt once called "the ruin of our categories of thought and standards of judgment."[50] Of course, there are many factors currently contributing to this production of intolerance, racism, and the diminishment of individual and collective agency. The forces promoting a deep-seated culture of authoritarianism run deep in American society and have been smoldering for some time.

Such factors extend from the current authority of celebrity culture, a growing anti-intellectualism in American society, and the dumbing down of curricula in schools to the transformation of the mainstream media into a stupefying mix of commercial propaganda and entertainment. The latter is particularly crucial as the collapse of journalistic standards that could inform the onslaught of information finds its counterpart in a government wedded to state secrecy and the aggressive prosecution of whistle-blowers,[51] the corruption of political language,[52] and the disregard for truth, all of which have contributed to a growing culture of political and civic illiteracy.[53] The deficits in knowledge and value that produce such detrimental forms of ignorance not only crush the ethical imagination, critical modes of social interaction, and political dissent, but also destroy those public spaces that promote thoughtfulness, thinking, and open dialogue, and serve as "guardians of truths as facts," as Arendt once put it.[54] Independent thinking, imagination, and memory always pose threats to authoritarian control, but in the United States these are not simply dangerous, but also in short supply. A consumer, market-driven culture is synonymous with a formative culture of passivity, illiteracy, and numbness, especially when buying, selling, and self-interest are what define the parameters of leadership, agency, and citizenship.

The Privatization of Space and Time

Space, time, and even language are subject to the forces of privatization and commodification and provide a breeding ground for authoritarianism. Public space has been replaced by malls and a host of commercial intrusions. Commodified and privatized, public space is now regulated through market values rather than public values, just as communal values are replaced by the competitive notion of survival of the fittest. Time is no longer connected to long-term investment in community, the development of social well-being, and goals that benefit young people and the common good. On the contrary, time is now connected to short-term investments and quick financial gains. More broadly, time is now defined by "the non-stop operation of global exchange and circulation"[55] and the frenetic perpetuation of an impoverished commercial culture that depoliticizes people and tethers them to consumer-related options. Under neoliberalism, time presents itself as a form of tyranny, an unquestioned necessity, and in speeding up the flows of work, leisure, knowledge, and everyday life it spawns a new kind of violence in which the flow of money replaces the flow of thoughtfulness, atomization replaces a notion of shared solidarity, spectacle undermines historical memory, privatization seeks to erase all notions of the public good, and preventable precarity replaces any sense of security and long-term planning.

In the age of demagogues, time itself has become a burden more than a condition for contemplation, self-reflection, and the cultivation of community. The extended arc of temporal relations in which one could imagine long-term augmentation of the common good has given way to a notion of time in which the horizon is contained within the imperative of increasing short-term profit for the financial elite irrespective of the consequences that doing so may visit upon others. What is lost in this merging of time and the dictates of neoliberal capital are the most basic elements of being human, along with the formative culture and institutions necessary to develop a real, substantive, and sustainable democracy. As Christian Marazzi observes:

> Taking time means giving each other the means of inventing one's future, freeing it from the anxiety of immediate profit. It means caring for oneself and the environment in which one lives, it means growing up in a socially responsible way. [Taking time means] questioning the meaning of consumption, production, and investment [so as to not] reproduce the preconditions of financial capitalism, the violence of its ups and downs, the philosophy

> according to which "time is everything, man is nothing." For man (sic) to be everything, we need to reclaim the time of his existence.[56]

Civic death and disposability are the new signposts of an authoritarian society in which historical memory is diminished and ethical evaluations become derided as figments of the liberal past. Dispossession and depoliticization are central to the discourse of neoliberalism in which language molds identities, desires, values, and social relationships. As Doreen Massey observes, under neoliberalism citizens are reconfigured as consumers, customers, and spectators while relentlessly indoctrinated to behave as if only self-interest matters.[57] In this instance, social and communal bonds are shredded, important modes of solidarity are attacked, and war is waged against any institution that embraces the values, practices, and social relations endemic to a democracy.

This retreat into private silos has resulted in the inability of families, individuals, and communities to connect their personal and collective victimization with larger public issues. Detached from any concept of the common good, they are left alone to face a world of increasing uncertainty in which it becomes difficult to imagine anything other than living day to day, meal to meal. In this context, there is little room for thinking critically and acting collectively in ways that are imaginative and courageous. In such a historical moment, a necessary sense of crisis is replaced by what appears to be something Erin Ramlo calls a "drugged complacency."[58] How else to expain the paucity of opposition to the endless lies of right-wing talk radio, or to a congress dominated by extremists that wage a constant war against Black voting rights, women's rights, and the social provisions of the welfare state.

Surely, the celebration and widespread prevalence of ignorance in American culture does more than merely testify "to human backwardness or stupidity"; it also "indicates human weakness and the fear that it is unbearably difficult to live beset by continuous doubts."[59] Yet, what is often missed in analysis of political and civic illiteracy is the degree to which these handicaps not only result in a flight from politics, but also produce a moral coma that supports emerging systems of terror and authoritarianism. Democratic forms of governance are on their death bed, particularly since as Paul Rosenberg argues "Having run out of ideas how to govern, the American right has turned against the very concept of governing."[60]

Neoliberal Attacks on Civic Literacy

At another point in U.S. history, Trump's presidential campaign might have been treated as a practical joke or publicity stunt, as when Abbie Hoffman attempted to levitate the Pentagon. But at a time when the ravages of deindustrialization and despair are mediated by a society that has lost any recognition of itself, the toxic promises of Trump's authoritarianism provide convincing, simple, and quick fixes. Trump's enduring popularity is not new to American history, but a culture that thrives on instant pleasure, is hypnotized by banal celebrities, and regards thinking as an act of stupidty gives it a new meaning and popular impetus. Put differently, manufactured ignorance is producing a nationwide crisis of agency, memory, imagination, and independent thinking.

As Noam Chomsky, Richard Hofstadter, and Susan Jacoby have made clear, ignorance is not simply about the absence of knowledge, it is a kind of ideological sandstorm in which reason gives way to emotion, and a willful limitation of critical thought spreads through the culture as part of a political project that both infantilizes and depoliticizes the general public.[61] Trump is simply the most visible embodiment of a corporate-indoctrinated society that is relentlessly programmed to be suspicious of, bored by, or contemptuous of independent thought. Trump is the quintessential symbol of the merging of a war-like arrogance, militant economic self-interest, and a narcissistic unworldliness that is disconnected from the problems of the real world. Donald Trump is far from the kind of clownish fiction some writers have described him to be. And while liberals such as Michael Tomasky have pointed to his appeal to racial resentment, his gladiatorial style, and his ability to combine a discourse of hatred and elements of conservative fundamentalism with a flair for entertainment,[62] this type of analysis shies away from talking about Trump's presence on the political landscape as an indication and warning of emerging forms totalitarianism in America today.[63]

Trump is the embodiment of a party and economic order in which informed judgments, moral responsibility, and collective action disappear from the world of politics.

Trump's often insulting, humiliating, misogynist, and racist remarks signify more than the rantings of a privileged white man who is comfortable in front of a camera. Trump represents the new face of what Hannah Arendt once called the "banality of evil."[64]

Unapologetic about the racist nature of his remarks, unreflective about a savage economic system that is destroying the planet and the lives of most of its inhabitants, and unaware of his own "criminal" participation in furthering a culture of intolerance and cruelty, he is typical of an expanding mass of pundits, anti-public intellectuals, and right-wing fundamentalists who live in a historical void and for whom emotion overtakes reason. Trump's call for a multibillion-dollar wall between Mexico and the United States is about more than a waste of resources; it is part of a racialized propaganda of ultra-nationalism, punishment, cruelty, and disposability that informs all totalitarian regimes. Trump may be incapable of understanding "the complex realities of immigration and immigration reform in the United States," but what he does understand is that pandering to anxiety and nativism resonates with the deepest impulses of white racial and economic hegemony, authoritarianism, and fear.[65]

The logic of disposability gains a sordid legitimacy in Trump's discourse. Immigrants are positioned as the enemies of civilization and relegated to zones of ideological and political abandonment, caught between the arbitrary registers of life and death, visibility and invisibility. Within this hate-filled discourse, any appeal to civic literacy is lost in the dark recesses of ignorance and the looming shadow of the police state.

In these threatening times, illiteracy is a political tool designed primarily to wage war on language, meaning, thinking, and the capacity for critical thought. Chris Hedges is right in stating that "the emptiness of language is a gift to demagogues and the corporations that saturate the landscape with manipulated images and the idiom of mass culture."[66] Words such as love, trust, freedom, responsibility, and choice have been deformed by a market logic that narrows their meaning to either a relationship to a commodity or a reductive notion of self-interest. We don't love each other, we love our new car. Instead of loving with courage and compassion, and desiring a more just society, we love owning commodities.

At the same time, illiteracy bonds people and offers the pretense of a community forged in hate, fear, and insecurity. Mark Slouka is instructive here. He writes:

> What we need to talk about, what someone needs to talk about, particularly now, is our ever-deepening ignorance (of politics, of foreign languages, of history, of science, of current affairs, of pretty much everything) and not just our ignorance but our complacency in the face of it, our growing fondness for it. A generation ago the proof of our foolishness, held up to our faces, might still have elicited some redeeming twinge of shame—no longer. Today, across vast swaths of the republic, it

> amuses and comforts us. We're deeply loyal to it. Ignorance gives us a sense of community; it confers citizenship; our representatives either share it or bow down to it or risk our wrath.[67]

Clearly, attacks on reason, evidence, science, and critical thought have reached perilous anti-democratic proportions in the United States. A number of political, economic, social, and technological forces now work to distort reality and keep people passive, unthinking, and unable to act in a critically engaged manner. Politicians, right-wing pundits, and large tracts of the American public embrace positions that support Creationism, capital punishment, torture, and the denial of human-preventable climate change. Even at the end of Barack Obama's presidency, 62 percent of Trump's supporters believed that Obama was a Muslim.

In such situation, literacy disappears not just as the practice of learning skills, but also as the foundation for taking informed action. Divorced from any sense of critical understanding and agency, the meaning of literacy is narrowed to completing basic reading, writing, and numeracy tasks assigned in schools. Literacy education is similarly reduced to strictly methodological considerations and standardized assessment, rooted in test taking and deadening forms of memorization, and becomes far removed from forms of literacy that would impart an ability to raise questions about historical and social contexts. While critical literacy in and of itself guarantees nothing, it is an essential step toward democratic agency, the ability to narrate on behalf of oneself and others, and the ethical and social capacity to challenge authority. Civic literacy is the bedrock of any democratic society and its decline suggests that the prospect of totalitarianism is becoming the crisis of our time. The increasing atomization of society, the commodification of thought, the rise of the surveillance state, the transformation of schools into dead zones of the imagination, the war on communities of color and immigrants—all of these anti-democratic tendencies in American society point to a social order in which tyranny destroys everything that makes civil society possible. Trump's message is simply a more strident version of what the financial elite who donate to both political parties have been saying for years: everything should be understood, ordered, and solved by way of the market. In this view of America, militant self-interest rules, independent critical thought is dangerous, and dissent is the sign of the enemy. In this age of political zombies, the Terror Wars have been internalized. Terror becomes an organizing principle of society—a culture of terror based on a fear of the other, fear of criticism, and fear of democracy itself.

There are hints of this type of proto-fascism in Trump's claim that dissenters are "bad people," and so "bad for our country."[68] Trump and his followers want to eliminate the heartbeat of democracy—dissent, representative government, and civically engaged citizens. That is, they are against the strong idea of democracy with its call for equality and social and economic justice. We should be reminded here, as Zygmunt Bauman and Carlo Bordoni point out, that for Fascism and Nazism, democracy is "the most serious threat that could be faced by any form of civilization, and it was precisely because they wanted to prevent the masses from erasing the social order that they imposed control through authoritarianism and totalitarianism, extreme and illiberal forms of personal control, aimed at uniformity and conformity."[69]

Similarly, emerging authoritarians such as Donald Trump seek to accelerate a social and political re-ordering in which human bonds can only be shaped within a racially distorted, economically rigged, aggressively policed set of hierarchies. All social relations are dominated by a white financial elite's vantage point of combative self-interest. Matters of empathy and shared responsibilities are viewed a weaknesses, all of which Trump made clear on his TV show, *The Apprentice*. There is more at stake in the current menace of totalitarianism than the curse of the inability to think. At stake is the militarized financialization of all social relations and spaces, a kind of blind death march in which coercion, violence, foreclosure, and greed become the organizing principles of all aspects of social life.

With few exceptions, political authorities in the United States embrace insecurity by design, mobilize anxiety through appeals to fear, promote a rigid friend/enemy and us-or-them world in which mistrust and rage replace understanding, dialogue, and kindness. War becomes a totalizing metaphor serving largely to expand and hasten criminalization and militarization of everything. Waging war has become a psychology, an emotional lever, a rational fix, a swindle of fulfillment, a source of power, and a manufactured release for the fear, insecurity, and powerlessness that many people experience on a daily basis. Political actors such as Marco Rubio, Paul Ryan, and others are emblematic of what Eisenhower once defined as leaders who construct a "life of perpetual fear and tension."[70] As Eisenhower notes, these are politicians who keep "humanity hanging from a cross of iron"—the military-industrial complex—by supporting policies that not only threaten humanity through a runaway arms buildup, but also seem indifferent to this plain fact:

> Every gun that is made, every warship launched, every rocket fired signifies, in the final sense, a theft from those who hunger and are not fed, those who are cold and are not clothed. This world in arms is not spending money alone. It is spending the sweat of its laborers, the genius of its scientists, [and] the hopes of its children.[71]

The Menace of Totalitarianism

For Hannah Arendt, the inability to think, to be thoughtful, and to assume responsibility for one's actions not only spoke to a regrettable type of civic and political illiteracy, but was crucial for creating the formative cultures that permitted authoritarian tendencies to fully consolidate into totalitarian regimes. Absent any residue of moral responsibility, political indignation, and collective resistance, atrocities committed in a systemic way now emerge, in part, from a society in which acts of conscience have become taboo and passive spectatorship normal. Of course, thinking critically and acting independently largely take place in public spheres that instill convictions rather than destroy them, and encourage critical capacities rather than shut them down.

What Donald Trump represents is not genuinely investigated by a corporate media system that benefits from the ratings and revenues that his antics generate. As mentioned in the previous chapter, media executives like CBS head Les Moonves boast that Trump's hate-mongering, irrespective of the larger consequences for many Americans, increases his profit. "Sorry," says Moonves. "It's a terrible thing to say. But, bring it on, Donald. Keep going."[72] Matt Taibbi nails it when he says, "Trump found the flaw in the American Death Star. It doesn't know how to turn the cameras off, even when it's filming its own demise."[73] And this may be the darkest and most noxious aspect of what Donald Trump truly represents: the demise of democracy, but not as murder so much as an assisted suicide. "Mankind, which in Homer's time was an object of contemplation for the Olympian gods, now is one for itself," wrote Walter Benjamin. "Its self-alienation has reached such a degree that it can experience its own destruction as an aesthetic pleasure of the first order. This is the situation of politics which Fascism is rendering aesthetic."[74]

Bigot, con man, bully, TV character, Trump has in almost every way become an Imperial Wizard of the spectacle. Following in the footsteps of previous authoritarian strongmen, he mimics their "exaltation of the masses," bombastic in-your-face politics, belittling threats and mockery, the call to sacrifice, promises of greatness, mass rallies, the appeal to raw power, constant references that bolster a notion of racial purity and exceptionalism, and the use of highly orchestrated media ritual, all of which are on full display with his godlike displays of wealth.

In addition, the new totalitarianism is echoed in the resurgence of religious intolerance that runs through U.S. society like an electric current and is personified in the media celebration of bigots such as Kentucky clerk Kim Davis, who insists that her private religion gives her the public right to both deny marriage license to gays and disavow the separation of church and state. Far from being seen as an oddball outlier, Davis reflects a sizable number of religious followers who have the backing of the Republican Party.

Totalitarianism throws together authoritarian and anti-democratic forms that represent a new moment in American history. Economic fundamentalism governs increasing sectors of society, and in doing so it creates draconian policies against women, communities of color, Latinos, immigrants, workers, the elderly, and the economically disadvantaged. Marked by vast inequalities in wealth and power, it imposes massive hardships and suffering for much of the American public, and it does so with little regard for the culture of cruelty it advances. Militarization dismisses injustice by reinforcing the immediacy of armed authority and martial law over the rights and diversity inherent to civilian democracy. In this scenario, an increasing number of behaviors are criminalized, militarism feeds the punishing and incarceration state, and a kind of hyper-masculinity parades as the new model for legitimating aggression and violence in multiple spheres.

As American society moves from a culture of questioning to a culture of shouting, it restages politics and power in ways that are truly unproductive, frightening, and antidemocratic. Writing about Arendt's notion of totalitarianism, Jerome Kohn provides a commentary that contains a message for the present age, one that points to the possibility of hope triumphing over despair—a lesson that needs to be embraced at the present moment. He writes that for Arendt, "what matters is not to give oneself over to the despair of the past or the utopian hope of the future, but 'to remain wholly in the present.' Totalitarianism is the crisis of our times insofar as its demise becomes a turning point for the present world, providing us with an entirely new opportunity to realize a common world, a world that Arendt called a 'human artifice,' a place fit for habitation by all human beings."[75] If Trump is the manifestation of an emerging self-destructive totalitarianism, the movement for solidarity and change developing among a diverse range of national networks including the Black Lives Matter movement, fast food workers, environmentalists, and a range of other social justice groups, points to an alternative, diversified, and sustainable future.

Trump signifies the marshaling of self-destructive white anxiety, bigotry, and intolerance to the service of an exclusionary grid of economic, military, surveillance, police, and corporate self-interest. Rather than view Trump as an eccentric clown, perhaps it is time to portray him in a historical context connected with the West's totalitarian past, a story that needs to be publicly retold and remembered. By making such connections and telling such stories, we strengthen ourselves and spread the insurgent call to prevent contemporary manifestations from gaining further ground.

The great writer James Baldwin once said we are living in dangerous times, that the society in which we are living is "menaced from within," and that young people have to "go for broke." And while he acknowledged that "going for broke" would mean meeting the "most determined resistance," he argued that it was necessary for young people to rise up and use their energy to reclaim their right to live with dignity, justice, equity, and a sense of possibility.[76] Baldwin got it right, and so do the young people who are now taking up this challenge and, in doing so, are imagining a future free of the menace of totalitarianism that now hangs like a punishing sandstorm over our current political moment.

II.

Landscapes of Violence in Dark Times

FOUR

POISONED CITY: FLINT AND THE SPECTER OF DOMESTIC TERRORISM

In the current age of free-market forces, privatization, commodification, and deregulation, Americans are now decreasingly bound by historical memory, connecting narratives, or modes of thinking that allow them to translate private troubles into broader systemic considerations. As Irving Howe once noted, "the rhetoric of apocalypse haunts the air," accompanied by a relentless spectacle that flattens time, disconnects events, obsesses with the moment, and leaves no traces of the past, resistance, or previous totalitarian dangers.[1] The United States has become a privatized "culture of fast time,"[2] a society in which the past is erased and the future appears ominous.

Under the rule of neoliberalism, the dissolution of historical and public memory "cauterizes democracy's more radical expressions."[3] By restaging the relationship between the state and economic power, neoliberal logics frame all aspects of conduct, modes of governance, and daily existence in exclusively economic terms. Neoliberalism has sabotaged the radical repositories of memory while also subjecting the dreams of social justice and full civic participation to the one-dimensional dictates of the market. The American public's vision of a good and just society is now haunted by the demands of a consumer-obsessed social order defined by possessive individualism, instant gratification, and a growing infantilism. The only subject of any value is the one propelled by the demands of constant consumption, self-promotion, and the relentless pursuit of financial gain. The self in the age of consumerism becomes an illusory figure indifferent to either social responsibility or democratic participation and governance. In the era of Donald Trump, American politics involves forgetting civil rights, full inclusion, and the promise of democracy. There is a divorce between thought and its historical determinants, a severance of events both from each other and from the conditions that produce them.

The recent crisis over the poisoning of the water supply in Flint, Michigan, and the ways in which it has been taken up by many analysts in the mainstream media provide a classic example of how public issues have been emptied of any substance or historical understanding. This is a politics that fails to offer a comprehensive mode of analysis, one that refuses to link what is wrongly viewed as an isolated issue to a broader set of social, political, and economic factors. Under such occurrences, shared dangers are isolated and collapsed into either insulated acts of governmental incompetence, cases of misguided bureaucratic ineptitude, or unfortunate acts of individual misconduct, and other narratives of depoliticized disconnection. In this instance, there is more at work than flawed arguments or conceptual straitjackets. There is also a refusal to address a savage neoliberal politics in which state violence is used to hurt, abuse, and humiliate those populations who are vulnerable, powerless, and considered disposable. In Flint, the unimaginable has become a living nightmare as 8,657 children under six years of age have been subjected to potential lead poisoning.[4] Flint provides a tragic example of what happens to a society when democracy begins to disappear and is surpassed by a state remade in the image of a cost-cutting corporation.

What happened to the children in Flint, Michigan, represents a genuine criminal act, or even worse, a case of domestic terrorism, and those responsible should be arrested and held accountable in a court of law. As of April 21, 2016, Stephen Busch and Michael Prysby, two officials from the Michigan Department of Environmental Quality (MDEQ) were charged with "five and six counts, respectively, including misconduct in office, tampering with evidence and violation of the Michigan Safe Drinking Water Act."[5] "Flint is a crime scene," says Jesse Jackson. "It should have duct tape around it. And it is a disaster zone."[6] As Robert Thompson, a practicing pediatrician and former director of the Department of Preventive Care at Group Health in Washington State observed in a personal email to me, "As contrasted to other instances of bureaucratic malfeasance, the Flint issue to me is perhaps the worst I have seen. Lead poisoning damage to the kids in Flint is NOT something that can be reversed. Those kids' brains are forever damaged and so to me this adds up to a flat out crime. I have dealt with lead poisoning as a clinician at Johns Hopkins when I was in training. In my opinion the governor committed a criminal act and should be sentenced to a term in jail. What he did is far worse than 'bureaucratic bungling' or the like."

To morally justify military violence against foreign leaders, the U.S. often evokes the fact that "they kill their own people," as was the case for attacking Iraq and Syria. The fact that governing bodies in the United States are now clearly responsible for poisoning low-income populations in Flint forecloses such morality and reveals the "dark side of a ruthless mode governance that hints at a more threatening reality."[7] This suggests analyzing the water crisis in Flint within wider contexts of power and politics, addressing it as a form of domestic terrorism—or what Mark Levine has called in a different context "a necropolitics of the oppressed."[8]

This is a form of systemic terror instituted intentionally by different levels of government in order to realize economic gains and achieve political benefits through practices that range through assassination, extortion, incarceration, violence, intimidation, or coercion of a civilian population.[9] Some of the more notorious expressions of U.S. domestic terrorism include the lynchings of Blacks following Reconstruction; the existence of COINTELPRO, the illegal counter-intelligence program designed to disrupt social movements and resistance leaders in the 1960s and 1970s; the assassination of Black Panther Party leader Fred Hampton by the Chicago Police Department on December 4, 1969, the Philadelphia Police Department's air-to-surface bombing of the African American naturalist group MOVE in 1985, resulting in the incineration of sixty-five homes and the killing of eleven adults and five children; the use of mass surveillance and mass arrest to counter the Occupy movement, the use of extortion by the local police and courts practiced on the largely poor Black inhabitants of Ferguson, and the more recent killings of Freddie Gray and Tamir Rice by the police—to name just a few incidents.

The growing acceptance of state violence, even its normalization, can be found in repeated statements by the Republican Party presidential candidate, Donald Trump, who has voiced his support for torture, mass deportations, internment camps, beating up protesters, and punishing women who have abortions. Such policies embody what Umberto Eco once called a cult of "action for action's sake"—a term he associated with fascism. Ominously, Trump's campaign of violence has attracted a commanding number of followers, including the anti-Semitic former Ku Klux Klan leader David Duke and other white hate groups, whom Trump hesitated to disavow in the face of public criticism. But a death-dealing state can operate in less spectacular but no less lethal ways. Cost-cutting negligence, malfeasance, omissions, the withholding of social protections, and denial of civil rights can also inflict untold suffering.

Connecting the Dots: From Katrina to Flint

At first glance, the tragedies that engulfed New Orleans as a result of Hurricane Katrina and the one that rocked Flint, Michigan, as a result of a water contamination scandal, appear to have little in common. In the aftermath of Hurricane

Katrina, the world was awash in shocking images of thousands of people in flooded low-income communities, mostly people of color, stranded on rooftops, isolated on dry roads with no food, or packed into the New Orleans Superdome desperate for food, water, medical help, fresh clothes, clean bathrooms, and a place to sleep. Even more troubling were images of the bloated bodies of the dead, some floating in the flood waters, others decomposing on the streets for days, and others found in their homes and apartments.

Flint also represents a different order of terrorism and tragedy. Whereas Katrina unleashed disturbing images of dead Americans in New Orleans, Flint unleashed inconceivable reports that thousands of children had been subjected to lead poisoning because of austerity measures sanctioned by Michigan's Republican governor, Rick Snyder, and imposed by Ed Kurtz, the unelected emergency manager of Flint. Such measures based on the need for fiscal discipline deny resources to the poor and elderly while gifting banks, multinational corporations, and the ultra-rich with generous tax breaks.

The economically disadvantaged communities of color in both New Orleans and Flint share the experience of disenfranchisement, and of potential exclusion from the institutional decisions that impact their lives. They live the consequences of neoliberal policies that relegate them to zones of abandonment expunged from the realm, democratic governance and accountability. Both communities find the state at war with them—and many more like them suffer from a machinery of domestic terrorism in which state violence is visited upon impoverished populations considered defective, criminal, ungovernable, and unworthy of human rights. Such populations have recently multiplied in the United States and suffer from what Richard Sennett has called a "specter of uselessness," one that renders disposable those individuals and groups who are most vulnerable to private exploitation, expulsion, predation, and state violence.

In New Orleans, state violence took the form of a refusal by the Bush administration to financially invest in infrastructure needed to protect against floods, a decision that was as much about saving money as it was about seamless consistency with the historic continuum of savage white racism, cloaked in the discourse of austerity, and willful indifference to the needs of the powerless and underserved in communities of color. In both New Orleans and Flint, the ruin caused by the politics of disposability was quickly used to further benefit conditions for markets and profits. Austerity politics were the basis for refusing to invest in protecting New Orleans, and the destruction following Katrina was used to justify multiple forms of privatization that were politically untenable prior to the storm, including vouchers, charters, and no-bid contracts.[10] Similarly, the human-made disaster in Flint and the Republican politics of austerity formed the basis for the emergency management of the communities and schools that created the conditions for the mass water poisoning.[11]

In Flint, austerity as a weapon of race and class warfare played out in a similar way. With the imposition of unelected emergency managers in 2011, democratically elected officials were displaced in predominantly Black cities such as Detroit and Flint, and rendered powerless to influence the formation and implementation of key policy decisions. These emergency managers are the front-line shock troops that represent a new mode of authoritarian rule wrapped in the discourse of financial exigency. As the editors of *Third Coast Conspiracy* observe:

> For more than decade now, Michigan governors have been appointing so-called "emergency managers" (EMs) to run school districts and cities for which a "state of financial emergency" has been declared. These unelected administrators rule by fiat—they can override local elected officials, break union contracts, and sell off public assets and privatize public functions at will. It's not incidental that the vast majority of the people who have lived under emergency management are black. Flint, whose population was 55.6% black as of the 2010 census (in a state whose population is 14.2% black overall), was under emergency management from December 2011 to April 2015. [Moreover] it was during that period that the decision was made to stop purchasing water from Detroit and start drawing water directly from the Flint River.[12]

Rather than invest in cities such as Flint and Detroit, Republican Governor Rick Snyder decided to downsize the budgets of these predominantly Black cities. For instance, in Detroit, "Snyder's appointed manager decided to push Detroit into bankruptcy . . . and gain the necessary legal footing to obliterate pensions, social assistance, public schools and other bottom-line city structures."[13] In Flint, emergency manager Kurtz followed the austerity playbook to downsize the city's budget and put into play a water crisis of devastating proportions. Under the claim of fiscal responsibility, a number of emergency managers succeeded in privatizing the parks and garbage collection, and in conjunction with the Snyder administration aggressively pushed to privatize the water supply. Clair McClinton, a Flint resident, summed up the larger political issue well. She writes: "And that's the untold story about the problem we have here. We don't have just a water problem. We've got a democracy problem. We've got a dictatorship problem. We've got a problem of being stripped of our democracy as we've known it over the years."[14]

The backdrop to Flint's lead-poisoning scandal is the nationwide epidemic of white police violence in Black communities, the restructuring of the global economy, the deindustrialization of manufacturing cities such as Flint, and the departure of the auto industries, all of which greatly reduced the city's revenues. Yet, these oft repeated events only constitute part of the story. As Jacob Lederman points out, Flint's ongoing economic and environmental crisis is the consequence of years of destructive free-market reforms:

> According to the Michigan Municipal League, between 2003–2013, Flint lost close to 60 million

> dollars in revenue sharing from the state, tied to the sales tax, which increased over the same decade. During this period, the city cut its police force in half while violent crime doubled, from 12.2 per 1000 people in 2003, to 23.4 in 2011. Such a loss of revenue is larger than the entire 2015 Flint general fund budget. In fact, cuts to Michigan cities like Flint and Detroit have occurred as state authorities raided so-called statutory revenue sharing funds to balance their own budgets and pay for cuts in business taxes. Unlike "constitutional" revenue sharing in Michigan, state authorities could divert these resources at their discretion. It is estimated that between 2003–2013 the state withheld over $6 billion from Michigan cities. And cuts to revenue sharing increased in line with the state's political turn.[15]

These policy changes and reforms provided a rationale for the well-oiled cogs of the neoliberal machine to use calamitous budget deficits of their own design to impose severe austerity measures, gut public funding, and cut benefits for autoworkers. As General Motors relocated jobs to the South in order to increase its profits, its workforce in Flint went from 80,000 in the 1970s to its current number, 8,000. These devastating economic conditions further deteriorated under a Snyder administration that was hell-bent on imposing its Republican game plan on Michigan, with the worst effects being visited on cities consisting largely of impoverished communities of color and immigrants, most of whom were loyal to the Democratic Party. Under the harsh restrictions imposed by the Snyder administration, public services were reduced and impoverishment spread to over 40 percent of the population. Meanwhile, schools deteriorated—with many closing—grocery stores vanished, and entire neighborhoods fell into living ruins.

Through the rubric of a financial crisis, intensified by neoliberal policies aimed at destroying any vestige of the social contract and a civic culture, the Snyder administration appointed a series of emergency managers to undermine and sidestep democratic governance in a number of communities, including those of Flint. In this instance, a criminal economy produced in Flint an egregious form of environmental racism that was part of a broader business-as-usual class war that served to further impoverish already disadvantaged communities of color while diverting the skimmings to the coffers of the rich and corporations. What emerged has been a kind of economic Jim Crow politics that transformed cities such as Flint into zones of social and economic abandonment. Michael Moore sums up the practice at work in Flint succinctly:

> When Governor Snyder took office in 2011, one of the first things he did was to get a multi-billion-dollar tax break passed by the Republican legislature for the wealthy and for corporations. But with less tax revenues, that meant he had to start cutting costs. So, many things—schools, pensions,

> welfare, safe drinking water—were slashed. Then he invoked an executive privilege to take over cities (all of them majority black) by firing the mayors and city councils whom the local people had elected, and installing his cronies to act as "dictators" over these cities. Their mission? Cut services to save money so he could give the rich even more breaks. That's where the idea of switching Flint to river water came from. To save $15 million! It was easy. Suspend democracy. Cut taxes for the rich. Make the poor drink toxic river water. And everybody's happy. Except those who were poisoned in the process. All 102,000 of them. In the richest country in the world.[16]

In spite of the dire consequences of such practices, Snyder's appointed officials proceeded to promote economic policies that exacerbated Flint's crumbling infrastructure, its high levels of violence, and its corroding and underfunded public school system. Similar policies followed in Detroit, where the schools were so bad that teachers and students reported conditions frankly impossible to imagine. For instance, Wisdom Morales, a student at one of the Detroit's public schools, said the following to Amy Goodman: "I've gotten used to seeing rats everywhere. I've gotten used to seeing the dead bugs. . . . I want to be able to go to school and not have to worry about being bitten by mice, being knocked out by the gases, being cold in the rooms."[17] Julie Bosman, in the *New York Times*, further highlights the rancid conditions of Detroit's destitute schools in the following statement:

> In Kathy Aaron's decrepit public school, the heat fills the air with a moldy, rancid odor. Cockroaches, some three inches long, scuttle about until they are squashed by a student who volunteers for the task. Water drips from a leaky roof onto the gymnasium floor. "We have rodents out in the middle of the day," said Ms. Aaron, a teacher of 18 years. "Like they're coming to class." Detroit's public schools are a daily shock to the senses, run down after years of neglect and mismanagement, while failing academically and teetering on the edge of financial collapse.[18]

Under Snyder, "emergency management" laws gave authoritarian powers to unelected officials in cities where Black majorities were also the objects of devastating forms of environmental racism and economic mass destruction. As Flint's economy was hollowed out and held ransom by the financial elite, communities of color and immigrants became more vulnerable to a host of deprivations, increasingly becoming more disposable. As this happened, families found themselves steadily losing control of their material possessions as well as the sanctity of their bodies, their health, and the minimal necessities required for civilized living in a Western nation. Given these conditions, exchange value became the only value that counted, and one outcome was that state institutions and policies meant to eliminate human suffering, protect the environment, and supply social provisions were transformed into machineries of social abuse, trauma, and terror. In both cities, impoverished populations experienced a threshold of disappearance as a consequence of a systematic dismantling of the state's political machinery, regulatory agencies, and political institutions whose first priority had been to serve citizens rather than corporations and the financial elite.

This particular confluence of market-forces and right-wing politics that privileges private financial gain over community needs and public values took a drastic and dangerous turn in Flint. As a cost-saving measure, Darnell Earley, the emergency manager appointed by Snyder and in charge of Flint in April 2014, went ahead and allowed the switch of Flint's water supply from Lake Huron to the Flint River. Water from Lake Huron had been treated at the Detroit Water Plant and had supplied Flint for fifty years. The switch was done in spite of the fact that the Flint River had long been a toxic dumping ground for the automobile factories, among other industries.[19] By pumping contaminated river water to the families of Flint, the state expected to skimp about $19 million over eight years. In short, peanuts for city budgets. Congressional hearings in March 2016 revealed that "Earley received a $44,000 raise and a promotion from Governor Snyder."[20]

As part of a cost-saving effort, the Republican administration refused to employ an anti-corrosive additive used to seal the lead in the pipes and prevent the toxin from reaching people's faucets. The cost of such a measure was only "$100 a day for three months." Yet refusal to do so has directly resulted in catastrophic consequences for the communities of Flint whose children were being poisoned daily with brain-damaging contaminants.[21]

As soon as switch began in 2014, Flint residents noticed that the water appeared filthy, tasted bad, and gave off an offensive smell. Many residents who bathed in the water developed severe rashes, some lost their hair, and others experienced a range of other unhealthy symptoms. The water was so corrosive that it leached lead from the city's aging pipe infrastructure, adding to its toxicity. Soon afterward a host of problems emerged. As Amy Goodman points out:

> First, the water was infested with bacteria. Then it had cancerous chemicals called trihalomethanes, or TTHMs. A deadly outbreak of Legionnaires' disease, which is caused by a water-borne bacteria, spread throughout the city, killing 10 people. And quietly, underground, the Flint River water was corroding the city's aging pipes, poisoning the drinking water with lead, which can cause permanent developmental delays and neurological impairment, especially in children.[22]

The genesis of the Flint water crisis reveals the disturbing degree to which the political economy of neoliberalism is deeply wedded to deceit and neglect. In the early stages of the crisis, according to Daniel Dale of the *Toronto Star*, people showed up at meetings "with brown gunk from their taps. . . . LeeAnne Walter's 4-year old son, Gavin, was diagnosed with lead poisoning," and yet the Snyder administration stated repeatedly that the water was safe.[23] Dale argues that the Snyder administration poisoned the people of Flint and that "they were deceived for a year and a half,"[24] and were not only exposed to disposable waste, but found themselves treated like disposable waste as well. In October 2014, the Michigan Department of Environmental quality underplayed the crisis and blamed cold weather and aging pipes for the problems that Flint residents were experiencing. The complaints grew, and in January 2015, the "Detroit water system offered to reconnect to Flint, waiving a $4 million connection fee. Three weeks later, Flint's state-appointed emergency manager, Jerry Ambrose, declines the offer."[25]

For more than a year, the Republican Snyder administration dismissed the complaints of parents, residents, and outside health officials who insisted that the water was unsafe to drink and constituted a major health hazard. The crisis grew dire, especially for the children. The horror of this act of conscious poisoning and its effects on the Flint population, both children and adults, is echoed in the words of Melissa Mays, who was asked by Amy Goodman if she had been affected by the toxic water. She responds with a sense of utter despair and urgency:

> Well, all three of my sons are anemic now. They have bone pain every single day. They miss a lot of school because they're constantly sick. Their

> immune systems are compromised. Myself, I have seizures. I have diverticulosis now. I have to go in February 25th for a consultation on a liver biopsy. Almost every system of our bodies have been damaged. And I know that we're not the only one. I'm getting calls from people that are so sick, and they don't know what to do.[26]

The health effects of lead poisoning can impact children for their entire lives, and the financial cost can be incalculable—to say nothing of the emotional costs to families. According to David Rosner and Gerald Markowitz, "As little as a few specks of lead [when] ingested can change the course of a life. The amount of lead dust that covers a thumbnail is enough to send a child into a coma or into convulsions leading to death . . . cause IQ loss, hearing loss, or behavioral problems like attention deficit hyperactivity disorder and dyslexia."[27] According to the Centers for Disease Control (CDC), "No safe blood lead level in children has been identified."[28] The damage caused by lead poisoning is horrific and many of its side effects are not revealed when the Flint crisis is analyzed. Marian Wright Edelman points to some of the effects often neglected in the mainstream press. She writes:

> Lead causes biological and neurological damage linked to brain damage, learning disabilities, behavioral problems, developmental delays, academic failure, juvenile delinquency, high blood

> pressure and death. Pregnant women, babies, and young children are especially vulnerable because of developing child brains and nervous systems.[29]

Unmournable Bodies[30]

In spite of a number of dire warnings from a range of experts about the risks that lead poisoning poses for children, the Snyder administration refused to act even when repeated concerns were aired. Internal emails revealed that the regional office of the EPA failed to act for months after it knew Flint residents were at risk for lead poisoning. Not only did people at the EPA know in early 2015 that Flint's water was contaminated with dangerously high levels of lead, they refused to take action until January 2016. Moreover, congressional hearings revealed that interns in the office of Susan Hedman, the former regional EPA head, testified that they "had been intimidated and told not to talk publicly about the Flint water crisis."[31] Another email made public at the hearings was from Debbie Baltazar, an EPA water chief for the region that included Michigan. She stated: "I'm not so sure Flint is the community we want to go out on a limb for," code for a blatant rationale for environmental racism.[32]

It gets worse. Edelman observed: "A state-employed nurse reportedly dismissively told a Flint mother whose son was diagnosed with an elevated blood lead level: 'It is just a few IQ points. . . . It is not the end of the world.'"[33] At the same congressional hearing, Marc Edwards, an expert in municipal water quality and a professor from Virginia Tech who first broke the Flint crisis as a public health disaster stated that the EPA's reaction to the Flint crisis was "unremorseful for their role in causing this man-made disaster . . . and completely unrepentant and unable to learn from their mistakes."[34]

Needless to say, there is more at work here on the part of Michigan officials than an obstinate refusal to acknowledge scientific facts or a willingness to suspend their cruel indifference to a major crisis and take the appropriate government action. Those who complained about the water crisis and the effects it was having on the city's children and adults were met initially with a "persistent tone of scorn and derision."[35] In September 2016, Marc Edwards issued a statement indicating that the level of corrosiveness in the Flint water supply caused lead to leach into the Flint River. The Department of Environmental Quality dismissed his findings. Edwards responded later in an interview in *The Chronicle of Higher Education* with the damning charge that in "Flint the agencies paid to protect these people weren't solving the problem. They were the problem."[36]

Testifying in March 2016 at a congressional hearing on the Flint crisis, Edwards provided a harsh criticism of the regional EPA and stated: "Records show that people at the EPA knew in early 2015 that Flint's water had dangerously high lead levels. But it did not take any formal action, beyond pushing Michigan officials to do something, until January 2016."[37] When local physician Dr. Mona Hanna-Attisha reported elevated levels of lead in the blood of Flint's children, she was dismissed as a quack and "attacked for sowing hysteria."[38] When the Federal EPA warned that the state was "testing the water in a way that could profoundly understate the lead levels," they were met with silence.[39]

The *New York Times* added fuel to the fire engulfing key governmental officials by noting that "a top aide to Michigan's governor referred to people raising questions about the quality of Flint's water as an 'anti-everything group.' Other critics were accused of turning complaints about water into a 'political football.' And worrisome findings about lead by a concerned pediatrician were dismissed as 'data,' in quotes."[40] As a last straw, government officials blamed both landlords and tenants for neglecting to service lead-laden pipes that ran through most of the city.[41] What they failed to mention was that the state's attempt to save money by switching Flint's water supply from Lake Huron to the Flint River and by refusing to add an anti-corrosive chemical to the water were what caused the pipes to bleed lead. Many states have lead-laden pipes, but the water supplies are treated in order to prevent corrosion and toxic contamination.

Comparably, Katrina revealed what right-wing Republicans and Democrats never wanted the public to see: the needless suffering and deaths of residents, the elderly, the homeless, and others who were the most powerless to fight against the ravages of chronic political and economic deprivation that rendered them an ignorable drain on the system, and ultimately disposable. Flint's politicians perpetrated a different order of crime—and one more consciously malevolent—creating a generation of children with developmental disabilities for whom there will more than likely be no adequate services now, while they are children, or when they become adults. These are the populations the Republicans and some right-wing Democrats have been teaching us to disdain since the 1980s: those framed as moochers, morally lax, and undeserving of the social, political, and personal rights accorded to white middle-class and ruling elites. Both Katrina and Flint also laid bare a new kind of politics in which entire populations, even children, are considered disposable, an unnecessary burden on state coffers, and consigned to fend for themselves. In the case of Flint, children were knowingly poisoned while people who were warning the Snyder administration and local residents about the toxicity levels were derided and shamed. Also laid bare was the neoliberal mantra that government services are wasteful and that market forces can take care of everything. This is a profit-driven politics that strips government of its civic functions, worsens already massive inequality, and makes clear how a three-decades-long policy of business-as-usual social neglect fermented into lethal and malicious malfeasance.

How else to explain that while Snyder eventually admitted to the scandal, he not only tried to blame the usual suspect, inefficient government, but once again made clear that the culture of cruelty underlying his neoliberal policies is alive and well. This was evident in his refusal to discontinue charging residents extremely high bills for poisoned water and to continue sending shut-off notices to past-due accounts despite widespread condemnation. Communities of color in places like Flint and Ferguson, and countless other cities in the United States, have long been considered expendable populations, whose preventable misery has not presented ethical dilemmas for white-dominated institutions of law enforcement, criminal justice, political administration, or the economic forces that relentlessly pressure the system to favor financial elites. Social death now works in tandem with physical death as the provisions considered basic to Western civilization are taken away, regardless of the irreparable damage it may cause, even to pregnant women, children, and the elderly.

The confluence of finance, militarization, and corporate power has not only destroyed essential collective structures in support of the public good, such forces have also devastated American democracy. A society that finds it more profitable to poison children than to give them a decent life is a society at war with itself. A society that chooses to incarcerate people rather than to educate them is a society at war with itself. A society that admits economic self-interest over social responsibility as the guiding national principle is one where politics is emptied out, authoritarianism prevails, and the processes of national decomposition accelerate. Americans are now living in an age of organized forgetting, an age in which a flight from responsibility is measured in increasing acts of corruption, violence, trauma, and the struggle to survive.

Decaying schools, poisoned water, racist law enforcement, and the imposition of emergency managers on cities largely populated by impoverished communities of immigrants and people of color represent more than "the catastrophe of indifference;" there is also a chronic case of criminal impunity in which communities disadvantaged by class, color, and residency status are divorced from the grid of privilege and protection and thereby rendered voiceless, politically invisible, and criminally suspect.[42] The Flint lead-poisoning scandal is not an isolated crime. Nor is it a function of an anarchic lawlessness administered by blundering politicians and administrators. Rather, it is a lawlessness that thrives on and underwrites the power and corruption of the financial elite. Such lawlessness owes its dismal life to a failure of conscience and a politics of disposability in the service of a "political economy which has become a criminal economy."[43] Flint is symptomatic of a mode of politics and governance in which the categories of citizenship and democratic representation, once integral to a functioning polity, are no longer recognized. As a result, vast populations are subject to conditions that confer upon them the status of the living dead. Under the auspices of life-threatening austerity policies, not only are public goods defunded and the commons devalued, but the very notion of what it means to be a citizen is manipulated and redefined in terms of consumerism. At the same time, politics is hijacked by corporate power and the ultra-rich, making it "unappealing and toxic—full of ranting and posturing, emptied of intellectual seriousness, and pandering to an uneducated and manipulable electorate and a celebrity-and-scandal-hungry corporate media."[44] Nowhere has this been more repugnantly exemplified than in Donald Trump's rise to political power in the United States.

What happened in Flint is not about the failure of electoral politics, nor can it be attributed to bureaucratic mishaps or the bungling of an incompetent Republican administration. As *Third Coast Conspiracy* points out, the Flint crisis is necessarily understood through the lens of disposability, one that makes visible new modes of governance for those populations, particularly the working class, that are "rendered permanently superfluous to the needs of capital, and are expelled from the labor process, waged employment, and, increasingly, from what remains of the welfare state."[45] These are racialized populations—impoverished communities of color that are both the victims of what Michelle Alexander calls the new Jim Crow, and ones that are subjected to "the systems that orchestrate the siphoning of resources away from some populations and redirect them toward others. These systems do more than just define which lives matter and which lives don't—they materially make some lives matter by killing others more."[46]

As democratic institutions are hollowed out, powerful forms of social exclusion and homelessness organized at the intersection of race and poverty come into play, producing without apology "the most conspicuous cases of social polarization, of deepening inequality, and of rising volumes of human poverty, misery and humiliation."[47] How else to explain the criminal inaction on the part of the Republican administration in Flint once they learned that the residential drinking water was poisoning thousands of people?

Cruel Hypocrisy

A number of emails from various administration officials later revealed that Snyder had received numerous signs that the city's water was contaminated and unsafe to drink long before he had made a decision to switch back to the Detroit water system. Unfortunately, he acted in bad faith by not taking any action. A few months after the initial water switch, General Motors discovered that the water from the Flint River was causing their car parts to erode and negotiated with the state to have the water supply at the corporate offices switched back to the Detroit water system. General Motors made this revelation in October 2014, and yet it took an entire year before state authorities admitted the problem and warned people not to drink, bathe in, or cook with the contaminated water. In our current neoliberal system, corporate products get better treatment than our communities and our kids.

Similarly, a Flint hospital noticed that the water was damaging its instruments and decided to set up its own private filtering system. A local university did the same thing.[48] David Rosner and Gerald Markowitz observed that "10 months before the administration of Governor Snyder admitted that Flint's water was unsafe to drink, the state had already begun trucking water into that city and setting up water coolers next to drinking fountains in state buildings" in order for state workers to be able to drink a safe alternative to Flint's visibly filthy water.[49] At the beginning of 2015, "an Environmental Protection Agency official had notified the state about lead contamination, only to be ignored by the Snyder administration and taken off the investigation by his EPA superiors."[50]

It was only after a lead scientist from the EPA and a volunteer team of researchers from Virginia Tech University conducted a study of Flint's water supply and concluded that it was unsafe that the Snyder administration came clean about the poisoned water supply.[51] They were met with resistance. The Michigan Department of Environmental Quality had tried to discredit the research findings of the group. As one of the volunteers, Siddhartha Roy, pointed out in an interview, "We were surprised and shocked to see [the government] downplaying the effects of lead in water, ridiculing the results that all of us had released, and even questioning the results of a local Flint pediatrician. They tried to discredit us researchers."[52] But it was too late. The scientists may have been vindicated, but not before close to 9,000 children under the age of 6 had been poisoned. A disproportionate number of them are children of color.

Historical Memory and the Politics of Disappearance

These acts of state-sponsored violence have reinforced the claim by the Black Lives Matter movement that Snyder's actions represent a racist act, that it is part of "systemic, structurally based brutality," and that "the water crisis would never have happened in more affluent, white communities like Grand Rapids or Grosse Pointe."[53] Not only do impoverished communities of color suffer the most from such practices of environmental racism, but economically disadvantaged children of color in particular suffer needlessly, not just in Flint, but all over the United States. This is a crisis that rarely receives national attention because most of the children it impacts live in marginalized communities. Some health experts have called lead poisoning a form of "state-sponsored child abuse" and a "silent epidemic in America." As Nicholas Kristof makes clear:

> In Flint, 4.9 percent of children tested for lead turned out to have elevated levels. That's inexcusable. But in 2014 in New York State outside of New York City, the figure was 6.7 percent. In Pennsylvania, 8.5 percent. On the west side of Detroit, one-fifth of the children tested in 2014 had lead poisoning. In Iowa for 2012, the most recent year available, an astonishing 32 percent of children tested had elevated lead levels. (I calculated most of these numbers from C.D.C. data.). Across America, 535,000 children ages 1 through 5 suffer lead poisoning, by C.D.C. estimates. "We are indeed all Flint," says Dr. Philip Landrigan, a professor of preventive medicine at the Icahn School of Medicine at Mount Sinai. "Lead poisoning continues to be a silent epidemic in the United States."[54]

A wide-ranging multi-part *USA Today* investigation in March 2016 revealed that lead poisoning constitutes a serious crisis that extends far beyond Flint. According to reporters Alison Young and Mark Nichols, in "almost 2,000 additional water systems spanning all 50 states . . . testing has shown excessive levels of lead contamination over the past four years. The water systems . . . collectively supply water to 6 million people. About 350 of those systems provide drinking water to schools or day cares. [Moreover] at least 180 of the water systems failed to notify consumers about the high lead levels as federal rules require."[55] This is a preventable national crisis resulting from cost-cutting austerity measures imposed by both Republicans and Democrats. Congress, for instance, in 2012 slashed funding for lead programs at the Centers for Disease Control by 93 percent; in addition, lobbyists for the chemical industry have worked assiduously to prevent their corporate clients from being regulated.

America has a long economic history of recklessly plundering the environment, profiting from poisonous consumer goods such as lead paint, lead gasoline, and addictive toxins such as nicotine and alcohol. Moreover, it has an equally long history of scientists both studying and calling for prevention, but too often unsuccessful in their efforts to fight legions of corporate lobbyists who keep laws in place that allow businesses to continue to destroy the ecosystem. Contemporary lead poisoning is not simply about a failure of governance, deregulation, and corporate malfeasance, however important; it is also the toxic by-product of a form of predatory political economy that places financial self-interest above life-and-death environmental and human consequences.[56]

As Rosner and Markowitz argue, the poisoning of African American and Latino children represents a broader political and economic crisis fed by a "mix of racism and corporate greed that have put lead and other pollutants into millions of homes in the United States."[57] But pointing to a mix of bigotry and corporate greed does not tell the entire story either about the crisis in Flint or the broader crisis of environmental racism. And solutions demand more than fixing the nation's infrastructure, replacing the country's lead pipes, curbing the power of polluting corporations, or publicizing what amounts to a widespread public health crisis.[58] Flint, like Ferguson, signals a much broader deterioration of social justice, agency, memory, and democracy occurring in communities across the country, and reveals how corporate gentrification and disinvestment from society leads to political pathologies, mass suffering, and authoritarianism.

The Politics of Domestic Terrorism

Snyder's decision to keep quiet for over a year about the contaminated water was comparable in my view to an act of domestic terrorism—a form of institutional abuse and violence perpetrated by the state against powerless families. Historical memory might serve us well here. After the 9/11 attacks in 2001, various environmental protection and intelligence agencies warned that "water supplied to U.S. communities is potentially vulnerable to terrorist attacks . . . The possibility of attack is of considerable concern [and] these agents . . . inserted at a critical point in the system . . . could cause a larger number of casualties."[59] If we expand the definition of terrorism to include instances in which the state inflicts deliberate suffering on its own populations—a central aspect of Native Americans' ignored historical narrative—the poisoning of Flint's water supply represents a form of domestic terrorism. As Frank Joyce observes, "in the annals of institutional white racism," U.S. hate groups have called for poisoning the water supply in cities largely inhabited by Blacks. He writes:

> A 2012 editorial by *Detroit News* Editor Nolan Finley, Michigan's white supremacy spokesman in chief, is worth noting. His nasty little "tongue-in-cheek" editorial is headlined, *Michigan Is Breeding Poverty*. It begins, "Since the national attention is on birth control, here's my idea: If we want to fight poverty, reduce violent crime and bring down our embarrassing drop-out rate, we should swap contraceptives for fluoride in Michigan's drinking water."[60]

Reverend William J. Barber is right in arguing that we need a new language for understanding and protecting ourselves from terrorism. Not only is terror one of America's chief exports, it is also as part of a long legacy that extends from whites' genocide of indigenous peoples and enslavement of people of color to "racist police shootings of unarmed black adults and youth and males and females in Chicago . . . Charlotte, and New York."[61]

What is happening in Flint is an expression of a broader narrative and set of policies and values bound up with a politics of disposability that has become one of the distinctive features of neoliberal capitalism. The politics of disposability embodies a particularly savage violence that marks some people, such as Mexican immigrants, as disposable in both material and symbolic terms, authorizing "the lives of some while disallowing the lives of others."[62] João Biehl observes that disposability thrives on the energies of the dead and works through "a machinery of inscriptions and invisibility [producing] zones of abandonment [that] accelerate the death of the unwanted."[63]

Disposability has a long history in the United States, but it has taken on a greater significance under neoliberalism and has become an organizing principle of the authoritarian state, one that has intensified and expanded the dynamics of racialized class warfare. Privatization, commodification, and deregulation are now merged with what historian David Harvey has called the process of "accumulation by dispossession."[64] Extracting real estate, capital, labor, time, and profits from the impoverished and powerless are now central features of financial predation and austerity, key methods for the wealthy to continue to hoard profits during times of recession. How else to interpret the right-wing call to impose higher tax rates on the economically disadvantaged while subsidizing tax breaks for mega-corporations and the ultra-rich? How else to understand right-wing tolerance for CEOs making 350 times as much as their workers while 250,000 people die each year from poverty—more than from heart attacks, strokes, and lung cancer combined.

Disposability and preventable human suffering now engulf large swaths of American communities, often pushing them into situations that are not merely degrading but also life-threatening. The top .01 percent of Americans, approximately 16,000 of the richest families, "now own the same as the total wealth of 256,000,000 people."[65] Paul Buchheit rightly labels the ultra-rich in the United States "the real terrorists," for it is the ultra-rich who buy off the politicians and lobbyists responsible for making economically disadvantaged children disposable; it is the ultra-rich who are responsible for gutting the welfare state; it is the ultra-rich who are responsible for tweaked tax laws that permit corporations to stash wealth in offshore accounts; it is the ultra-rich who are responsible for corrupting politics, for militarizing the police, and for producing a culture of surveillance and war. In addition, it is the ultra-rich—like the Koch brothers—who fund right-wing front groups that are increasingly fascistic, groups that stoke hate, racism, militarism, Islamophobia, ignorance, xenophobia.[66] War and terror as a form of state violence are part of the regime of cruelty let loose upon the children and adults in Flint, revealing all too clearly how in an authoritarian state, officials' impunity from social justice becomes normalized, without apology.

What the Flint catastrophe reveals is a survival-of-the-fittest ethic that replaces any reasonable notion of solidarity, social responsibility, and compassion for the Other. Flint makes clear that rather than considering the lives of Black children just as sacred as those of white kids, our current system considers harming them defensible. Chris Hedges concurs that "the crisis in Flint is far more ominous than lead-contaminated water. It is symptomatic of the collapse of our democracy. Corporate power is not held accountable for its crimes. Everything is up for sale, including children."[67] Cities like Flint and Ferguson hold a mirror to the fact that America is indeed at war with itself, for they reveal the civilian casualties of racist class war—the people, families, and whole communities whose existential struggle is to convince the rest of the country, and the world, that *their lives matter too*. Under a regime of neoliberalism, impoverished communities are not only increasingly defunded and abandoned, they are under siege, and their modes of resistance have been cauterized, subject to criminalization, harassment, surveillance, and police violence.

As we have learned from the scandalous condition of the public schools in Detroit and many other collapsing public institutions in the United States, the victims are mostly the children who are forced to spend their days in economically ravaged schools and communities, and live in environments contaminated with health-compromising toxins. The characteristics of this wartime regime are all around us: the domination of financial self-interest, the elimination of social safety nets, the criminalization of communities of color and the economically disadvantaged, the impunity of police violence, the internalization of the Terror Wars and its invasive surveillance machine, the selling off of public goods to private and corporate interests, increasing debt, the continued impoverishment of larger segments of the population, the relentless perpetration of environmental racism, and growing unemployment for large numbers of young people.

At work here are systemic attempts to eliminate public spheres—institutions whose first allegiance is to the noncommercial values of the common good rather than to the manipulation of every human activity into an opportunity for profitable extraction. But there is more. Neoliberal capitalism thrives on producing subjects, identities, values, and social relations that cohere with the imperatives of the market, and in doing so it undermines the public's capacity for democracy. It works through a false language and logic of common sense that treats people as customers of corporate-offered choices. It works through a vocabulary and ideological scaffolding in which individuals are "enjoined to become consumers rather than workers," customers rather than citizens.[68] It celebrates self-interest in order to construct commercial images of ourselves and our relationship to the larger world, further depoliticizing the polity. In the process, the system indoctrinates all who come in contact with its media, entertainment, products, and financial processes to accept that they have to face the world alone and that all relationships are subordinated to self-promotion, self-interest, and money.

A small group of ultra-wealthy people now dominate all aspects of American life, and relentlessly pursue their own self-interests through the coded language of economic growth and national security. In the process, everyone else is forced to witness the ecological assault on the planet, the impunity of corporate and police crime, the elevation of greed, and growing authoritarianism, that have led to forms of mass destruction and degradation that are add odds not just with acceptable notions of democracy and human rights, but with acceptable notions of Western Civilization. America is at war with itself, and cities like Flint and Ferguson are just two of countless places where this is evident. Such a war announces the death of politics as a practice of democracy in the United States. As Jean and John Comaroff observe:

> [T]here is a strong argument to be made that neoliberal capitalism in its millennial moment, portends the death of politics by hiding its own ideological underpinnings in the dictates of economic efficiency: in the fetishism of the free market, in the inexorable, expanding needs of business, in the imperatives of science and technology. Or, if it does not conduce to the death of politics, it tends to reduce them to the pursuit of pure interest, individual or collective.[69]

The policy decisions that led to the poisoning of Flint point to the disintegration of public values, the hardening of culture, and the emergence of a kind of self-righteous brutalism that accepts the chronic suffering of others as a natural expense of a free market system. What Flint exemplifies is that the United States is awash in a culture of cruelty fueled by a pathological disdain for community, public values, and the common good, all of which readily capitulate to the characteristics assigned to warfare and terrorism. In such settings, public and historical memory withers, only to be matched by "a weakening of democratic pressures, a growing inability to act politically, [and] a massive exit from politics and from responsible citizenship."[70] Rather than inform the social imagination, memory under the reign of neoliberalism has become an obstacle to power, a liability that is constantly under assault by the anti-public intellectuals and cultural apparatuses that fuel what I have called the disimagination machines now dominating American culture.[71]

Memory must once again become the contested activity of self-criticism, renewal, and collective struggle. Resistance is no longer simply an option. The promise of shared rule has been eclipsed and given way to the promise of a large stock portfolio for some and the despair and anxiety of facing daily the challenge of simply trying to survive for hundreds of millions more. One consequence is that a market economy expands into a market society, making it easier to normalize the notion that capitalism and everyday life are inseparable. As authoritarian power becomes more concentrated, it pushes democracy into a twilight existence where corporate domination and militarization become more menacing, and where organized and collective resistance become an urgent necessity.

Flint reveals the omissions, lies, and deceptions that thrive in such a twilight, and provides an opening to harness the increasing sense of injustice, inequality, and moral outrage, and mobilize it strategically through insurgent forms of pedagogy and politics. Doing so is a crucial part of a sustained struggle to re-democratize the economy and society. Flint is a wake-up call to make the moral poverty of power both visible and accountable. Moral outrage over the poisoning of the children and adults of Flint must draw upon history to make visible the long list of acts of violence and domestic terrorism that have come to mark the last three decades of neoliberal governance and corruption. Flint speaks to both a moral crisis and a political crisis of legitimation.

Democracy has lost its ability to breathe and must be brought back to life. The political scandal of Flint provides a space of intervention, and we are seeing glimpses of it in the reaction of youth of color all over the United States who are organizing to connect acts of violence to widespread structural abuse and ideological motivations. Flint offers us a time of reflection, and a recognition that with shared convictions, hopes, and collective struggle, history can be ruptured and opened to new possibilities.

Flint calls out for resistance not only socially and politically, but economically. The need has never been greater for an alternative to a predatory financial system whose means and ends are not only completely divorced from "the general welfare of the population," but are used to discipline and punish both the larger public and its most powerless populations.[72] Today we are witnessing a new kind of fidelity to a distinctively radical politics. What young, progressive, movement-oriented young people are making clear is that economics cannot drive politics, violence cannot be the organizing principle of the state, and markets cannot define the present and future.[73]

There has never been a more important time to rethink the meaning of politics, justice, struggle, collective action, and the development of new political parties and social movements. The Flint crisis demands a new language for nascent modes of creative long-term resistance, a wider understanding of politics, and a new urgency to develop types of collective struggle rooted in more diverse social formations. Americans need a new discourse to resuscitate historical memories and methods of resistance to address the connections between the escalating destabilization of Earth's biosphere, impoverishment, inequality, police violence, mass incarceration, corporate crime, and the poisoning of low-income communities.

But most importantly, if the ideals and practices of democratic governance are not to be lost, educators, artists, intellectuals, young people, and emerging political formations such as the Black Lives Matter and Prison Abolition movements need to continue producing the critical formative cultures capable of building new social, collective, and political institutions that can both fight against the impending authoritarianism in the United States and imagine a society in which democracy is viewed no longer as a remnant of the past, but as an ideal worthy of continuous struggle.

FIVE

APPETITE FOR DESTRUCTION: AMERICA'S OBSESSION WITH GUNS

On October 1, 2015, nine people were killed and seven wounded in a mass shooting at a community college in Roseburg, Oregon. Two months later there was another mass shooting that left fourteen people dead and more than twenty wounded in San Bernardino, California. Mass shootings have become routine in the United States and speak to a society that lives by violence while relying on it as a tool to feed the coffers of the merchants of death. Violence runs through American society like an electric current, offering instant pleasure from all markets of commercial entertainment, whether it be Hollywood, TV, or video game products that glorify killing.

At a policy level, violence drives a gargantuan arms industry and a militaristic foreign policy, and is increasingly the punishing state's major tool to enforce its hyped-up brand of domestic terrorism, especially against immigrants and people of color. The United States is utterly wedded to a neoliberal culture in which cruelty is viewed as a virtue, while mass incarceration is treated as the default welfare program and chief mechanism to "institutionalize obedience."[1] At the same time, dog-eat-dog competition replaces any notion of solidarity, and a transcendental sense of self-interest pushes society into the abyss of depoliticization and mindless consumerism. All of these forces coalesce in new modes of authoritarianism that re-order a society saturated in state violence, daily gun massacres, racism, fear, militarism, bigotry, and massive inequities in wealth and power.

According to the *New York Times*, the United States currently endures one gun massacre per day, a trend that has been consistent for decades.[2] Such shootings are more than another tragic expression of unchecked violence in the United States, they are symptomatic of a society engulfed in fear, militarism, and a growing disdain for human life. Sadly, these shootings are not isolated incidents: "The United States sees an average of 92 gun deaths per day—and more preschoolers are shot dead each year than police officers are killed in the line of duty."[3] Given the bloodbath that goes hand in hand with U.S. gun culture, what is under-discussed is the scope and extent of the gun violence impacting children, their families, and their communities. For example, over a recent three-year period, on average, one child under 12 years old was killed every other day by a firearm, which amounts to 555 children slaughtered by gunfire in the United States over a three-year period. Gun violence does not spare the youngest of children. The *New York Times* reported that during one week in April 2016, four toddlers who had access to guns killed themselves and one two-year-old in Milwaukee shot her mother after a gun slid out from under the driver's seat. In what can only be described as a statistic that speaks to an insane level of preventable bloodshed, "shootings by preschoolers [are] happening at a pace of about two per week." These are shootings by children so young they can barely speak or tie their shoelaces.[4]

An even more atrocious statistic was noted in data provided by the Centers for Disease Control and Prevention (CDC), which stated that "2,525 children and teens died by gunfire in [the United States] in 2014; one child or teen death every 3 hours and 28 minutes, nearly 7 a day, 48 a week."[5] Such figures indicate that America is at war with itself on multiple levels, and that our children are increasingly forced to live in theaters of violence, injury, terror, and trauma. In this scenario, the gun business, gun culture, and the insane political lobby that advances them, give more support to shooters than to young people and life itself.

The predominance of a relatively unchecked gun culture and a politically obscene culture of violence is particularly evident in the power of the gun lobby to successfully pressure the passage of legislation in eight states that allows students and faculty to carry concealed weapons "into classrooms, dormitories and other buildings" on college campuses.[6] In spite of the rash of recent shootings on university campuses, Texas lawmakers, for instance, passed one such "campus carry bill" taking effect in August 2016. To add insult to injury, Texas also passed an "open carry bill" that allows registered gun owners to carry their guns openly in public. Such laws not only reflect "the seemingly limitless legislative clout of gun interests," but also a rather deranged return to the violence-laden culture of the "Wild West." As in the past, individuals will be allowed to walk the streets while openly packing heat, as a measure of their love of guns and their reliance upon a quick resort to lethal violence should a situation call for bloodshed.

This return to the deadly practices of the "Wild West" is neither a matter of individual choice nor some far-fetched, yet allegedly legitimate, appeal to the Second Amendment. On the contrary, mass violence in America has to be placed within a broader historical, economic, and political context in order to understand the totality of forces that create it.[7] Focusing merely on the mass shootings, or the passing of potentially dangerous gun legislation, does not get to the roots of America's love affair with violence and the ideologies and criminogenic institutions that produce it. Violence has a long and incontrovertible history in America.[8] As Angela Davis reminds us, "a broader way of thinking about such [violence] would require . . . a fuller understanding of . . . its historical context, and would require us to ask questions about the way our lives today bear the historical imprint of earlier eras," such as the brutal murder of Emmett Till by white racists and the 1963 terrorist bombing of a church in Birmingham, Alabama, carried out by four known Ku Klux Klansmen and segregationists.[9] Atrocious as that act was, it was far from an exception. In her autobiography, Angela Davis states that white terrorists attacked Black families so frequently where she lived that her neighborhood was referred to as "Dynamite Hill."[10]

Imperial policies that promote aggression all across the

globe are now matched by increasing levels of lawlessness and state repression, all of which mutually fuel each other. On the home front, civil society is degenerating into a military organization, a space of domestic terrorism and war-like practices, organized primarily for purposes of social control, state violence, and surveillance. For instance, as Steve Martinot observes, the police now use their discourse of command and power to criminalize behavior and create a culture of intimidation in which militaristic principles replace legal standards. He also points out that in addition, their use of military weapons and surveillance tools furthers the drift toward a permanent martial-law mentality that consolidates authoritarianism over a rule of law centered on democracy, fairness, and social justice. Martinot writes:

> This suggests that there is an institutional insecurity that seeks to cover itself through social control, for which individual interactions with the police are the means. Indeed, with their command position over people, the cops act out this insecurity by criminalizing individuals in advance. No legal principle need be involved. There is only the militarist principle. When the pregnant woman steps away from the cop, she is breaking no law. To force her to ground and handcuff her is far from anything intended by the principle of due process in the Constitution. The Constitution provided for law enforcement, but not for police impunity. When police shoot a fleeing subject and claim

> they are acting in self-defense (i.e. threatened), it is not their person but the command and control principle that is threatened. To defend that control through assault or murderous action against a disobedient person implies that the cop's own identity is wholly immersed in its paradigm. There is nothing psychological about this. Self-worth or insecurity is not the issue. There is only the military ethic of power, imposed on civil society through an assumption of impunity. It is the ethos of democracy, of human self-respect, that is the threat.[11]

Violence feeds on corporate-controlled disimagination machines that celebrate it as a sport while upping the pleasure quotient for the public. Americans do not merely witness violence, they also pay to be entertained by it. This kind of toxic irrationality and lure of bloodshed is mimicked in America's aggressive foreign policy, in the sanctioning of state torture, and in the gruesome killings of civilians by drones. As David L. Clark pointed out to me in a private email correspondence, "bombing make-believe countries is not a symptom of muddled confusion but, quite to the contrary, a sign of unerring precision. It describes the desire to militarize nothing less than the imagination and to target the minutiae of our dreams." State repression, unbridled self-interest, empty consumerism, and an expansive militarism have become the organizing principles of American society, producing an indifference to the common good, compassion, a concern for others, and equality. As the public collapses into the individualized values of a banal consumer culture and the lure of private possessions, American society flirts with forms of irrationality that are at the heart of everyday aggression and the withering of public life.

Americans love violence. In part, this is borne out by Donald Trump's appeal to aggression throughout his campaign and the popularity he mobilizes with his calls to fisticuffs and incitements to physical abuse. But Trump is only symptomatic of a Republican Party that has nurtured resentment among white voters against "those long shunted to the margins, whether by virtue of race, religion, or gender."[12] Such aggression is reinforced by a history of "school shootings and gang warfare, police killings of unarmed civilians, open-carry laws, . . . assassinations and assassination attempts," and a country immersed in "entertainment habits" in which many Americans find "diversion in murder and mayhem."[13] All aspects of everyday life extending from movies and video games to police encounters with communities of color, to the rhetoric used against immigrants, appear to "drip with blood."[14] At the same time, cruel policies that produce economic dislocations, the elimination of crucial social provisions, and the collapse of welfare take their toll in the form of substance abuse, crumbling marriages, the elimination of basic health services, extensive periods of unemployment, and increasing death rates not just for those on the bottom of the economic ladder but also for middle-aged Americans. This is a kind of silent violence that goes unnoticed but has a profound effect in fueling a country at war with its own citizens.

America is at war with itself, and wartime values no longer suggest a pathological entanglement with a kind of mad irrationality or danger. On the contrary, they have become normalized. For instance, the United States government is willing to lock down a major city such as Boston in order to search for terrorists, but refuses to pass bills for gun control that would significantly lower the number of Americans who are killed or maimed each year as a result of gun assaults. As Michael Cohen observes, it is truly a symptom of irrationality when politicians can lose their heads over the threat of terrorism, even sacrificing civil liberties, but ignore the fact that "30,000 Americans die in gun violence every year (compared to the 17 who died [in 2012] in terrorist attacks."[15] As the specter of terrorism is used by the American government to consolidate an increasingly invasive surveillance state, suspend civil liberties, and advance the normalization of authoritarianism, the fear of personal and collective violence has no rational bearing on addressing the morbid acceleration of gun-related and other forms of unnecessary violence in the United States. In fact, the fear of terrorism appears to fuel, recuperate, and expand a toxic culture of violence produced, in part, by the booming gun and weaponry market.

Corporations are enriched by America's fascination with guns and violence, and directly market a wide range of entertainment products that suggest a false sense of power and security. In this logic one not only kills terrorists with drones, but also makes sure that patriotic Americans are individually armed so they can be ready when the enemy reaches their neighborhood. "If you see something, say something," may be the official state line posted in urban subways and buses, but the implicit market line is "If you see something, be prepared to shoot something."

Rather than conduct national debate that would limit consumer gun production and ownership, various states increase its likelihood by passing laws that allow "guns at places from bars to houses of worship."[16] Florida's "Stand Your Ground" law, based on the notion that one should shoot first and ask questions later, demonstrates that America is a nation at war with itself on multiple levels. This obsession with guns and violence has produced a pathology that reaches the highest levels of government and serves to further consolidate authoritarian forces. For example, the U.S. government's warfare state is propelled by a military-industrial complex that cannot spend enough on weapons of death and mass destruction. War planes such as the F-35 Joint Strike Fighter cost up to $228 million each—an obscene amount of taxpayer money—and are plagued by mechanical problems, and yet are supported by the military and defense establishment. As Gabriel Kolko observes, such war-like behaviors "reflect a pathology and culture that is expressed in spending more money regardless"[17] of how it contributes to running up the debt or, for that matter, thrives on "the energies of the dead."[18] Militarism provides more ideological support for policies that protect gun owners and sellers rather than ones that protect children. The Children's Defense Fund is right in asking, "Where is our anti-war movement here at home? Why does a nation with the largest military budget in the world refuse to protect its children from relentless gun violence and terrorism at home? No external enemy ever killed thousands of children in their neighborhoods, streets and schools year in and year out."[19]

There is a not-so-hidden structure of politics at work in this type of sanctioned irrationality. Advocating for gun rights provides a convenient discourse for ignoring a "harsh neoliberal corporate-state order that routinely generates pervasive material suffering, social dislocation, and psychological despair—worsening conditions that ensure violence in its many expressions."[20] American society is driven by unrestrained market values in which economic actions and financial exchanges are divorced from social costs, further undermining any sense of social responsibility. In addition, a massive military-industrial-surveillance-complex, fueled by the Terror Wars, along with America's insatiable *Appetite for Destruction* (to quote the title of the 1987 hit Guns N' Roses album that has sold tens of million of copies worldwide) as entertainment further normalizes the massacres that have been occurring on a daily basis for decades in the United States. American politicians now attempt to govern the effects of systemic violence while ignoring its underlying causes. In this case, a society inundated in violence gains credence when its political leaders seem to have given up on the notions of the common good, social justice, and equality.

In the face of a one-massacre-per-day average, the public relations disimagination machine kicks into overdrive, claiming that guns are not the problem, and that the causes of such crime can be largely attributed to the mentally unfit.

But this is not the case. Vanderbilt University researchers, Dr. Jonathan Metzl and Kenneth T. MacLeish, publishing in the *American Journal of Public Health*, observe:

> Fewer than 6 percent of the 120,000 gun-related killings in the United States between 2001 and 2010 were perpetrated by people diagnosed with mental illness. Our research finds that across the board, the mentally ill are 60 to 120 percent more likely than the average person to be the victims of violent crime rather than the perpetrators. . . . There are 32,000 gun deaths in the United States on average every year, and people are far more likely to be shot by relatives, friends or acquaintances than they are by lone violent psychopaths.[21]

It may not be an exaggeration to claim that the U.S. government has blood on its hands because of the refusal of Congress to rein in a gun lobby that produces a growing militarism that sanctions a love affair with the unbridled corporate institutions, financial interests, and mass-produced cultures of violence. The Oregon community college shooting was the forty-first school shooting in 2015, and there have been 142 incidents of violence on school properties since 2012. Yet, violence continues unchecked while politicians beholden to the industry refuse to enact legislation to curb the proliferation of guns, refuse to pass legislation to compel background checks (which 88 percent of the American people support), and even refuse to ban consumer access to military-grade assault rifles. In part, politicians' refusal is due to the fact that they receive a torrent of donations from gun lobbyists who inject huge amounts of cash into their campaigns. For example, in 2015, the gun lobby spent $5,697,429 while those supporting gun control paid out $867,601. In an op-ed in the *New York Times* Gabrielle Giffords pointed out that in the 2012 election cycle the National Rifle Association (NRA) "spent around $25 million on contributions, lobbying and outside spending."[22] Money does more than corrupt politics, it also is responsible for people being shot, killed, and terrorized.

Many Americans are obsessed with owning guns, and corporations cash in on the obsession. Nearly 300 million firearms are known to be in the possession of Americans. Among these millions of guns are powerful weapons such as 9mm Glock semi-automatic pistols, AR15 assault rifles, and even military-grade sniper rifles. Collective anger, frustration, anxiety, and resentment increasingly characterize a society in which people are out of work, young people cannot imagine a decent future, everyday behaviors are criminalized, income inequality is worsening, and the police are viewed as occupying armies. This is not only a recipe for both random violence and mass shootings; it makes such acts appear routine and commonplace.

Fear has become a public relations strategy used by both the national security state and the gun business. When you live in a country where you are constantly exposed to views that the government is an enemy and that nobody can be trusted, and where a discourse of intolerance, particularly against people of color, immigrants, and social justice advocates, spews out daily from thousands of right-wing radio stations and major TV networks, a climate of anxiety and fear pushes people right into the gun stores, just as it pushes them into the supermarkets before a big snowstorm or hurricane. In such circumstances, genuine fears and concerns for safety are undermined. These include the fear of impoverishment, lack of meaningful employment, the absence of decent health care, poor schools, police violence, and the militarization of society, all of which further legitimize and fuel the machinery of insecurity, violence, and death. Fear degenerates into willful ignorance while any semblance of rationality is erased, especially around the logic of gun control. As Adam Gopnik observes:

> Gun control ends gun violence as surely an antibiotics end bacterial infections, as surely as vaccines end childhood measles—not perfectly and in every case, but overwhelmingly and everywhere that it's been taken seriously and tried at length. These lives can be saved. Kids continue to die en-masse because one political party won't allow that to change, and the party won't allow it to change because of the irrational and often paranoid fixations that make the massacre of students and children an acceptable cost of fetishizing guns.[23]

President Obama is right in stating that the violence we see in the United States is "a political choice we make."

While he takes aim at the gun lobby, especially the National Rifle Association, what Obama fails to address is that extreme violence is systemic in American society and has become the foundation of politics, and therefore must be understood within a broader historical, economic, cultural, and sociological context. To be precise, politics has become an extension of violence driven by a culture of fear, cruelty, and hatred justified by the politicians whose services are bought by industry lobbyists. Moreover, violence has long been a source for a wide variety of profitable entertainment products ranging from film, TV, and video games to shooting ranges and sport hunting.

Weapon industries undermine American democracy, and their influence speaks to a deeper political and ethical corruption in the United States. As Rich Broderick insists, American society "embraces a soulless free-market idolatry in which the value of everything, including human beings, is determined by the bottom line," and in doing so, this market fundamentalism perpetuates a theater of cruelty fed by an echo chamber "of paranoia, racism, and apocalyptic fantasies rampant in the gun culture."[24] The lesson here is that the culture of violence cannot be abstracted from the violence of business.

Sick as it sounds, shooting children in schools, in the streets, in jails, in detention centers, and other places has become something of a national pastime. One wonders how many innocent children have to die in the United States before it becomes clear that the revenue made by the $13.5 billion gun industry, with a $1.5 billion profit, is fueling a national bloodbath by using lobbyists to pay off politicians, wage a mammoth propaganda campaign, and induct young children into the culture of violence.[25] What is clear is that as more guns find their way into the hands of more people, a savage killing machine is unleashed that targets the most vulnerable, the economically disadvantaged, and communities of color.

The widespread availability of guns is responsible for the shooting and killing of children and adults in Chicago, Boston, Ferguson, New York City, and other major cities. The Law Center to Prevent Gun Violence reports that "in 2010, guns took the lives of 31,076 Americans in homicides, suicides and unintentional shootings. This is the equivalent of more than 85 deaths each day and more than three deaths each hour. [In addition], 73,505 Americans were treated in hospital emergency departments for non-fatal gunshot wounds in 2010."[26] It is heartbreaking to contemplate the almost 30,000 young people killed in a ten-year period, which amounts to "nearly 3,000 kids shot to death in a typical year."[27] According to a Carnegie-Knight News21 investigation:

> For every U.S. soldier killed in Afghanistan during 11 years of war, at least 13 children were shot and killed in America. More than 450 kids didn't make it to kindergarten. Another 2,700 or more were killed by a firearm before they could sit behind the wheel of a car. Every day, on average, seven children were shot dead. A News21 investigation of child and youth deaths in America between 2002

> and 2012 found that at least 28,000 children and teens 19 years old and younger were killed with guns. Teenagers between the ages of 15 and 19 made up over two-thirds of all youth gun deaths in America.[28]

Even worse, the firearms industry is pouring millions into marketing campaigns designed to interest children in guns at an early age. Reporting on such efforts for the *New York Times*, Mike McIntire writes:

> The industry's strategies include giving firearms, ammunition and cash to youth groups; weakening state restrictions on hunting by young children; marketing an affordable military-style rifle for "junior shooters" and sponsoring semiautomatic-handgun competitions for youths; and developing a target-shooting video game that promotes brand-name weapons, with links to the Web sites of their makers. . . . Newer initiatives by other organizations go further, seeking to introduce children to high-powered rifles and handguns while invoking the same rationale of those older, more traditional programs: that firearms can teach "life skills" like responsibility, ethics and citizenship.[29]

As the move from a welfare state to a warfare state accelerates, violence and the impunity of authorities become normalized. America's moral compass and its highest democratic ideals have begun to wither, and the institutions that were once designed to "protect and serve" people now increasingly serve to suppress them. Gun laws matter, social responsibility matters, and a government responsive to its people matters, especially when it comes to limiting the effects of a mercenary gun culture. But more has to be done. The dominance of gun lobbyists must end; the reign of money-controlled politics must end; the proliferation of high levels of violence in popular culture and the ongoing militarization of American society must end. At the same time it is crucial, as those in the Black Lives Matter movement insist, that Americans refuse to endorse the kind of gun control that criminalizes young people of color.

"Moderate" calls for reining in gun culture do not go far enough, because they fail to address the roots of the violence causing so much carnage in the United States, especially among children and teens. For example, Hilary Clinton's much publicized call for controlling the gun lobby and for background checks, however well intentioned, has nothing to say about the perpetration of violence by the federal government, the financial elites, the defense industries, or an economy that is built on corruption and class war. Moreover, none of the calls to eliminate gun violence in the United States link it to the racial caste system and the fact that bullets hit more victims in communities of color than in white ones. More specifically, the call for gun rights also conveniently ignores criticizing a popular culture and corporate-controlled media that use violence to attract viewers, increase advertising revenue, and produce highly profitable products that adrenalize kids by giving them a point-of-view experience of slaughtering people.

While it would be wrong to suggest that the violence that saturates commercial entertainment directly causes violence in the larger society, it is arguable that such violence not only produces an insensitivity to real-life suffering but also functions to normalize violence both as a source of pleasure and as a practice for reflexively addressing social problems. When young people and others begin to believe that a world of aggression, vengeance, and intimidation is the only world they inhabit, the culture and practice of real-life violence is more difficult to scrutinize, resist, and transform. Many critics have argued that a commercial culture that endlessly markets killing runs the risk of blurring the line between the world of fantasies and the world we live in. What such critics often miss is that when violence is celebrated in its myriad registers and platforms in a society, even though it lacks any sense of rationality, a formative culture can begin to give rise to forms of fascism. A culture that thrives on violence runs the risk of losing its capacity to separate politics from violence. In addition, the deterioration of popular and mainstream culture into a theater of cruelty is "part of the larger degeneration of democracy."[30] A. O. Scott recognizes such a connection between gun violence and popular culture, but he fails to register the deeper significance of the relationship. He writes:

> [It] is absurd to pretend that gun culture is unrelated to popular culture, or that make-believe

> violence has nothing to do with its real-world correlative. Guns have symbolic as well as actual power, and the practical business of hunting, law enforcement and self-defense has less purchase in our civic life than fantasies of righteous vengeance or brave resistance. . . . [Violent] fantasies have proliferated and intensified even as our daily existence has become more regulated and standardized—and also less dangerous. Perhaps they offer an escape from the boredom and regimentation of work and consumption.[31]

Commercial culture invests in violence as entertainment and relentlessly markets it to a society addicted to an endless barrage of sensations, the lure of instant gratification, and a pleasure principle steeped in graphic images of others' suffering, mayhem, and bloodshed. Violence is now represented without the need for either subtlety or critical examination. Even worse is the "unprecedented visibility of extreme violence," which now feeds the 24/7 spectacle of media culture and increasingly reinforces what Etienne Balibar calls "death zones of humanity." He writes:

> In the face of the cumulative effects of different forms of extreme violence or cruelty that are displayed in what I called the "death zones" of humanity, we are led to admit that the current mode of production and reproduction has become a mode of *production for elimination*, a reproduc-

> tion of populations that are not likely to be productively used or exploited but are always already *superfluous*, and therefore can be only eliminated either through "political" or "natural" means—what some Latin American sociologists provocatively call *población chatarra*, "garbage humans," to be "thrown" away, out of the global city. If this is the case, the question arises once again: what is the rationality of that? Or do we face an absolute triumph of *irrationality*?[32]

Relieved of the pedagogical necessity to instruct, violence is split from its moral significance, just as it becomes more plentiful and lurid in order to infuse the pleasure quotient with more novelty. Americans now live in "a culture of the immediate" which functions as "an escape from the past" and a view of the future as one of menace, insecurity, and potential danger.[33] In an age of organized forgetting, the present becomes the only register of hope, politics, and survival. Americans now "look to the future with worry and suspicion and cling to the present with the anguish of those who are afraid of losing what they have," all the while considering those deemed "other" as a threat to their security.[34] One result is that trust and mutual respect disappear, democratic public spheres are foreclosed, and democracy becomes a cover for the swindle of false promises and deferred fulfillment.

Another consequence is the merging of pleasure and cruelty in commercial pornographies of violence.[35] One telling example of this can be found in those films in which the use of waterboarding has become a prime staple of torture. While the Obama administration banned waterboarding as an "enhanced" interrogation method in January 2009, it thrives in numerous prominent Hollywood films, including *Safe House*, *Zero Dark Thirty*, and *GI Jane*. In an ethically challenged world in which nothing seems to matter more than money, pleasure and gratification slide into boredom, shielding a pornographic violence from any sense of moral and social accountability. The use and legitimation of torture by the government is not limited to corporate-made films; Donald Trump announced on ABC's *This Week* that he would bring back waterboarding, because it "is peanuts compared to what they do to us."[36] It appears that moral depravity and the flight from social responsibility and human rights have no limits in an authoritarian political landscape.

Gun violence in America is inextricably tied to economic violence, as when hedge fund managers invest heavily in companies that make high-powered automatic rifles, 44-40 Colt revolvers, laser scopes for semi-automatic handguns, and expanded magazine clips.[37] The same mentality that trades in profits at the expense of human life gives the United States the shameless title of being the world's largest arms exporter. According to the Stockholm International Peace Research Institute (SIPRI), "Washington sold 31% of all global imports during the 2010–2014 period."[38] In a later interview on *This Week with George Stephanopoulos*, the host asked Trump if he would authorize torture. Trump replied that he would "authorize something beyond waterboarding."[39] Trump's public support for torture embodies a "more disturbing reality," one that regards violence as one of the "defining characteristics of our age."[40] This epidemic of the domestication of the unimaginable connects the spreading of violence abroad with the violence waged at home. It also points to the violence reproduced by politicians who would rather support the military-industrial-gun-complex and arms industries than address the most basic needs and social problems faced by the American people. There is more at work here than the marriage of politics and depravity; there is also the gathering threat of totalitarianism. How else to explain the existence, for example, of the ongoing war on women's reproductive rights, one that allows Donald Trump to state that women who have abortions should be punished (though he later under pressure retracted the statement)? The fact that such a cruel act could be thought, never mind uttered in a public forum, points to an ideological climate conducive to the rise of authoritarianism in America.

Rather than arming people with more guns, criminalizing every aspect of social behavior, militarizing the police, and allowing the gun lobby to sanction putting semi-automatic weapons in the hands of children and adults, the most immediate action that can be taken is to institute effective gun-control laws. As Bernardine Dohrn has argued:

> We want gun control that sanctions manufacturers, distributors and adults who place, and profit

> from, deadly weapons in the possession of youth. We want military-style weaponry banned. We want smaller schools with nurses and social workers, librarians and parent volunteers—all of which are shown to contribute to less disruption and less violence. Let's promote gun-control provisions and regulations that enhance teaching and learning as well as justice and safety for children, not those that will further incarcerate, punish and demonize young people of color. We've been there before.[41]

And Dohrn's suggestions would be only the beginning of real reform, one that goes right to the heart of abolishing the violence at the core of American society. The United States has increasingly become a society that is indifferent to the welfare of its citizens as the success of big corporations has become a higher priority than the subsistence of the one in six Americans who live in misery below the poverty line. Guns are certainly a major problem in the United States, but they are symptomatic of a much larger crisis, one that suggests not only that democracy is broken in the United States but that the country has tipped into forms of domestic and foreign terrorism characteristic of a new and deadly form of authoritarianism. We have become one of the most violent cultures on the planet, and regulating guns does not get to the root of the problem. Zhiwa Woodbury touches on this issue when he writes:

> In truth, the gun issue is an easy chimera that allows us to avoid looking in the mirror. It is much easier for us to imagine that this is an unfortunate political or regulatory issue than it is to ask what our own complicity in this ongoing, slow motion slaughter of innocents might be. Think about this. We are a country of approximately 300 million people with approximately 300 million firearms—a third of which are concealable handguns. Each one of these guns is made for one purpose only—to kill as quickly and effectively as possible. The idea that some magical regulatory scheme, short of confiscation, will somehow prevent guns from being used to kill people is laughable, regardless of what you think of the NRA. Similarly, mentally ill individuals are responsible for less than 5% of the 30,000+ gunned down in the U.S. every year.[42]

And trends show the nation drifting in the wrong direction. The increasing intolerance embraced by many, especially right-wing Republicans, make it clear, as John Pilger has argued, that in America "an insidious modern fascism is now an accelerating danger."[43] It is difficult to watch how Trump's rise and the corporate media benefit from each other, particularly as his fascistic assaults and actions become more aggressive. What is truly crucial to recognize is that there are ideological, economic, social, political, and sociological forces at work in the United States that have created the culture for authoritarian populism and its embrace of symbolic and material violence to thrive. Surely, two of the major crises of our times are the crisis of agency and civic literacy, on the one hand, and the withering of public values, trust, and democratic public spheres on the other. The distinguished historian of German history Fritz Stern is right in observing that we are experiencing "the struggles for democracy once again" and that "Trump is the best example of the dumbing down of the country and the terrifying weight of money."[44] Moreover, with the rise of a "new religiosity" of politics, America is in the midst of a frightening "new, illiberal age."[45]

Chomsky has argued that Stern's commentary on Nazi Germany, in which he states that Hitler's Germany marked "a historic process in which resentment against a disenchanted secular world found deliverance in the ecstatic escape of unreason," bears a resonance with the contemporary world that is "unmistakable."[46] The accelerating normalization of authoritarianism and the advance of intolerance in the United States parallels the violent pathologies of previous societies, their descent into hyper-nationalism, the collapse of democratic politics, the repression of dissent, the fanning of xenophobia and fear, the repeated demonization and attacks on immigrants, the concentration of power in the hands of the few, and the propaganda that only individuals are responsible for the systemic assaults they have to weather. With consumerism and commercial media serving as forms of soma, memory no longer serves as a moral witness.

Amidst the resurgence of a new style authoritarianism

in the U.S., American memory is voided of the violence and "conscious cruelty" associated with past totalitarian societies. In its new forms, the threats it poses go unrecognizable and are tolerated as politics as usual, only with less civility. Under such conditions, the social fragments, solidarity is replaced by shark-like competition, and state violence and its spectacle of violence become normalized. We live in a time of predatory monsters, and Donald Trump is simply symptomatic of the financial class he represents and the history we refuse to learn from.

In the current historical conjuncture, violence has arisen from the breakdown of public space, the erasure of public goods, the imposition of martial authority, and a growing disdain for the common good. Gratuitous violence is no longer limited to simulations in entertainment and video games, it has become increasingly central to a society that capitalizes on fear and fetishizes hyper-violent and punitive practices and social relations. Brutal masculine authority now rules American society and wages a war against women's reproductive rights, civil liberties, people of color, Latinos, and immigrants. Americans now inhabit a society run by a small financial elite that refuses to acknowledge that the racialized class war it is waging infects our language, values, social relations, safety, and the long-term prospects for sustainability itself. War has become an all-embracing ideal that feeds intolerance and consolidates an authoritarian state. When violence becomes fully normalized as an organizing principle of society, the political economy of war prevails and democracy becomes a mechanical farce.

The political apparatus that has become dependent on the cash of wealthy elites is restrained from confronting the conditions that undermine the national economy, the environment, communities of color, and the quality of everyday life. Despite society's increasingly diminished capacity to challenge authority, the system that permits such violence must be held accountable. The condemnation of violence clearly cannot be limited to police brutality. Violence does not come only from the police. In the United States there are other dangers emanating from state power that punishes whistle-blowers, intelligence agencies that encourage the arrest of those who protest against the abuse of corporate and state power, and commercial media that trade in ignorance, lies, and falsehoods, all the while demanding and generally "receiving unwavering support from their citizens."[47]

Yet, the only reforms we hear about are for safer gun policies, mandatory body cameras worn by the police, and more background checks. Well-intentioned as these reforms may be, they do not get to the root of the problem. The crisis we face goes far beyond threats to public security posed by armed law enforcement employees; the crisis we face is driven by a racialized political economy that puts profit over people, and has proven itself willing to wage war to keep things that way. Such a system produces politicians to support the militarization of everyday life, to tolerate torture, to bow down to the arms industries, and to let the nation be shaped by those with the money to pay their way through, be it the fracking industry or the gun industry.

These utterly corrupted politicians are killers in suits,

whose test of courage and toughness was captured in one of the recent Republican Party presidential debates when Hugh Hewett, a reactionary right-wing talk show host, asked Ben Carson, a surgeon trained to save lives, if he was ruthless enough to order military operations that would "kill innocent children by not the scores, but the hundreds and the thousands."[48] As if willingness to kill innocent children is now an accepted prerequisite for presidential leadership. This is what the internalization of the Terror Wars has come to: an increasingly intolerant authoritarian present accelerating toward an increasingly violent and fascistic future. Noam Chomsky is right to argue that we "live in critical and dangerous times" in which both humanity and the planet are at risk.[49]

Violence in the United States will not stop merely by holding politicians responsible. America has become a society in which the illegitimacy of violence is matched by the illegitimacy of politics. What is needed is the development of mass movements willing to resist and replace a predatory system that will assume increasingly intolerant and violent forms of social domination if left unchallenged. Democracy and justice are in grave danger, and the challenge is to energize and advance them not by reforming the system, but by replacing it. This will only take place with the development of an insurgent politics that succeeds in placing children and communities above the profits made from peddling guns, and in subordinating authorities to the job description democracy scripts for them: the job of public servants. In a substantive democracy, formative cultures, public spheres, and economic structures must be in the hands of the people, not big business and the wealthy. Americans don't need reform; they need social movements that go to the heart of the problems they face; they need a democratic, nonviolent revolution. Only then might we begin to achieve a society that realizes our highest ideals of democratic socialism.

III.

Scenes of Terrorism and the War on Youth

SIX

SANDRA BLAND'S AMERICA

On July 9, 2015, a young African American woman was pulled over by a white police officer for failing to signal while changing lanes in her car. What happened next has become all too common and illustrates the racial dimension to the many everyday theaters of engagement where America is at war with itself. Texas State Trooper Brian Encinia pulled Sandra Bland out of her car and pinned her to the ground after she allegedly became combative with him. A video of Encinia's humiliating arrest obtained by ABC 7 "doesn't appear to show Bland being combative with officers but does show two officers on top of Bland."[1]

In an alternate video released by the Texas Department of Public Safety, Encinia becomes increasingly hostile toward Bland and the interaction quickly escalates into a confrontational shouting match.[2] As it does, the armed male officer commands the female civilian to put out her cigarette.

Bland maintains her right to smoke and says: "I am in my car, why do I have to put out my cigarette?"

Encinia then opens the driver's door and quickly attempts to physically remove her. He then states: "I'm going to drag you out of here."

Bland says: "Don't touch me, I'm not under arrest."

Encinia then pulls out his Taser, aims it at Bland, and says: "I will light you up."

Spokespeople for the Texas State Troopers later conceded that "Encinia did not follow proper procedure." Waller County District Attorney Elton Mathis said after viewing the video that Bland was not "compliant" with the officer's directions.[3] Encinia alleges that after Bland was handcuffed, she swung her elbows at him and kicked him in the chin, though video documentation provides no evidence to support his allegation. Neither the police video nor the one taken by a bystander show the officer being kicked. Even more troubling is the fact that the police video had a number of glitches suggesting that it had been tampered with, though the Department of Public Safety indicated the glitches were the result of posting it and later released another version of the video.[4]

A witness reported that he saw "the arresting officer pull Bland out of the car, throw her to the ground and put his knee on her neck while he arrested her."[5] In the video, Bland can be heard questioning the officer's methods of restraint. She says: "You just slammed my head to the ground. Do you not even care about that? I can't even hear."[6] At one point, Bland indicates she has been hurt. "You're about to break my wrist," she says, "You're a real man now, you just slammed me, knocked my head into the ground, I got epilepsy, you motherfucker," to which Encinia responds, "Good."[7]

Brian Encinia arrested Sandra Bland for assaulting an officer, a third-degree felony, and interned her at the Waller County, Texas, jail. On July 13, 2015, she was found dead in her cell. Encinia's behavior echoes the comments of a former policeman who was interviewed on CBC. When asked about Bland's treatment by the police, he stated that the problem is the total militarization of policing: "suspects" are viewed as "the enemy," and anything that is done to them is therefore justified. This suggests something more than the increasing militarization of police arsenals; it points to the increasing militarization of police mentalities fueled by the adoption of the Terror Wars, a mentality that was popularized with heroic fanfare with the martial-law lockdown of Boston during the police hunt for the Tsarnaev boys.

Quite unbelievably, the Waller County Jail reported that Sandra Bland took her own life while in its custody. It appears inconceivable that a young woman who was starting a new job, an outspoken civil rights activist who went to church and was close to her family, would take her own life after being arrested for changing lanes without using a blinker. Bland often posted videos in which she talked about important civil rights issues. In one such posting she stated: "I'm here to change history. If we want a change, we can really truly make it happen."[8]

Ms. Bland's family and friends believe that foul play was involved, and rightly so.[9] Adding to the uncertainty is the fact that the head sheriff of Waller County, "Glenn Smith, who made the first public comments about Bland's in-custody death, was suspended for documented cases of racism when he was chief of police in Hempstead, Texas, in 2007. After [he completed] his suspension, more complaints of racism came in, and Smith was actually fired as chief of police in Hempstead."[10] Smith's well-documented racist behavior was made public by Judge DeWayne Charleston, the first African American justice of the peace in Waller County, Texas, who has called for Smith to resign as sheriff. He writes:

> You know, as I understand it, it was a pretty big media event back then. It was some years ago. When he was the chief of police, he had pulled—among other incidents that he was held accountable for, he pulled some African Americans over. I think he had a couple of his men with him. And they were searched in the street. They were—they had their pants pulled down and underwear pulled down and privates exposed, and they began to strip these guys in public. And there was testimony that he or one of his men began to ridicule the parts of their anatomy. And when it came to the attention of the city council, he was voted to be terminated. This was just part and parcel of their effort to intimidate, ridicule and malign, with an incredible sense of impunity. And I think that what happened to Sandra Bland is just an extension of that culture.[11]

Bland's death seems to fit quite well with the legacy of racism that Smith brought with him to his new job in Waller Country. Moreover, the claim that Bland took her own life seems highly improbable, given the political and racist ideological conditions in which her death took place. But just as improbable, if not unbelievable, is that this young Black woman's death was directly related to her being pulled over by white police for changing lanes without using a signal. Bland was not pulled over for a driving infraction, she was pulled over because she was Black, she was in Texas, and the police on patrol were white men.

America is at war with itself, and the armed state authorities who targeted Sandra Bland treated her like an enemy. The injustice of her death is indicative of a country where police immunity is now integral to the authoritarian state, and lethal violence against unarmed civilians is the new norm for a society shaped by the invisible legacies of the white enslavement economy, Jim Crow, the incarceration state, the drug wars, and the increasing militarization of everything, including the war on communities of color. For people of color and immigrants, routine encounters with authorities can result in jail, gun-shot casualty, detention, deportation, or death. There is more at stake here than the fact that, as federal statistics indicate, the police are "31 percent more likely to pull over a black driver than a white driver."[12] There is the violence that propels a deeply racist and militarized society, a violence that turns on young people and adults alike who are considered disposable and a threat to the public.[13] This type of harassment is integral to a form of domestic terrorism in which Blacks are beaten, arrested, incarcerated, and too often killed. This is the new authoritarianism of the boot-in-your face racism, one in which the punishing state is the central institution for both enforcing what Michelle Alexander calls a "racial caste system" and maintaining the economic hegemony of the financial elite. How much longer can this war go on? As Karen Garcia points out, "When police officers can stalk, threaten, harass, assault, arrest, injure and kill black people for the crime of merely existing, I think it's high time that the USA declares itself a state sponsor of terrorism."[14]

How many more people of color are going to be killed, injured, or terrorized by U.S. authorities, be they local police, state troopers, U.S. Border Patrol, or Immigration and Customs Enforcement? How many more names will join the list of those whose deaths have sparked widespread protests: Trayvon Martin, Michael Brown, Eric Garner, Freddie Gray, Renisha McBride, Aiyana Jones, Sakia Gunn, Sandra Bland, and 17-year-old Laquan McDonald, among others? Is it any wonder that one funeral director in Chicago stated that "young people in the city do not expect to live late into their adult life"?[15] "A 13-year-old Chicago boy who appeared in an award-winning public service video about the effect of gun violence on the city's black youth," reported the *New York Times* on March 28, 2016, "was shot in the back and critically wounded, officials said Monday."[16] For families of color living in Chicago and many other cities, this kind of unspeakable tragedy is but one of many such threads woven into the fabric of everyday life.

Police violence against people of color, especially Blacks, is not an aberration, it is a constant in a long history structured and defined by the legacy of whites' enslavement and human trafficking of people of color, white slave patrols and "militia tenants," the Second Amendment, convict leasing, lynching, and what Douglas A. Blackmon calls "the re-enslavement of Black Americans from the Civil War to World War II," followed by the period of the new Jim Crow.[17]

Sandra Bland's tragic case has joined those of Freddie Gray, Tamir Rice, Laquan McDonald. But these are only the well-publicized incidents. The data suggest that the number of such killings is astronomical. *The Progress Report* recently noted that two new projects are now keeping count in real time. "According to *The Guardian*, 637 people have been killed by the police" from the beginning of the year to July 22, 2015, it states. In addition, the *Washington Post* "is tracking police shootings and counts 535 of those. That's almost three people shot and killed by the police every day this year."[18]

Yet, those who profit from mainstream media are clearly more committed to building revenue from advertisers than they are to in-depth reporting on the violence waged against people of color in the United States. What is clear is that this violence reveals a form of racialized social control waged by a political economy increasingly divested from all forms of social responsibility. And if one measure of a democratic society is how a nation treats its most vulnerable, the United States has failed miserably.

The combat mentality of the Terror Wars is increasingly internalized in the form of a war of suspicion, neglect, intimidation, militarization, and violence, particularly in already disadvantaged communities like Ferguson and

Flint, and hundreds of others that endure similar oppressive conditions but never quite make it to the national news. Racism and police militarization have forced the nation to re-acquaint itself with an all-too-familiar kind of terror, the home-grown violence used by whites against Black people for the most trivial of infractions. The killing of Black people by armed whites (in and out of uniform) is part of a history of racial atrocity that dates back to the colonial days of legal enslavement.

What is different today is that such acts of domestic terror are now increasingly seen by the U.S. public after they are recorded by civilian witnesses.[19] New technologies and an ever-present screen culture now enable individuals to record such violence and broadcast it through social media. While this process makes visible the depravity of state violence, the images are sometimes co-opted by the mass media, commodified, and disseminated in ways that further exploit people's lives and communities, as William C. Anderson argues.[20] But it does more. It also sends a clear and chilling message to the American public, one that is as dangerous as it is intimidating.

Americans now live in an empire of images that serve not only to consolidate the dynamics of oppressive power, but also to empty words of any meaning. Such a process is often driven by a disimagination machine that denudes the images themselves of any substantive meaning other than adrenalizing viewers' feelings of anxiety and reinforcing their sense of powerlessness as spectators. The merging of screen culture and the spectacle of violence (beginning with the September 11, 2001, attacks on the Pentagon and World Trade Center) suggests something unique about the deadly power and battle of images in contemporary global culture. A cinematic politics of the visceral has replaced the more measured and thoughtful commentary on human suffering and alienation bequeathed by a post–World War II generation of intellectuals, artists, and others working in the public interest. Representations of bodies in fear, panic, vulnerability, and pain increasingly override narratives of social justice; pure entertainment, as a return to the hyper-real, enshrines audio-visual representations of the gruesome, opening up a new phase in the contemporary use of images as mechanisms of social control, coercion, and psychological war. Open authoritarianism now accelerates the alliance between political intolerance, violence, and insecurity—an alliance that cannot be understood outside of how the spectacle undermines community and delegitimizes social relations.

The senseless killing of unarmed Blacks by armed authorities is now on full display, given the ways in which events are screened, photographed, and recorded with dash cams, body cameras, and other mobile technologies. Violence in real time merges with the spectacles of violence that now dominate almost all aspects of entertainment, gaming, popular culture, and the mainstream media. The intersection between screen culture and state violence has also ushered in a new regime in which screen culture and visual politics create spectacular events just as much as they record them. But emerging alongside this "repositioning of visual communication practices, utilities, and techniques is a culture that circulates and intensifies anthropologically threatening images."[21] As acts of violence against communities of color and the modalities of the spectacle converge, a new species of technological magic is produced in which shock becomes the structuring principle in creating certain conditions of reception for the images and discourses of crime, terrorism, security, and power. What is especially disturbing about this war of images is that not only is it being shaped by the confluence of state and corporate power, but it reinforces the reckless polarities between safety and victims. Various right-wing groups further manipulate the situation to implicate Black youth with a culture of criminality, an implication that drives whites into gun shops and strengthens the political power of notorious right-wing groups like the National Rifle Association. Understanding the dynamics between the spectacle of media, politics, and the everyday violence of the racial caste system is all the more significant since, as novelist and cultural critic Marina Warner puts it, "in the realm of culture, the character of our representations matter most urgently. . . . The images we circulate have the power to lead events, not only [to] report them, [and] the new technical media have altered experience and become interwoven with consciousness itself."[22]

The new brutalism captured by screen culture was on full display in the widely reported condemnation of the wealthy white dentist who illegally tracked and killed Cecil the lion for sport. This senseless killing is deeply disturbing not only because of the savage death of such a beautiful animal, but also because of its wider implications regarding the culture and spectacle of violence in the United States. The public outrage triggered by Cecil's killing appeared immense next to the much smaller degree of publicity and public indignation over the criminal death of Sandra Bland. While brutal displays of violence still matter, they simply matter less when they occur within or against communities of color. The insurgent purpose of the Black Lives Matter and the Flint Lives Matter movements is to rebel against political formations based on a sliding scale of social worth. Such political formations are the direct descendants of centuries of enslavement, apartheid, and racial terrorism; and are strengthened, not diminished, by the internalization of the war on terror, spectacle media, and the new authoritarianism.

As mentioned previously, missing from most of the accounts of such police violence against Blacks in urban areas is that the data emerging around how often police officers kill civilians is shocking and egregiously indefensible, and points to what amounts to a state of siege one would find in a war zone.

Perhaps too many people in the United States have succumbed to a kind of political and moral coma now that violence is increasingly normalized as both a form of entertainment and as a mechanism to impose a life of hardship and misery on those whose lives are considered not to matter. Violence in the United States has become cheap entertainment divorced from ethical culture, and in this sense it mimics a market for which ecological and social costs are a joke. Screen culture is dominated by violence against people of color, women, immigrants, refugees, and a range of those Others considered to be criminal moochers and parasites, what Giorgio Agamben calls the detritus of "bare life." At the same time, the spectacle of violence produced by the disimagination machine as against those considered inferior, weak, or disposable, is one of the few dependable ways remaining for spectators of the mainstream media to feel any emotion at all. Such violence defines large swaths of popular culture, rampant in Hollywood films and endlessly produced in a military-corporate video culture that transforms the most extreme scenes of bloodletting into a cash crop. Violence has become America's national sport and its chief mode of entertainment. Senseless killings are now increasingly being recorded, publicly posted via the Internet, and absorbed as fodder for the spectacle of violence. (And it is precisely to this sick Western sensibility that ISIS disseminates its own sickening "faces of death" videos.)

While rich white men hunt and kill endangered animals for fun, armed authorities stop and harass people of color and immigrants with impunity, as was the case with Sandra Bland and many others. At the same time, the wealthiest few enjoy the handsome benefits of a predatory political economy that administers their domination in the form of what a recent Princeton University study calls an oligarchy. This is the face of the new authoritarianism, which has its Hollywood counterpart in the film *American Psycho* and its political counterpart in the image of Donald Trump. As James Baldwin once remarked, we live in truly dangerous times, endlessly recorded in an age when images appear to have been emptied of any substantive meaning beyond their ability to hold the attention of distracted spectators just long enough to be sold—click by click, byte by byte, moment by moment—to advertisers.

In Sandra Bland's America, local police and other authorities appear to recognize that images no longer provide the ultimate referent for revealing oppressive violence as much as they function to massage the machinery of aesthetic depravity. In Sandra Bland's America, racial violence, like economic violence, has become so commonplace and pervasive that justice is no longer measured by holding those who perpetrate the violence accountable. Police, like bankers, seem to operate in a realm of almost complete impunity. All that seems to matter is that the grievances of people victimized by police or financiers be noted publicly, as if that is the furthest measure of justice that neoliberalism will tolerate against itself. Far too few Americans are politically mobilized by the ongoing shootings, beatings, killings, foreclosures, evictions, harassment, and mass poisoning—as is the case in Flint—of people of color in a society in which any vestige of a culture of compassion, trust, and justice has been transformed into a culture of war and violence.

In a nation where militarism is pervasive and possessing guns is viewed as a sacred right, violence has morphed into the primary modality for addressing problems at home and abroad. Bomb first, then seek political solutions, especially if Muslims are involved. Shoot first, deal with innocent-until-proven-guilty later, especially in long-abandoned communities of color. One consequence of such modalities is that state violence is increasingly accepted, rendered trivial, and shamelessly legitimized in terms of either self-defense or national security. State violence fueled by the internalization of the Terror Wars, the militarization of everyday life, and an increasingly open political racism is now ubiquitous and should be understood as a form of domestic terrorism. However, such theaters of violence are not disconnected; they are structural aspects of an accelerating political climate change in which the combined impact of relentless corporate pressure, invasive surveillance capacity, militarized police, and brazen political intolerance produce manifestations of proto-fascistic power, manifestations of which Donald Trump is a clear and evolving example.[23] Terrorism, torture, and state violence are not part of a bygone era; they are defining characteristics of Sandra Bland's America—an America that is increasingly armed, intolerant, and authoritarian.

As police choked Eric Garner to death, he told them that he could not breathe. His words now apply to democracy itself, which is suffering from a critical loss of the civic oxygen that gives it life. Sandra Bland's America has become a place where democracy cannot breathe. At the same time, American gun culture, which celebrates violence as an antidote to practically all problems, imposes its own trajectory of terrorism. Witness the people killed and wounded in a Colorado movie theater by John Holmes, the nine killed in a church by a white bigot in Charleston, South Carolina, five service members killed in Chattanooga military facilities, and the more recent attack by a lone gunman, a drifter, who opened fire in a Louisiana movie theater, killing two women and injuring nine others before killing himself. This relentless plague of gun violence, coupled with state repression, suggests the United States has become something akin to a failed state. "How Often Do Mass Shootings Occur?," asked a *New York Times* headline in December 2015, "On Average, Every Day, Records Show."[24] And James Alan Fox, a criminologist at Northeastern University, said his research showed that there has not been a spike: "the number of such shootings has roughly held steady in recent decades."[25]

The mainstream press seems especially interested in stories where the victims can be viewed as assailants, as in the case of Trayvon Martin and Michael Brown, but are less interested when the suspect is a white cop. When the victims of police violence cannot be tarred with labels such as super-predators or thugs,[26] as was the case with Tamir Rice, demonizing discourse becomes useless and such acts of state terrorism simply fade out of view. Tamir was only 12 years old when shot to death by a policeman who, in his previous police assignment in another city, was labeled unstable. Even more tragic is the fact that the City of Cleveland blamed the boy for his own death, and attempted to sue his family to collect $500 for their son's "last dying expense."[27]

As Marian Wright Edelman has written, the police killing of Tamir Rice goes to the heart of a particular kind of abomination in the United States, one in which children have become collateral damage in the Terror Wars, an internalization of which the growing militarization and weaponization of the police is just one component. She writes:

[Tamir Rice was] a 12-year-old sixth grader who loved drawing, basketball, playing the drums, and performing in his school's drumline. Sometimes his teacher had to remind him not to tap a song on his desk with his fingers. When Tamir, a mere boy child, was shot and killed last November, who was there to protect him? Not Cleveland police officer Timothy Loehmann—the man who shot him. Tamir was sitting outside a recreation center near his home holding a friend's toy gun when Loehmann careened up in his squad car with his training officer. The surveillance video shows Loehmann took less than two seconds between getting out of the barely-stopped car and shooting Tamir. Worse, this child was left mortally wounded on the ground in agony for nearly four minutes while neither Loehmann nor his trainer Frank Garmback administered any first aid. An FBI agent who happened to be nearby responded to the police activity and was the first one to try to give Tamir help. When Tamir's 14-year-old sister ran to see and comfort him she was tackled by a police officer, handcuffed, and put in the back of a squad car unable to comfort her stricken brother. When Tamir's mother arrived at the same time as the ambulance the police wouldn't let her get close to her son and she said they threatened to handcuff and arrest her too if she didn't calm down. She was then denied entrance to the back of the ambulance

> to ride with or hold the hand of her son on the way to the hospital. I can only imagine the deep terror of both mother and child isolated from each other. Tamir died from his injuries the next day. Who was there to protect Tamir?[28]

National concern with the killing, poisoning, and incarceration of immigrant children and youth of color has been underwhelming. Why is it that there was almost no public outcry over the case of Kalief Browder, a young Black man, who was arrested for a crime he did not commit and incarcerated at the notorious Rikers Island, where he spent more than 1,000 days, two years of that time in solitary confinement, waiting for a trial that never happened? Shortly after being released he committed suicide.[29] Would this have happened if he were white, were middle class, and had access to a lawyer? Is his story different from that of other youth of color in Ferguson, Flint, Baltimore, New Orleans, or Cleveland? These are questions asked in Sandra Bland's America.

Not surprisingly, the all-powerful evocation of terrorism is reserved only for those acts that threaten the government-sponsored status quo, but not those perpetrated by the state or corporations against the population. So, for example, the ugly history of white people lynching, bombing, and killing Blacks in the United States is not understood, taught, or remembered as part of the homeland's history of terrorism. The financial acts of economic mass destruction that robbed millions of Americans of their homes and life savings and plunged the nation into years of recession, acts that directly assaulted national security, are not considered terrorism.

What needs to be recognized, as Robin D. G. Kelley points out, is that the killing of unarmed people of color by the police is a matter that speaks not simply to the need for reforming protocols of law enforcement and the culture that shapes them, but to the need for massive organized resistance against a war that is being waged on U.S. soil. "War?" asks Robin D. G. Kelley:

> Yes, war. The immediate and sustained resistance to the police following Mike Brown's murder revealed the low intensity war between the state and Black people, and the disproportionate use of force against protesters following the grand jury's decision escalated the conflict. To the world at large, Ferguson looked like a war zone because the police resembled the military with their helmets, flak jackets, armed personnel carriers, and M-16 rifles. But African-American residents of Ferguson and St Louis proper, and in impoverished communities across the country, did not have to endure tear gas or face down riot cops to know that they were already living in a war zone.[30]

The call for police "reform," echoed throughout the dominant media, is meaningless. We need to change a system steeped in violence, racism, economic corruption, and institutional rot. What is becoming a matter of public knowledge is that the police can kill people of color and immigrants, young and old, and do it with almost perfect impunity, just as bankers can commit theft and fraud and never face criminal charges. Exceptions are few, but they exist. For example, there is the case of Russell Rios, 19, who was shot in the back of the head by Police Sgt. Jason Blackwelder, who was convicted of manslaughter by a jury; there is also the case of Officer Randall Kerrick, who shot Jonathan Ferrell, 24, a former college football player, "as he attempted to get help after being involved a car crash late at night in Charlotte, North Carolina."[31] Kerrick currently faces charges for manslaughter. More recently, police officers have been indicted for the death of Freddie Gray, and there is an impending grand jury verdict regarding the police officer who killed Laquan McDonald. It should be no surprise that two of the officers responsible for Gray's death have been cleared. Other indictments are pending in some highly publicized shootings. Yet, such indictments are rare and the authorities involved are rarely convicted by the courts. This was made clear recently when juries refused to indict the police officers responsible for such tragic deaths as those of Tamir Rice and Sandra Bland, regardless of the public outcries both before and after the decisions.[32] The case of Tamir Rice is particularly disturbing since it was documented on video. Responding to the prosecutor's claim that Tamir's death was the result of a "tragic series of errors and miscommunications," a hard-hitting *New York Times* editorial suggested that there was a certain irony and profound act of deception in the comment, given that the real issue was that the "Cleveland police were dangerous and profoundly out of control."[33] Moreover, it noted that for the prosecutor to reduce the unnecessary and brutal shooting of Tamir Rice to a "miscommunication" served largely to "sidestep the history of violent, discriminatory police actions that led up to this boy's death. They also have the reprehensible effect of shifting the responsibility for this death onto the shoulders of this very young victim."[34] In such nefarious environments, it is understandable why some are in the streets calling for revenge.

Yet, we don't need revenge, we need justice—and that means structural change. This is particularly evident when people in positions of power commit egregious acts of violence or abuse and are not held to the same legal standard as the rest of the country. In this case, the Cuyahoga County prosecutor decided that the white rookie Cleveland cop, Timmy Loehmann, who shot Tamir just seconds after confronting him, will not face criminal charges. Identical verdicts of acute injustice have resulted in similar failures to indict white cops involved in the deaths of Michael Brown and Sandra Bland.[35]

Ending state and corporate criminal misconduct is certainly acceptable as a short-term goal to save lives, but if we are going to prevent the United States from becoming a full-fledged authoritarian enterprise dedicated to the interests of the rich, then the vicious neoliberal financial and police state must be resisted, dismantled, and rebuilt in a subordinate position to a community-centered civilian democracy. Such resistance is beginning with the emergence of the Black Lives Matter movement, along with youth movements such as the Black Youth Project, Millennial Activists United, We Charge Genocide, and other groups.[36]

America is at war with itself, and the atrocity of war is apparent in the ever-increasing flood of intolerable corporate crime and state violence.[37] More and more people are being locked up, jailed, beaten, harassed, raped, and violated because they are impoverished, vulnerable, and considered invisible and voiceless.[38] It will take national networks like Black Lives Matter—acting in solidarity with many other social justice movements—to build the political insurgency required to compel change. Until then, people of color, immigrants, Muslims, and the economically disadvantaged will continue to live in Sandra Bland's America, one in which they are not safe in their own neighborhoods, not safe on public streets, highways, schools, or any other areas in which the police and other armed authorities are at large.

SEVEN

PARIS, ISIS, AND DISPOSABLE YOUTH

Written with Brad Evans

"There's a nagging sense of emptiness. So people look for anything; they believe in any extreme—any extremist nonsense is better than nothing."
—J. G. Ballard

"We do not lack communication. On the contrary, we have too much of it. We lack creation. We lack resistance to the present."
—Gilles Deleuze & Felix Guattari

Youth in the Firing Line

There is a revealing similarity between the coordinated attacks in Paris in 2015, in which more than 130 people were killed and hundreds wounded, and those of September 11, 2001, when airplanes filled with passengers were flown into the Pentagon and the World Trade Towers, killing thousands. Yet, what they have in common has been largely overlooked in mainstream and alternative media coverage. While both assaults have been rightly viewed as desperate acts of religious terrorism, what has been missed is that both acts of violence were committed largely by young men. This is not a minor issue, because unraveling this similarity provides the possibility for addressing the conditions that make such attacks possible.

While French President François Hollande did say soon after the Paris assault that "youth in all its diversity" was targeted, he did not address the implications of the attacks' heinous and wanton violence. Instead, he embraced the not so "exceptional" discourse of militarism and vengeance, a discourse that allowed 9/11 to metastasize into global Terror Wars, a tragic mistake that has cost millions of lives and displaced millions more. The call for more killing, retribution, and revenge extended the violent landscape of everyday oppression by shutting down any possibility for understanding the conditions that gave birth to the atrocities committed by young people against civilians.

In an altogether familiar and expected way, Hollande channeled the Cheney/Bush/Rumsfeld response to an act of terrorism, and in doing so further paved the way for the advance of the mass surveillance state, the collapsing of the state/army distinction, and the emergence of a police state, all the while legitimizing a culture of fear and demonization that unleashed a new wave of racism and Islamophobia in continental Europe and beyond. What Hollande and others who are calling for increased military action have also missed is that "the kind of brutal policies pursued by the Bush administration and Rumsfeld and Cheney utterly failed. They strategically failed on the ground in that they achieved nothing in terms of stabilizing Iraq or dealing with the threat of Islamic extremism."[1] And they failed intellectually in that they offered no prospect for arresting the cycle of violence and revenge. Such is the definition of political nihilism.

There is a hidden politics here that prevents a deeper understanding, not only of the failure of the government's responses to attacks like the ones witnessed in Paris, but also of how such warlike strategies legitimize, reproduce, and quicken further acts of violence, moving governments closer to the practices of a security state. As Ian Buruma points out, hysteria not only produces fear, it also puts into play the conditions of mass violence in which "a Western government allows its policemen to humiliate and bully Muslims in the name of security, [which means] the more ISIS is likely to win European recruits."[2] In such circumstances, violence becomes the key organizing principle for societies, and intimidation becomes the foundation for indoctrinating subjects to accept previously unacceptable social conditions, such as the militarization of police, the suspension of civil rights, and open authoritarianism. Judith Butler is right in arguing that the fear and rage at the heart of such responses "may well turn into a fierce embrace of a police state."[3] In this instance, violence in fact is exonerated as an intolerable act and sets the conditions for the "purer" forms of violence to come.

But what does it mean that young people are now in the firing line? How does this force a change in our understanding and perception of the political stakes for the violence? And how might understanding such actions reveal both the contemporary political climate and what it might mean in terms of our shared political futures? Working from the understanding that youths have become a notable, if under-theorized object for power and violence in today's battlefields, this chapter addresses these questions and the necessity for rethinking the politics of violence dominating our current political moment. Moving beyond conventional understandings of the violence, which neatly map it out in terms of civilization versus barbarity, it is our contention that both sides have effectively created a Gordian knot that only the recourse to violence can sever. Indeed, once we recognize that the conflicts today are also fought over the site of imagination itself, it becomes imperative to offer a fundamental rethinking of how to name and break the cycle of bloodshed if we are not to permit ourselves, as Noam Chomsky warns, to be led cheerfully over a cliff like a bunch of lemmings.[4]

A War Waged on Youth and by Youth

While politicians, pundits, and the mainstream media acknowledged that the Paris attackers largely targeted places where young people gathered—the concert hall, the café, and the sports stadium—what they missed was that these acts of violence were also part of a strategic war on youth. This incident was part of a larger war waged on youth and by youth. For ISIS, the war on youth translates into what might be called hard and soft targets. As targets in the hard war, young people are subject to intolerable forms of violence of the sort seen in the Paris attacks. Moreover, there is a kind of doubling here, because once they are lured into the discourse of absolute religious righteousness and sacrificial violence, they are no longer targeted or defined by their deficits. On the contrary, they now reconfigure their sense of agency, resentment, and powerlessness in the image of the sacred warrior who now targets the young people of the enemy. The movement here is from an intolerable sense of powerlessness to an intolerable notion of violence defined through the image of a potential killing machine. In this script, the hard war cannot be separated from the soft war on youth, and it is precisely this combination of tactics that is missed by those Western forces contributing to the Terror Wars.

The soft war represents another type of violence, one that trades in both fear and a sense of certainty and ideological purity born of hyper-moral sensibilities, which narrates the victim as a mere necessity to the wider sacred claim. As symbols of the future, youth harbor the possibility of an alternative and more liberating world view, and thus constitute a threat to the fundamentalist ideology of ISIS. Hence, they are viewed as potential targets subject to intolerable violence—whether they join militant groups or protest against such organizations. It is precisely through the mobilization of such fear that whatever hope they might have for a better world is undermined or erased. The soft war constitutes an attack on the imagination, designed to stamp out any sense of agency, thoughtfulness, and critical engagement with the present and the future.

The use of violence by ISIS is deftly designed to both terrorize and indoctrinate young people. Their strategy is to create a situation in which France and other governments, influenced by structural racism and xenophobia, will likely escalate their repressive tactics toward Muslims, thereby radicalizing more young people, and persuading them to join the war. Put differently, when Hollande calls for pitiless vengeance he is creating the conditions that will enable an entire generation of Muslim youth to become sacrificial agents and the pretext for further violence. When violence becomes the only condition for possibility, it suppresses political agency and allows it to become either a target or the vehicle for targeting others. War is a fertile ground for resentment, anger, and violence because it turns pure survivability into a doctrine, and produces subjects willing to accept bloodshed as the best solution to address the conditions that cause an endless cycle of humiliation, intimidation, and powerlessness.

But the soft war does more than trade in a culture of coercion and fear. It also relies on a pedagogy of seduction, persuasion, and identification. ISIS capitalizes on the endless barrage of images depicting the violence waged by Western nations against Iraq, Syria, Afghanistan, and other Muslim nations. ISIS speaks directly, relentlessly, and fluently to the desperation, humiliation, and loss of hope that many young Muslims experience in the West. The spectacle of violence is its defining organizational principle. Many youth in the West are vulnerable to ISIS propaganda because they are constantly subject to widespread discrimination, and because of their religion continue to be harassed, dismissed, and humiliated. Much of this is further exacerbated by the expanding Islamophobia produced by right-wing manifestations in Europe and the United States. Donald Trump's call for banning Muslims from entering the United States is an egregious example.[5] Humiliating Muslims in the name of national security simply provides a powerful recruiting tool to win over young people from Europe and North America. The rampant spread of Islamophobia in the United States and Europe, coupled with the relentless bombing of ISIS strongholds in Lybia, Iraq, and Syria, "won't break the spell of [the] Islamist revolution for frustrated, bored, and marginalized young people" in the slums of Paris, New York, or other Western cities.[6]

All the while, the suffering and impoverishment of Muslim youth are ignored while their resentment is dismissed as a variant of ideological and political extremism devoid of both historical forces and personal experiences. Heiner Flassbeck rightly argues that ISIS is particularly adept at highlighting the conditions that produce this sense of resentment, anger, and powerlessness and at knowing how to strategically address the vulnerability of Muslim youth to join ISIS, luring them with the promise of community, support, and visions of an Islamic utopia. He writes:

> For as much as we know, they grew up in human and social conditions that few of us can even imagine. They grew up fearing attracting attention to themselves and being branded as potential terrorists if they were a bit too religious (in the eyes of the West) or frequented Arab circles a bit too often. They also saw that the West shows little reserva-

> tion in bombing what they considered their "home countries" and killing hundreds of thousands of innocent people in order to guarantee the 'safety' of its citizens. . . . The sad truth is that thousands of young men grow up in a world in which premeditated killings take place on an almost daily basis when army personnel from thousands of miles away push a button. Is it really surprising that some of them lose their wits, strike back and create even more violence and the death of many innocent people?[7]

When the conditions that oppress youth are ignored in the face of the ongoing practices of state terrorism—the attacks waged on Muslim youth in France and other countries, the blatant racism that degrades a religion as if all terrorists are Muslims, forgetting that all religions produce their own share of terrorists—there is little hope for developing the insight and vision to address such conditions before they erupt into a nihilistic form of rage. Abdelkader Benali gives credence to this argument when he notes:

> I know from my own experience that the lure of extremism can be very powerful when you grow up in a world where the media and everyone around you seems to mock and insult your culture. And European governments are not helping fight extremism by giving in to Islamophobia cooked up by right-wing populists. What I see is a lack of courage to

> embrace the Muslims of Europe as genuinely European—as citizens like everyone else.[8]

Very few voices are talking about the 2016 massacres in Paris as part of what can be called the war on youth. In that case, ISIS targeted places where young people gather, sending a message that suggests that young people will have no future unless they convert to the ideological fundamentalism that drives terrorist threats. This was an attack not simply on the bodies of youth but also on the imagination and on tolerance of heterogeneity, an attempt to kill any sense of a better and more just future. When this script is ignored or derided as an unrealistic fantasy, war, militarism, violence, and revenge too often define the first and only option for governments and young people to consider. Likewise, it is the systemic violence against the hope and imagination of young Muslims that offers the strongest recruitment incentive to join organizations where claims to an almighty God and other absolutes offer to restore a sense of meaning, belonging, and communal power.

The Everyday War

The seeds of terrorism do not lie simply in ideological fundamentalism; they also lie in conditions of oppression, war, racism, poverty, the abandonment of entire generations of Palestinian youth, the dictatorships that stifle young people in the Middle East, and the racism that youth of color, Latinos, and immigrants endure everyday in the United States. For too many people, youth are now the subject and object of a continuous state of siege warfare, transformed either into criminalized antagonists, jihadi enemies, or the collateral damage that comes from the ubiquitous war machines. There are few safe spaces for them any more, unless they are hidden in the gated enclaves and protectorates of the wealthy few. In an age of intensifying violence, civil wars, and increasing terrorism in the West, it is crucial for those wedded to a future with human rights to examine the state of youth globally, especially those marginalized by class, race, religion, ethnicity, and gender, in order to address those underlying forces that produce the conditions of violence, ideological fundamentalism, militarism, and massive political and economic inequalities. This is a crucial project that would also necessitate analyzing and distinguishing the ever-expanding global war machines that thrive on violence and exclusion from those governmental processes that might offer a transformation for the better.

Surely there is more to the future than watching young people be killed by drones and gun massacres. Maybe it is time to ask important questions about the choices different youth are making: Why are some youth joining militant religious organizations? And what has led others to resist state violence and terrorism in all of its forms, framing this violence as an indecent assault on individuals, groups, and the planet itself?

Maybe it is time to ask ourselves what it means when a society ignores young people and then goes to war because they engage in terrorist acts or are its victims. One thing is clear: there will be no sense of global safety unless the conditions that produce young people as both the subjects and objects of violence are addressed. Safety is not guaranteed by war, militarism, and vengeance. In fact, this response becomes the generative principle for violence to both continue and escalate. As Flassbeck rightly argues:

> Safety cannot be guaranteed. Airplanes, public buildings and politicians can be protected, but there is no way to guarantee the safety of citizens. Those who oppose the "system" that, in their eyes constitutes a destructive and life-threatening force may strike anywhere. To them, it makes little difference who dies, as long as their actions create death, destruction, fear and, of course, more violence as a reaction. Safety can only be achieved if we start to realize and admit to ourselves that these angry young men are a product of our world. They are not just strangers that are driven by some perverted ideology. They are the result of a long series of misjudgments from our part and from our callousness when it comes to identify potential suspects and hit them with bombs and drones in order to restore "order" and "safety."[9]

Western powers cannot allow the fog of violence to cover over the bankruptcy of militaristic responses to terrorism. Such responses function largely to govern the effects of acts of terrorism by ISIS while ignoring its wider systemic dimensions. Dealing with the barbarity of ISIS requires political contextualization and serious engagement, not just more bloodshed. However abhorrent we might find their actions, it is patently absurd for any leader not to recognize that media is a theater of operations in which ISIS is heavily invested. ISIS strategically deploys the editorial production values of our own commercial entertainment to propagate high-definition films featuring raw, up-close dehumanization of its enemies as an act of psychological warfare. That these videos reach the minds of people in West only serves to reinforce the ongoing damage caused by the internalization of the Terror Wars.

John Pilger ventures to take this observation a step further by noting the historical parallels with the Khmer Rouge that terrorized Cambodia. As Pilger writes, this movement was the direct outcome of a U.S. bombing campaign: "The Americans dropped the equivalent of five Hiroshimas on rural Cambodia during 1969–73. They leveled village after village, returning to bomb the rubble and corpses. The craters left monstrous necklaces of carnage, still visible from the air. The terror was unimaginable."[10] The outcome was the emergence of a group largely made up of radical young men, driven by a dystopian ideology, all dressed in black, sweeping the country in the most violent and terrifying of ways. The historical comparison is all too apparent: "ISIS has a similar past and present. By most scholarly measures, Bush and Blair's invasion of Iraq in 2003 led to the deaths of some 700,000 people—in a country that had no history of jihadism."[11]

If a nation continually bombs a people, invades and occupies their land, appropriates their resources, harms their children, imprisons and humiliates their families, and tears apart the fabric of the social order, there is direct responsibility for the inevitable backlash to follow. It actually produces the very conditions in which violence continues to thrive. The rush to violence only kills more innocent people, and is only strategically useful as a recruiting tool for those who thrive on power derived from coercion and fear. The charge to violence simply accelerates the internalization of the Terror Wars and the normalization of militant authoritarianism inherent in the surveillance state, a lock-down society, and a heavily policed social order used to manage forms of racial and economic privilege—including the privilege to commit crimes of financial fraud and predation without risk of arrest or prison.[12]

But the willingness to embrace violence does more than perpetuate a war on youth; it also eliminates what might be called a politics of memory, the legacy of an insurrectional democracy, and in doing so deepens the invasiveness of the militaristic state.[13] The call for lethal violence in the face of the murderous attacks in Paris eviscerates from collective consciousness the mistakes made by "President Bush who declared 'a war on terror' after 9/11, a statement that led us to the Patriot Act, the invasions of Afghanistan and Iraq, and Guantánamo."[14] The consequences of that rush to war are difficult to fathom. As Bret Weinstein observes, Bush responded in a way that fed right into the terrorists' playbook:

> The 9/11 attack was symbolic. . . . It was designed to provoke a reaction. The reaction cost more than

> 6,000 American lives in the wars in Iraq and Afghanistan, and more than $3 trillion in U.S. treasure. The reaction also caused the United States to cripple its own Constitution and radicalize the Muslim world with a reign of terror that has killed hundreds of thousands of Iraqi and Afghani civilians.[15]

How different might our futures look now had an alternative response been pursued at that particular moment? Continuing the cycle of aggression and revenge, the response ramped up the violence and derided anybody who called for "addressing some of the social, cultural, and economic problems that create a context for extremism."[16] The Soviet occupation of Afghanistan, the failure of the U.S. war in Vietnam, the conjured U.S. destruction of Iraq, and the futility of the military attacks on Libya and Syria all testify to the failure of wars waged against foreign societies, especially people in the Middle East. As Peter Van Buren dryly observes,

> We gave up many of our freedoms in America to defeat the terrorists. It did not work. We gave the lives of over 4,000 American men and women in Iraq, and thousands more in Afghanistan, to defeat the terrorists, and refuse to ask what they died for. We killed tens of thousands or more in those countries. It did not work. We went to war again in Iraq, and now in Syria, before in Libya, and only created more failed states and ungoverned spaces

> that provide havens for terrorists and spilled terror like dropped paint across borders. We harass and discriminate against our own Muslim populations and then stand slack-jawed as they become radicalized, and all we do then is blame ISIS for Tweeting.[17]

The ongoing Terror Wars and the ethos of militarism that has driven them into the normalized fabric of everyday politics is seen by many of its victims as an act of terrorism because of the dreadful toll it takes on noncombatants, and who can blame them? When the United States orders drone strikes that result in the bombing of hospitals, wedding parties, and innocent children, regardless of the humanitarian signatures, the violence becomes a major selling point for recruitment into ISIS and other groups committed to pursuing revenge.[18]

When Donald Trump calls for the banning of Muslims from the United States, his inflammatory and racist rhetoric is appropriated into Al-Shabaab videos as a recruiting tool.[19] When the practice of moral witnessing disappears, along with the narratives of suffering on the part of the oppressed, politics collapses, and the turn to violence and terrorism gains ground, especially among impoverished youth. When the West forgets that "UN data shows that Muslim avoidable deaths from deprivation in countries subject to Western military intervention in 2001–2015 now total about 27 million," such actions further serve to both create more fear of the "Other" and generate more resentment and hatred by those who are relegated to the shameless and morally reprehensible status of collateral damage.[20]

The ongoing call for war writes over historical consciousness and public memory. While memory can be used selectively, history is more pedagogical and "takes the form of record, endlessly rewritten and retested against old and new evidence."[21] Social memory without a critical historical consciousness aligns itself with a self-serving and destructive species of historical amnesia. The pedagogical dimensions embedded in its practice of forgetting ensure that any intervention in the present will be limited by erasing any understanding of the past that might cultivate a renewed sense of political identification, social responsibility, and those forms of ethical and political commitments that bear on the immediacy of a world caught in the fog of war and the thoughtlessness of its conditioning. As such, those who forget the past ignore precisely the similarities mentioned above, whether we are discussing the Western actions that created Pol Pot and his Khmer Rouge or the direct role that America's unjustified acts of war, occupation, mass destruction, terror, torture, and killing in Iraq have had in the formation of the Islamic State in Iraq and Syria.[22] Chris Floyd is right to remind us:

> Without the American crime of aggressive war against Iraq —which, by the measurements used by Western governments themselves, left more than a million innocent people dead—there would be no ISIS, no "Al Qaeda in Iraq." Without the Saudi

> and Western funding and arming of an amalgam of extremist Sunni groups across the Middle East, used as proxies to strike at Iran and its allies, there would be no ISIS. Let's go back further. Without the direct, extensive and deliberate creation by the United States and its Saudi ally of a world-wide movement of armed Sunni extremists during the Carter and Reagan administrations, there would have been no "War on Terror"—and no terrorist attacks in Paris.[23]

Joseph G. Ramsey is also correct in insisting that those who focus only on the immediate suffering and trauma of those young people killed and injured in Paris, while failing to acknowledge the broader historical context out of which this intolerable bloodshed emerged, "neither do justice to the situation, nor do they help us to achieve a framework for response, in thinking or in action, that can in fact reduce, rather than escalate and increase, the dangers that these terrible events represent, and that they portend."[24] One way in which such violence can be escalated is by giving free rein to the cheerleaders of racism, impatience, and militarism. This is the "bomb first and think later" group that not only claims to hold the high moral ground, but also refuses adamantly to attend to any alternative understanding that addresses underlying causes. Unfortunately, the gospel of fear and sensationalism is being encouraged by mainstream corporate media outlets who in their search for higher advertising volume shamelessly encourage turmoil by providing coverage that lacks any meaningful context of the histories, places, cultures, traditions, and homes of the people we spend millions, if not billions, to bomb and destroy.[25]

How Fear Turns to Fascism

As Rabbi Michael Lerner has insightfully argued, fear and the desires it generates add momentum to the forces of fascism. Fear undermines historical memory due to its appeal to intense emotions and the itch for vengence. And, as Lerner writes, fear also guarantees these dynamics:

> Fascistic and racist right-wing forces will grow more popular as their anti-immigrant policies are portrayed as "common sense." In doing so, the politics of fear will inevitably lead to the empowering of domestic intelligence forces who are eager to invade our private lives and adamant in their call to receive greater support from the American public in the name of a disingenuous commitment to security. The call for tighter security and the allocation of increasing powers of surveillance to the government and its intelligence agencies will be supported by liberal leaders who seek to show that they too can be "tough."[26]

Violence born of such viscerally felt moments is always rooted in a pedagogical practice that mobilizes fear, pushes emotion over serious deliberation, and serves to legitimize a discourse that drowns out historical memory and ethical considerations. This is a discourse that is perpetrated as a form of indoctrination, one that uses crimes and catastrophes as free opportunities to tighten restrictions on civil liberties and further normalize martial law. In France and Belgium, for example, top government officials have now called for new sweeping security bills, increasing the antiterrorism budget, new powers for the police, and the expansion of wiretaps. "A Terror Attack," read a *New York Times* headline on March 31, 2016, "Then Far Right Moves In."[27] This is indeed the trend.

Capitalizing on the 2015 Paris massacres in a way that is nothing more than an act of political expediency, John Brennan, the head of the CIA, has criticized those who had exposed the illegal spying activities of the National Security Agency. The *New York Times* claimed he was using the tragedy in Paris to further his own agenda and had resorted to a "new and disgraceful low."[28] The *Times* also stated that Brennan was in fact a certified liar and that it was hard to believe anything he might say.[29] James Comey, the head of the FBI, made a similar case, suggesting that the encrypted messages used by Apple and Google customers were benefiting our enemies and that these companies should "make it possible for law enforcement to decode encrypted messages."[30] Authoritarian societies have little regard for freedom and will instigate any number of fears, however exaggerated, to create a security state and subordinate civil liberties to the demands of maintaining unchallenged martial hierarchy. This is a dangerous trade-off, and as William C. Anderson observes:

> The many tragedies at hand—from Paris to Beirut to Baga—are horrid, and chaos abounds. . . . That being said, in these weeks following the attacks in Paris, we should be vigilant and refuse to allow the types of politics and policy that were used to manipulate the public after 9/11 to arise. Violent terror attacks are a threat to one's physical existence (the freedom to live), but the draconian advances that come afterward threaten societies' freedoms as a whole in the most intricate of ways. What is life without freedom?[31]

While there is some evidence that the Paris attackers used encrypted messaging, this does not justify expanding the powers of the surveillance state. As Harvard University's Bruce Schneier observes, "the point remains that to use a tragedy to vilify encryption, push for surveillance expansion, and pass backdoor laws that will make everybody less safe—is nearly as gruesome as the attacks themselves."[32] While the mainstream media's criticisms of the call for expanded surveillance powers were well placed, they nevertheless failed to report when airing the comments of both Brennan and Comey that the U.S. government was spying not simply on terrorists, but on everyone. What's at stake here is the sacrifice of civil society for a martial one. In the wake of the Paris massacres, things done in the name of security increasingly drift toward practices associated with totalitarian states. We hear it in the in the words of Sarkozy, the former French president, who wants to put Syrian immigrants in detention camps. Marie Le Pen, the leader of France's most popular right-wing party, referred to the new migrants as "bacteria" and called for the country to annihilate Islamist fundamentalism, shut down mosques and expel dangerous "foreigners" and "illegal migrants."[33] In the United States, Republican politicians and candidates discuss the same issues with similarly hateful rhetoric.[34]

What is worth noting is that the emergence of such fascistic language is front and center in the various ways in which the discourse of bigotry has become a major manipulative tool of politicians in the United States. All of the Republican Party's leading presidential candidates resorted to racist and politically reactionary comments in the aftermath of the Paris killings that would seem unthinkable in a country that calls itself a democracy. When asked about Syrian refugees, Ben Carson referred to them as "rabid dogs."[35] Donald Trump echoed the Nazi practice of registering Jews and forcing them to wear a yellow star when he stated that, if elected president, he would force all Muslims living in the United States "to register their personal information in a federal database."[36] He also called for shutting down mosques in the United States. Marco Rubio, while getting a high degree of media attention as a Republican candidate, went even further arguing that he would not only shut down mosques but would shut down "any place where radical Muslims congregate, whether it be a café, a diner, an internet site—any place where radicals are being inspired."[37] Carson and Rubio have also called for policies that would eliminate abortions, even for women whose lives are at risk or who have been raped.[38]

The roots of anti-democratic practices reach deep in American society. Of course, all of the Republicans' fascistic proposals would do nothing more than legitimize and spread insidious acts of racism and xenophobia. How else to explain the rabid racism expressed by Elaine Morgan, a state senator in Rhode Island, when she stated in an email that "the Muslim religion and philosophy is to murder, rape, and decapitate anyone who is a non-Muslim."[39] There is more at stake here than an escalation of hate speech and Islamophobia; there is also the call for policies that make recruiting young people easier for ISIS and other religious combatant groups. As Peter Bouckaert, Human Rights Watch's emergencies director, points out:

> Every Syrian refugee who reaches the United States has gone through four levels of security review. These are the most carefully screened refugees anywhere in the world. And there have been no incidents with the hundreds of thousands of refugees that the U.S. has taken in over the years. The United States' values are built on being welcoming to refugees. And our most powerful tool in the war against Islamic extremism [is] our values. It's not our military planes and our bombs. The only way we can fight against this brutality, this barbarism, is with our values. And if we're going to shut the door on these refugees, we're giving a propaganda victory to ISIS . . . because they would

> love it if we shut the door on the people who are fleeing their so-called Islamic caliphate.[40]

The Violence of Anti-Public Intellectuals

Of course, it is not just rival Republicans who gush with war-mongering and racism. Bigotry is also to be found in public intellectuals such as Bernard-Henri Lévy and Neil Ferguson, who provide intellectual legitimacy to the marriage of militarism and racism. Lévy, a right-wing favorite of the mainstream media in France and the United States, argues that in the face of the Paris attacks, it is necessary to think the unthinkable, accept that everyone in the West is a target, allegedly because of our freedoms and our reluctance to go to war! For Lévy, caught in his own fog of historical denial, the greatest failing of the West is its aversion to all-out war.[41]

The real weakness is that Lévy finds genuine democracy dangerous, while refusing to recognize the anti-democratic intellectual violence he practices and supports. Lévy's militarism is matched by the historian Neil Ferguson's contemptuous claim in a *Boston Globe* op-ed: channelling Edward Gibbon, he argues that the Syrian refugees are similar to the barbaric hordes that contributed to the fall of Rome. Unapologetically, he offers a disingenuous humanitarian qualification before invoking his "war of civilizations" theses. He states the following regarding the Syrian refugees:

> To be sure, most have come hoping only for a better life. Things in their own countries have become just good enough economically for them to afford to leave and just bad enough politically for them to risk leaving. But they cannot stream northward and westward without some of that political malaise coming along with them. As Gibbon saw, convinced monotheists pose a grave threat to a secular empire.[42]

Ferguson also calls the Western countries weak and decadent for opening their gates to outsiders. Effectively inverting the humanitarian mantra of saving strangers, these types of comments reinforce a vision of a deeply divided world, demanding continued militarism and the insatiable call for war. Devoid of political imagination, such an analysis refuses to address the misery, suffering, and despair that, in fact, create the conditions that produce terrorists in the first place.

What makes such interventions so abhorrent is precisely the way they contribute to the production of *disposable futures*.[43] The future now appears to us as a terrain of endemic catastrophe and disorder from which there is no viable escape except to draw upon the logics of those predatory formations that put us there in the first place. Lacking an alternative image of the world, we are merely requested to see it as predestined and catastrophically fated. This is revealing of the nihilism of our times that forces us to accept that the only world conceivable is the one we are currently forced to endure: a world that forces us all to become witness to its spectacles of violence and demands we accept that all things are ultimately precarious by default. In this suffocating climate, the best we can hope for is to be connected to some fragile and precarious economic life-support system that may be withdrawn from us at any moment. Hope has dissolved into the pathology of social and civil death and the quest for mere survival. For if there is a clear lesson to living in these times, it is precisely that the water may be poisoned at any given moment, without any lasting concern for social responsibility. This is simply the natural order of things (so we are told) and we need to adapt our thinking accordingly.

Such a vision of the world is actually far more disturbing than the dystopian fables of the twentieth century. Our condition denies us the possibility of better times to come as the imagined and the real collapse in such a way that we are already living amongst the ruins of the future. All we can seemingly imagine is a world filled with unavoidable catastrophes, the source of which, we are told, remains beyond our grasp, thereby denying us any possibility for genuine systemic transformation in the order of things. How else can we explain the current fetish with the doctrine of resilience if not through the need to accept the inevitability of catastrophe, and to simply partake in a world that is deemed to be "insecure by design"? This forces us to accept narratives of vulnerability as the authentic basis of political subjectivity, regardless of the oppressive conditions that produce vulnerable subjects (thereby neutralizing all meaningful qualitative differences in class, racial, and gendered experiences). So we are encouraged to lament this world, armed only with the dim hope that perhaps at least the privileged elite might survive better than others.

Breaking the Cycle of Violence

Eliminating ISIS means eradicating the conditions that create it. This suggests producing a political settlement in Syria and stabilizing the Middle East and ending Western support for the various anti-democratic and dictatorial regimes throughout the Middle East and around the world. One obvious step would be for the West to stop funding and arming the ruthless dictators of Saudi Arabia and others who have been linked to providing financial and ideological support to terrorist groups all over the globe. It also demands an understanding that the war on terror is a war on youth, who are both its target and the vehicle for targeting others. Zygmunt Bauman's metaphor "Generation Zero" thus becomes more than an indication of the nihilism of the times.[44] It becomes the clearest discursive framing, as "0" symbolizes those who are targeted on account of their hopes and future aspirations.

The forms of violence we witness today are not only an attack on the present: such violence also points to an assault on an imagined and hopeful future. As such, youth connect directly to the age of precarity and uncertainty, its multiple forms of endangerment, the normalization of terror and the production of catastrophic futures. Vagaries in the state of war cannot be understood only by reference to juxtaposed temporalities—present horror as distinct from past horror or anticipated horrors to come. Rather, they must be addressed in terms of their projects and projections, their attempts to colonize and, failing that, eradicate any vestiges of the radical imagination. War is both an act of concrete violence and a disimagination machine; that is why the present landscape is already littered with corpses of the victims of the violence to come. The cycle of violence holds the potential to condemn our youth to a future that mimics the worst elements of the present.

We must also not forget the plight of the refugees who are caught in the strategic crossfire. As usual, it's those who are the most vulnerable in any situation who become the scapegoats. The refugee crisis must be resolved not simply by calling for open borders, however laudable that may be, but by making the countries that the refugees are fleeing from free from war and violence. We must eliminate militarism, encourage genuine political transformation, end neoliberal austerity policies, redistribute wealth globally, and stop the widespread discrimination against Muslim youth. Only then can history be steered in a different direction. There will be no safe havens anywhere in the world until the militaristic, impoverished, and violent conditions that humiliate and oppress young people are addressed. As Robert Fisk writes with an acute eye on new radically interconnected and violently contoured geographies of our times:

> Our own shock—indeed, our indignation—that our own precious borders were not respected by these largely Muslim armies of the poor was in sharp contrast to our own blithe non-observance

> of Arab frontiers. . . . Quite apart from our mournful Afghan adventure and our utterly illegal 2003 invasion of Iraq, our aircraft have been bombing Libya, Iraq and Syria along with the aircraft of various local pseudo-democracies for so long that this state of affairs has become routine, almost normal, scarcely worthy of a front-page headline. . . . The point, of course, is that we had grown so used to attacking Arab lands—France had become so inured to sending its soldiers and air crews to Africa and the Middle East to shoot and bomb those whom it regarded as its enemies—that only when Muslims began attacking our capital cities did we suddenly announce that we were "at war."[45]

The concept of violence is not taken lightly here. Violence remains poorly understood if it is accounted for simply in terms of who is victimized, by whom, and how. Intellectual violence is no exception, as its qualities point to a deadly and destructive conceptual terrain. As with all violence, there are two sides to this relation. There is the annihilative power of nihilistic thought that seeks through strategies of domination and practices of terminal exclusion to close down the political as a site for differences. Such violence appeals to the authority of a peaceful settlement, though it does so in a way that imposes a distinct moral blueprint of thought that already maps out what is reasonable to think, speak, and act. Since the means and ends are already set out in advance, the discursive frame is never brought into critical question.

And there is an affirmative counter that directly challenges authoritarian violence. Such affirmation refuses to accept the parameters of the rehearsed orthodoxy. It brings into question that which is not ordinarily questioned. Foregrounding the life of a person as key to understanding political deliberation, it eschews intellectual dogmatism with a commitment to the open possibilities in thought. However, rather than countering intellectual violence with a "purer violence" (discursive or otherwise), there is a need to maintain the language of engaged consciousness, civic courage, and critical pedagogy. By emphasizing the critical, we insist upon a form of thought that does not have war or violence as its object. If there is destruction, this is only apparent when the affirmative is denied. And by critical, we also mean and insist upon a form of thought that does not offer its intellectual soul to the seductions of economic or military power. Too often we find that while the critical gestures towards profane illumination, it is really the beginning of a violence that amounts to a death sentence for critical thought. Our task is to demand a politics that is dignified and open to the possibility of nonviolent ways of living. The doctrines of state violence and endless war need to be challenged on ideological and political grounds. The oppressive influence of such doctrines makes it all the more urgent to defend public spheres that advance investigative reporting, connect scholarship to social problems, and support work that, as James Risen puts it, challenges governments that "suppress the truth in the name of ceaseless war."[46]

We need to learn to live with violence less through

the modality of the sacred than through the critical lens of the profane. We need to own our violent histories so as to understand and transform the ways our subjectivities have been formed through the legacies of enslavement, human trafficking, genocide, colonization, war, and commercialization. This requires more of a willingness to interrogate violence in a variety of registers (ranging from the historical and concrete to the abstract and symbolic) than it does a bending to discourses of fate and normalization. We need to acknowledge our own shameful compromises with various manifestations of power. And we need to accept that intellectualism shares an intimate relationship with violence both in its complicity with violence and as an act of violence.

There is an echo of the pornographic here in the ethical detachment that now accompanies the spectacles of violence to which we are forced witnesses. We need then to reject what Leo Lowenthal has called the imperative to believe that "thinking becomes a stupid crime."[47] This does not require a return to the language of Benjamin's idea of "divine violence" as a pure expression of force regardless of its contestable claims to nonviolent violence.[48] We prefer instead to deploy the often abused term "critical pedagogy" as a meaningful political counter to vicissitudes of intellectual violence.

Intellectuals are continually forced to make choices, sometimes against our better judgment. The truth of course is that there are no clear lines drawn neatly separating what is left from what is right. And yet, as Paulo Freire insisted, we are inevitably drawn into an entire history of struggle the moment our critical ideas are expressed as force and put out into the public realm to the disruption of orthodox thinking. There is however a clear warning from history: our intellectual allegiances should be less concerned with ideological dogmatism. To the charges that critical pedagogy merely masks a retreat into cultural relativism, we may counter that there is no reciprocal relationship which doesn't respect difference, while at the same time recognizing that pedagogy is an act of intervention. Pedagogy always represents a commitment to the future, and it remains the task of educators to make sure that the future points the way to a more socially just world, a world in which the discourses of critique and possibility in conjunction with the values of reason, freedom, and equality function to alter, as part of a broader democratic project, the grounds upon which life is lived. This is hardly a prescription for either relativism or political indoctrination, but a project that gives education its most valued purpose and meaning, which in part is "to encourage human agency, not mold it in the manner of Pygmalion."[49]

Instead of accepting the role of the compromised intellectual as embodied in the likes of Lévy and Ferguson, we must acknowledge the urgent need for public intellectuals in the academy, art world, business sphere, media, and other cultural apparatuses to move from negation to hope. Now more than ever we need reasons to believe in this world. This places renewed emphasis on forms of critical pedagogy that enable citizens to reclaim their voices, speak out, exhibit ethical outrage, and create the social movements, tactics, and public spheres that will reverse the growing tide of political fascism on all sides. Such intellectuals are essential to any viable notion of democracy, as social well-being depends on a continuous effort to raise disquieting questions and challenges, use knowledge and analytical skills to address important social problems where possible, and redirect resources back to communities, families, and individuals who cannot survive and flourish without them. Engaged public intellectuals are especially needed at a time when it is necessary to resist the call to violence and its normalization through repetition.

It is time to remind ourselves that critical ideas are a matter of critical importance. Those public spheres in which critical thought is nurtured provide the minimal conditions for people to become worldly, take hold of important social issues, and alleviate human suffering in order to make more equitable and just societies. Ideas are not empty gestures, and they do more than express a free-floating idealism. Ideas provide a crucial foundation for assessing the limits and strengths of our senses of individual and collective agency and what it might mean to exercise civic courage in order to not merely live in the world, but to shape it in light of democratic ideals that would make it a better place for everyone. Critical ideas and the technologies, institutions, and public spheres that enable them matter because they offer us the opportunity to think and act otherwise, challenge common sense, cross over into new lines of inquiry and take positions without standing still—in short, to become border crossers who refuse the silos that isolate and determine the future of thought. Some intellectuals refute the values of criticality. They don't engage in debates; they simply offer already rehearsed positions in which unsubstantiated opinion and sustained argument collapse into each other. It is time then for critical thinkers with a public interest to make pedagogy central to any viable notion of politics. It is time to initiate a cultural campaign in which the positive virtues of radical criticality can be reclaimed, courage to truth defended, and learning connected to social change energized. Our task to implement a return of the political is a matter of critical urgency.

A global system that inflicts violence on young people all over the world cannot be supported. As Michael Lerner has argued, not only must the iniquitous and dangerous structural conditions for economic, political, and cultural violence be eliminated, but the subjective and psychological underpinnings of a hateful fundamentalism must be addressed and challenged through a public pedagogy that emphasizes an ethos of trust, compassion, care, solidarity, and justice.[50] Young people cannot inherit a future marked by intimidation, militarism, and suicide bombers, a world in which the very ideas of human rights, social justice, community, and sustainable democracy have been emptied of any substantive meaning. If they do, then the corrosive forces of nihilism and resentment will truly have won. Creating alternative futures requires serious and sustained investment in ending the cycle of violence, imagining better futures, and new ways of sustainable living in "one world in which many worlds fit," as the Zapatistas of Mexico envision it. By engaging in pedagogy and education with all our creative resources, social consciousness, and sense of global community, we deny the notion of an inevitably violent future being imposed on us by the rival tyrannies of economic and religious fanaticism. Through such engagement and denial, we endeavor to harness the insurgent power of imagination to arm youth worldwide, not with guns or spreadsheets, but with the confidence and solidarity to transform the world for the better.

IV.

Spaces of Resistance

EIGHT

MEMORIES OF FREEDOM AND THE PROMISE OF CRITICAL PEDAGOGY

America is at war with itself in multiple ways and on multiple fronts, all interconnected, with a racialized class war being the most out in the open. But this conflict is not unique to the United States. Across the globe, the tension between democratic values and market fundamentalism has reached a breaking point, ushering in a terrifying horizon of what Hannah Arendt once called "dark times."[1] Democracy is under assault, and undisguised manifestations of violent proto-fascism are being propelled to the forefront of national political life. As this occurs, we bear witness to a media system that is enriched by the repugnant escalation of intolerance and violence. Today it's immigrants, communities of color, Latinos, Muslims, and protesters. But the list is constantly under review, and if you are progressive and you are not already on it, you may be tomorrow. Given these conditions, it becomes frightfully clear that the conditions for totalitarianism and state violence are still with us, attacking multiculturalism, criminalizing protest, smothering critical thought, ridiculing social responsibility, foreclosing the ethical imagination, and dismissing democracy itself. As Bill Dixon observes:

> The totalitarian form is still with us because the all too protean origins of totalitarianism are still with us: loneliness as the normal register of social life, the frenzied lawfulness of ideological certitude, mass poverty and mass homelessness, the routine use of terror as a political instrument, and the ever growing speeds and scales of media, economics, and warfare.[2]

In the United States, the extreme right in both political parties no longer needs the comfort of a counterfeit ideology in which appeals are made to the common good, human decency, and democratic values. On the contrary, control is in the hands of relatively few ultra-wealthy individuals and corporations, while power is global and free from the limited politics of the weakened democratic state.[3] In fact, as authoritarian hierarchies consolidate, state and corporate power increasingly merge. These processes only serve to further normalize the militarization of local police forces, the increasing invasiveness of the surveillance state, and all of the resources brought to bear by a culture of national insecurity aligned with the war on terror. Informed judgment has given way to a corporate-controlled media apparatus that is enriched by the theatrical bullying and turmoil that bigoted intolerance clearly seems to generate, all the while reinforcing the racialized class war and value systems of the white-dominated financial elite.[4]

Following Arendt's description, a dark cloud of political and ethical misinformation has descended on the United States, creating a crisis of memory and agency.[5] As I have stressed throughout this book, intolerance has become something that now occupies a privileged, if not celebrated, place in America's increasingly authoritarian landscape. A new kind of infantilism and culture of ignorance now shapes daily life as agency devolves into a kind of anti-intellectual cretinism evident in the babble produced by Fox News, celebrity culture, the cult of high-stakes testing, and the politicians and pundits who support creationism, argue against climate change, and denounce almost any form of reason. There is a growing body of scientific evidence that concludes that the financial elite and ultra-rich "are, on average, less likely to exhibit empathy, less likely to respect norms and even laws, more likely to cheat, than those occupying lower rungs on the economic ladder."[6] It should not be surprising that when a group of narcissistic and militantly self-interested billionaires use their power and influence to reorder society, public goods are defunded in favor of private rights, just as citizenship is dismissed in favor of consumerism. Intolerance reorders society in ways that serve to further gentrify education and democracy, as civil rights, privacy, and civic power fold before the trump card of national security played out on a daily basis.

Politics has become synonymous with a culture of warfare, just as systemic economic predation and state-sponsored violence increasingly find legitimation in the discourses of fear and insecurity. Too many people today accept the notion that their fate is solely a matter of individual responsibility, irrespective of wider structural forces. This much-promoted ideology, favored by the rich, suggests that human relations boil down to competition and combat. People today are expected to inhabit a set of economic relations in which the only obligation is to fight for one's own self-interest. Yet there is more at work here than a flight from social responsibility, community, and the common good. Also lost is the importance of those social solidarities, modes of community, public spheres, and cultural apparatuses crucial for a sustainable democracy-centered society.

The egalitarianism of democracy and its promise of social protections are among the first forms of collateral damage lost to a new corporate Gilded Age and its fantasy worlds of passive consumption, free social media celebrity, and entertainment for the masses, along with more privatization, deregulation, and wealth for the few. At the same time, the civic and formative cultures that make social protections and community central to democratic life are in danger of being eliminated altogether. As militarization and market-centered authoritarianism tighten their grip on all aspects of society, democratic institutions and public spheres are being choked off, downsized, and defunded. As these institutions vanish—including public defenders, housing, schools, and libraries—there is also a serious erosion of the discourses of community, social justice, equality, compassion, economic cooperation, environmental preservation, and the common good. As Wendy Brown points out:

> Neoliberal rationality takes aim at the very idea of a public good as it strives to make a world in the image of the sentence famously uttered by Margaret Thatcher, one of its most ardent and unabashed proponents: "There is no such thing as society . . . [only] individual men and women." Neoliberalism thus calls for formerly public goods to be privatized in at least three senses. First, they are outsourced to nongovernment for-profit providers, hence submitted to calculations of profit rather than public benefit. Second, they are marketed and priced as individual consumer rather than public goods. Thus do toll roads and fee-per-use transport, school voucher programs and high tuition institutions replace publicly funded transportation infrastructure and public education. Third, as both funding and accountability for formerly publicly-provisioned goods are devolved to the lowest and smallest units, these units themselves are forced into wholly entrepreneurial conduct: departments, teachers, students, office workers all have to protect and advance their own interests without regard for common or public ones.[7]

One outcome of a society at war with itself is that people are stripped of inspiring public spheres and the "thick mesh of mutual obligations and social responsibilities" to be found in any viable democracy.[8] This grim reality marks a failure in the power of the civic imagination, political will, and open democracy to resist the confluence of forces currently formed by the normalization of the Terror Wars and the relentless economic gentrification of the American people's social, justice, political, and education systems.[9]

We live in dangerous times. Global corporatism, war, violence, racism, an arms race, militarism, terrorism, climate change, the threat of nuclear weaponry, and the rise of authoritarian societies internationally pose a dire threat not just to human rights and democracy, but to humanity itself. Matters of education, civic literacy, civil rights, and pedagogies that support the social contract, equality, justice, and the common good are crucial in the struggle against authoritarianism. Within this climate, education has to be seen as more than a credential or a pathway to a job, and pedagogy more than a methodology or teaching to the test. One of the challenges facing the current generation of educators and students is the need to reclaim the role that education has historically played in developing political literacies and civic capacities, both of which are essential prerequisites for democracy. Education must also be viewed as a form of moral witnessing and as a crucial element of historical memory. In this case, educational struggles of the past are resuscitated and critically engaged for the variety of ways in which they connect teaching to social responsibility, learning to social change, and knowledge to modes of individual and social agency. There is a need to use education to mobilize students to be critically engaged agents, attentive to addressing important social issues, and acutely alert to the responsibility of deepening and expanding the meaning and practices of a vibrant democracy.

If we are to survive ourselves, education has to be seen as more than a credential or a pathway to a job. It has to be viewed as crucial to understanding and overcoming the current crises of agency, democracy, environment, and historical memory. Central to such a challenge is the question of what education should accomplish in a democracy. What work do educators have to do to create the economic, political, and ethical conditions necessary to endow young people with the capacities to think, question, doubt, imagine the unimaginable, and defend education as essential for inspiring and energizing the citizens necessary for the existence of a robust democracy? In a world in which there is an increasing abandonment of egalitarian and democratic priorities, what will it take to educate young people to challenge authority and in the words of James Baldwin "rob history of its tyrannical power, and illuminate that darkness, blaze roads through that vast forest, so that we will not, in all our doing, lose sight of its purpose, which is after all, to make the world a more human dwelling place."[10]

What role might education and critical pedagogy have in a society in which the social is individualized, emotional life is redirected into "retail therapy," and quality education is only for those who can afford it? Progress, particularly economic progress, is defined through a simple culture of metrics, measurement, and efficiency: that which benefits the ultra-rich.[11] In a social order drowning in a new love affair with empiricism and data reified by the marketplace, that which is not measurable is ignored. Lost here are the registers of community, cooperation, care for the other, the radical imagination, democratic vision, and a commitment for economic and social justice.

The great Spanish painter Goya once created an engraving titled *The Sleep of Reason Produces Monsters*. Goya's title is richly suggestive, particularly in regard to the role of education and pedagogy in mentoring students to recognize, as my colleague David Clark points out, "that an inattentiveness to the never-ending task of critique breeds horrors: the failures of conscience, the wars against thought, and the flirtations with irrationality that lie at the heart of the triumph of every-day aggression, the withering of political life, and the withdrawal into private obsessions."[12]

Given the accumulation of pathologies and multiple crises that haunt our current political moment, much of American society appears to be drifting—willingly—toward social intolerance and authoritarianism. Educators need a new language for addressing the changing contexts and issues facing a world in which there is an unprecedented convergence of resources—financial, cultural, political, economic, scientific, military, and technological—that are increasingly used to concentrate powerful and diverse forms of control and domination. Such a language needs to be insurgent without being dogmatic and needs to recognize that pedagogy is always political, because it is connected to the struggle over agency. In this instance, making the pedagogical more political means being vigilant about those very "moments in which identities are being produced and groups are being constituted, or objects are being created."[13] At the same time it means educators need to be attentive to those practices in which critical modes of agency and particular identities are being denied. For example, the Tuscon Unified School District board not only eliminated its famed Mexican American Studies Program, but also banned a number of Chicano and Native American books it deemed dangerous. The ban included Shakespeare's play *The Tempest*, and *Pedagogy of the Oppressed* by the Brazilian educator Paulo Freire. These acts of censorship provide a particularly disturbing case of the war that is being waged in the United States against the very spaces and pedagogical practices that endow critical thinking with political agency.

Such actions suggest the need for faculty to develop forms of critical pedagogy to challenge a growing number of anti-democratic practices and policies while also resurrecting a radical democratic project that provides the basis for imagining a life beyond a social order immersed in inequality, environmental degradation, and the normalization of militarization and war as supreme symbols of white hegemony, patriotism, and national strength. Under these circumstances, education becomes more than an obsession with crunching market data, accountability schemes, auditing, and market values. It becomes part of a politically and morally bankrupt formative culture in which intolerance prevails and provides the new baseline for prepping society to further succumb to the dictates of self-interested power—totalitarianism.

At a time of increased repression, it is all the more crucial for educators to reject the notion that the university is simply a site for advancing the culture of business. At issue here is the need for educators to recognize the power of education to challenge the various threats being mobilized against the ideas of justice and democracy. It is equally crucial that they fight for those public spheres, ideals, values, and policies that offer alternative modes of identity, thinking, social relations, and public sovereignty to which democracy is faithfully dedicated.

In both conservative and progressive discourses, pedagogy is often treated simply as a set of strategies and skills used in order to teach pre-specified subject matter. Thus, pedagogy becomes synonymous with teaching as a technique or the practice of a craft-like skill. Any viable notion of critical pedagogy must grasp the limitations of this definition and its endless imitations, even when they are claimed as part of a radical discourse or project. In opposition to pedagogies of repression that assault the imagination and impose disciplinary practices on young people through harsh modes of accountability, critical pedagogy investigates and challenges the relationships among knowledge, authority, power, and the possibility of liberation from domination.[14]

What makes pedagogy critical is, in part, the recognition that it is always a deliberate attempt to influence how and what knowledge and subjectivities are produced within particular sets of social relations. This approach to critical pedagogy does not reduce educational practice to the mastery of methodologies; it stresses, instead, the importance of understanding what actually happens in classrooms and other educational settings by raising questions. What is the relationship between learning and social change? What does it mean to know something? How are different forms of knowledge valued? How should one align their desires? Pedagogy is always about power, because it cannot be separated from how subjectivities are formed, desires mobilized, how some experiences are legitimized and others are not, or how some knowledge is considered acceptable while other forms are excluded from the curriculum.

Paulo Freire believed that pedagogy could be a form of intervention in the service of genuine social liberation. As such, he also believed that it was impossible to separate the teaching of content, theories, values, and social relations from how one is formed ethically and politically. Consequently, he rejected the notion that education is neutral, just as he embraced a notion of the educator that was generous, self-reflective, professionally competent, and willing to provide the conditions for students "to question, doubt, and criticize."[15]

For Freire, citizens do not develop as a consequence of technical efficiency, nor do they develop under pedagogical conditions that smother the imagination or disable the conditions for engaging students in critical dialogue. To the contrary, he was passionate that one of the tasks of pedagogy in relation to social change is to energize and inspire people to become critically engaged citizens willing to struggle for the promise of a real democracy. Learning to think analytically about the world around them is inextricably related to the ability of students to think critically about themselves in relation to the struggle for liberation, and in solidarity with the struggles of others as they relate to the advancement of the larger common good. For Freire, the classroom and any other viable pedagogical space is one in which students come to terms with their own power, forge solidarities with others, resist oppression, and cultivate their own sense of agency under conditions in which they engage dangerous memories and historical context, and embrace the right to dream, imagine, and co-author new social realities. Freire is quite clear about what it means to be a critical educator. He writes:

> I am a teacher who stands up for what is right against what is indecent, who is in favor of freedom against authoritarianism, who is a supporter of authority against freedom with no limits, and who is a defender of democracy against the dictatorship of right or left. I am a teacher who favors the permanent struggle against every form of bigotry and against the economic domination of individuals and social classes. I am a teacher who rejects the present system of capitalism, responsible for the aberration of misery in the midst of plenty. I am a teacher full of the spirit of hope, in spite of all signs to the contrary. I am a teacher who refuses the disillusionment that consumes and immobilizes. I am a teacher proud of the beauty of my teaching practice, a fragile beauty that may disappear if I do not care for the struggle and knowledge that I ought to teach. If I do not struggle for the material conditions without which my body will suffer from ne-

> glect, thus running the risk of becoming frustrated and ineffective, then I will no longer be the witness that I ought to be, no longer the tenacious fighter who may tire but who never gives up.[16]

Pedagogy, as Freire taught, is a moral and political practice because it offers particular visions of civic life, community, the future, and how we might advance representations of ourselves and others, fully conscious of the forces that seek to dominate society and deny the possibilities for collective sovereignty. But it does more; it also "represents a version of our own dreams for ourselves, our children, and our communities. But such dreams are never neutral; they are always someone's dreams, and to the degree that they are implicated in organizing the future for others they always have a moral and political dimension."[17] It is in this respect that any analysis of pedagogy must begin with a discussion of educational practice as a particular way in which a sense of identity, place, worth, and above all, value, are informed by practices that organize knowledge and meaning in the service of a greater collective good.[18] Central to my argument is the assumption that politics is not only about the exercise of economic and political power, but also, as Cornelius Castoriadis points out, "has to do with political judgments and value choices,"[19] indicating that questions of civic education and critical pedagogy (learning how to become a skilled citizen) are central to sustaining and winning the struggle for political agency and democracy. Critical to such an understanding is a recognition of the importance of culture as a condition of existence that shapes the values, desires, and identities of everyone and, as such, functions to make the political more pedagogical. At the heart of politics are pedagogical institutions and spheres, each of which, as Raymond Williams once noted, "actively and profoundly teaches" in order to make individuals both the subjects and objects of power.[20]

Critical pedagogy is useful because it emphasizes critical reflection, bridging the gap between learning and everyday life, understanding the connection between power and difficult knowledge, and extending democratic rights and identities by drawing from the shared resources of history and theory. However, among many educators and social theorists, there is a widespread refusal to recognize that education takes place not only in schools, but also through what can be called the educative nature of the culture. That is, there is a range of creative forces, including music, poetry, philosophy, visual arts, technological arts, and other forms of cultural work that engage in forms of public pedagogy central to the tasks of either expanding and enabling political and civic agency or shutting them down. At stake here is the crucial recognition that pedagogy is crucial to social change because it is about altering the way people see things. As the late Pierre Bourdieu reminded us, "the most important forms of domination are not only economic but also intellectual and pedagogical, and lie on the side of belief and persuasion."[21] In an age dominated by video and electronically produced spectacles, authoritarianism makes education central to its enforcement of political hierarchy; that is, education is viewed as a serious sphere in the struggle over the production of values, identities, and modes of agency that conform to the status quo.

People have to invest something of themselves in how they are addressed or recognize that any mode of education, argument, or idea has to speak to their conditions and provide a moment of recognition. Thus, there can be no authentic politics without a pedagogy of identification. Lacking this understanding, pedagogy all too easily becomes a form of symbolic and intellectual violence, one that assaults rather than educates. One can see these effects in forms of high-stakes testing and empirically driven teaching approaches that dull the critical impulse and produce what might be called dead zones of the imagination. These forms of pedagogical oppression do more than deaden the imagination and produce crippling modes of conformity, they also produce long-term stress in children, as well as anxiety and depression in students.[22] We also see such violence in schools whose chief function is indoctrination. Such schools often employ modes of instruction that are punitive and mean-spirited, mostly driven by regimes of memorization, depoliticization, and compliance. Pedagogies of repression are largely disciplinary and have little regard for analyzing contexts and history, making knowledge meaningful, or expanding upon what it means for students to be critically engaged agents.

Expanding critical pedagogy as a mode of public education suggests being attentive to and addressing modes of knowledge and social practices in a variety of sites that not only encourage critical thinking, thoughtfulness, and meaningful dialogue but also offer opportunities to mobilize instances of moral outrage, social responsibility, and collective action. Such mobilization opposes glaring material inequities and the growing cynical belief that today's culture of investment and finance makes it *impossible* to address many of the major social problems facing the United States, Canada, Latin America, and the larger world. Most importantly, such work points to the link between civic education, critical pedagogy, and modes of oppositional political agency that are pivotal to creating a politics that promotes democratic values, relations, autonomy, and progressive social change. Hints of such a politics were evident in the various approaches developed by the Quebec student protesters, the now dormant Occupy movement, the student movements in Chile, and the pedagogical strategies currently being developed by the Black Lives Matter movement in the United States.

Borrowing a line from Rachel Donadio, these young protesters are raising important questions, such as "What happens to democracy when banks become more powerful than political institutions?"[23] What kind of society allows economic injustice and massive inequality to run wild by allowing drastic cuts in education and public services? What does it mean when students face not just tuition hikes, but a lifetime of financial debt while governments in Canada, Chile, and the U.S. spend trillions on weapons of death and needless wars? How do we understand police violence against communities of color as part of a broader form of domestic terrorism linked to the rise of mass incarceration and the punishing state?[24] What kind of education does it take both in and out of schools to recognize the emergence of various economic, political, cultural, and social forces that counter the dissolution of democracy and resist the normalization of new forms of undisguised intolerance, social control, and authoritarian rule?

Rather than viewing teaching as technical practice, pedagogy in the broadest critical sense is premised on the assumption that learning is not about processing received knowledge but actually transforming it as part of a more expansive struggle for achieving a democracy-centered society with an ever-progressing sense of how the collective good can be realized. The fundamental challenge facing educators within the current age of neoliberalism, militarism, and religious intolerance is to provide the conditions for students to address how knowledge is related to the power of both self-definition and social agency. In part, this suggests providing students with the skills, ideas, values, and authority necessary for them to protect and advance democracy, recognize and resist anti-democratic forms of power, and fight deeply rooted injustices in a society and world founded on systemic economic, racial, and gendered inequalities. I want to take up these issues by addressing a number of related concerns: teachers as public intellectuals, pedagogy as it relates to the project of insurrectional democracy, the politics of emancipation and responsibility, and finally, pedagogy as a form of collective resistance and educated hope.

The Responsibility of Teachers as Public Intellectuals

In an age of privatization and racialized class war, it has become increasingly difficult to acknowledge that educators and other cultural workers bear an enormous responsibility to re-energize democracy as a counteroffensive against the self-destructive forms of economic self-interest and militarization that currently threaten both civilizational sustainability and the biosphere upon which all life depends. Lacking a self-consciously democratic political focus or project, teachers are often reduced either to technicians or functionaries engaged in formalistic rituals, absorbed with bureaucratic demands and unconcerned with the disturbing and urgent problems that confront the larger society and the consequences of one's practices and research.

In opposition to this model, with its claims to and conceit of political neutrality, I argue that teachers and academics should combine the mutually interdependent roles of critical educator and active citizen. This requires finding ways to connect the practice of classroom teaching with issues that bear down on the lives of those within the larger society. It also requires finding ways to provide the conditions for students to view themselves as critical agents capable of making those who exercise authority and power answerable for their actions. The role of a critical education is not to train students solely for jobs, but also to educate them to question critically the institutions, policies, and values that shape their lives, their relationships to others, and their myriad connections to the larger world. As public intellectuals, teachers have a responsibility to their students and themselves both to imagine a better world, and to do everything possible to prevent a worse one from emerging.

The late Stuart Hall was on target when he insisted that educators, as public intellectuals, have a responsibility to provide students with "critical knowledge that has to be ahead of traditional knowledge: it has to be better than anything that traditional knowledge can produce, because only serious ideas are going to stand up."[25] At the same time, he insisted on the need for educators to "actually engage, contest, and learn from the best that is locked up in other traditions," especially those attached to traditional academic paradigms.[26] It is also important to remember that education as a form of informed hope is not simply about fostering critical consciousness, but also about teaching students, as Zygmunt Bauman has put it, to own their responsibilities, be they personal, political, or global.

Students should be made aware of the ideological and structural forces that cause preventable suffering while also recognizing that it takes more than awareness to resolve them. I think Tony Judt was right when he argued that intellectuals have a distinctive responsibility in a time of political upheaval, one that demanded that the work of academics, artists, and other cultural workers "be driven by an explicit set of contemporary concerns and civic commitments."[27] More specifically, he writes:

> I think it is fair . . . to demand that we discuss uncomfortable matters openly and without constraint at a time of self-censorship and conformity. Intel-

> lectuals with access to the media and job security in a university carry a distinctive responsibility in politically troubled times . . . to inform their work with explicit ethical engagement . . . and to demonstrate that the way in which he or she contributes to local conversation is in principle of interest to people beyond that conversation itself.[28]

What role might educators play in an America at war with itself? In the most immediate sense, they can raise their collective voices against the influence of corporations that are propagating a culture of violence, fear, anti-intellectualism, commercialism, and privatization. They can show how this culture of commodified cruelty and violence is only one part of a broader and all-embracing militarized culture of war, the arms industry, and a Darwinian survival-of the-fittest ethic that increasingly disconnects schools from public values, the common good, and democracy itself. They can bring all of their intellectual and collective resources together to critique and dismantle the imposition of high-stakes testing and the commercialization of creativity and learning.

They can speak out against modes of governance that have reduced faculty to the status of part-time Walmart employees, and they can struggle collectively to take back the governing of the university from a new class of managers and bureaucrats that now outnumber faculty, at least in the United States. This suggests that educators must resist those modes of corporate managment in which faculty are reduced to the status of clerks, technicians, entrepreneurs and a subaltern class of part-time workers with little power, few benefits, and excessive teaching loads. As Noam Chomsky has observed, this neoliberal business model is "designed to reduce labor costs and to increase labor servility" while at the same time making clear that "what matters is the bottom line."[29] Academics can work in solidarity with social movements like Black Lives Matter as they emerge, write policy papers, publish op-eds, and call for young people and others to defend education as a public good by advocating for policies that invest in schools rather than in the authoritarian police state and military-industrial complex.

In addition, such intellectuals can develop modes of pedagogy along with a broader comprehensive vision of education and schooling that are capable of winning struggles against those who would deny education its critical function, and this applies to all forms of dogmatism and political purity, across the ideological spectrum. As Paulo Freire once argued, educators have a responsibility not only to develop a critical consciousness in students but to provide the conditions for students to be engaged individuals and social agents. This is not a call to shape students in the manner that Pygmalion shaped Galatea, but an appeal to encourage human agency rather than to mold it. Since human life is conditioned rather than determined, educators cannot escape the ethical responsibility of addressing education as an act of intervention whose purpose is to provide the conditions for students to become the subjects and makers of history rather than passive spectators, disconnected objects, or mere consumers rather than producers of knowledge, values, and ideas.[30]

This is a pedagogy in which educators are neither afraid of controversy nor hesitant to make connections that are otherwise hidden, nor are they fearful about teaching students how to translate private issues into public considerations. One measure of the demise of vibrant democracy and the corresponding impoverishment of political life can be found in the increasing inability of a society to make private issues public, to translate individual problems into larger social issues. As the public collapses into the personal, the personal becomes "the only politics there is, the only politics with a tangible referent or emotional valence."[31] This is a central feature of neoliberalism as an educative tool and can be termed the individualization of the social. Under such circumstances, the language of the social is either devalued or ignored, as public life is often reduced to a form of pathology or deficit (as in public schools, public transportation, public welfare) and all dreams of the future are modeled increasingly around the dictates of an economy rigged to benefit the ultra-rich. Similarly, all problems, regardless of whether they are structural or caused by larger social forces, are now attributed to individual failings, matters of character, or personal ignorance. In this case, poverty is artificially reduced to matters concerning lifestyle, individual responsibility, bad choices, or flawed character.

Critical Pedagogy as a Project of Insurrectional Democracy

In opposition to dominant views of education and pedagogy, I argue for a notion of pedagogy as a practice of freedom—one that is rooted in a broader project of a resurgent and insurrectional democracy. This is a pedagogical practice that relentlessly questions the kinds of labor, practices, and forms of production that are enacted in both the public school and the university. While such a pedagogy does not offer guarantees, it does recognize that its own position is grounded in particular modes of authority, values, and ethical principles that must be constantly debated for the ways in which they both open up and close down democratic relations, values, and identities. Needless to say, such a project should be principled, relational, and contextual, as well as self-reflective and theoretically rigorous. By relational, I mean that the current crisis of schooling must be understood in the context of the broader assault that is being waged against all aspects of democratic public life. At the same time, any critical comprehension of those wider forces that shape public and higher education must also be supplemented by an attentiveness to the historical and conditional nature of pedagogy itself. This suggests that pedagogy can never be treated as a fixed set of principles and practices that can be applied indiscriminately across a variety of sites. On the contrary, it must always be aware of the specificity of different contexts, conditions, formations, and problems that arise in various spaces where education takes place. Such a project suggests recasting pedagogy as a practice that is indeterminate, open to constant revision, and constantly in dialogue with its own assumptions.

The notion of a neutral, objective education is an oxymoron. Education and pedagogy do not exist outside of relations of power, values, and politics. Ethics on the pedagogical front demand an openness to the Other, a willingness to employ a "politics of possibility" through a continual critical engagement with texts, images, events, and other registers of meaning as they are transformed into pedagogical practices both within and outside of the classroom.[32] Pedagogy is never innocent, and if it is to be understood and problematized as a form of academic labor, educators must not only critically question and register their own subjective involvement in how and what they teach, but also resist all calls to depoliticize learning. This suggests the need for educators to rethink the cultural and ideological baggage that they bring to each educational encounter; it also highlights the necessity of making educators ethically and politically accountable and self-reflective for the stories they produce, the claims they make upon public memory, and the images of the future they legitimize.

Critical Pedagogy and the Promise of a Democracy to Come

As a practice of freedom, critical pedagogy needs to be grounded in a project that not only problematizes its own location, mechanisms of transmission, and effects, but also functions as part of a wider project to help students think creatively about how existing social, political, and economic arrangements might be better suited to address the promise of a democracy to come. Understood as a form of educated hope, pedagogy in this sense is not an antidote to politics, a nostalgic yearning for a better time, or for some "inconceivably alternative future." Instead, it is an "attempt to find a bridge between the present and future in those forces within the present which are potentially able to transform it."[33] Unlike optimism, which suggests that change for the better will inevitably come about, educated hope believes that substantive changes for justice and a better future can only take place in collective struggle and that such change must begin by making power visible, connecting the dots, and confronting the conditions of injustice locally while thinking globally.

What has become clear is that the corporatization of education functions so as to cancel out the teaching of democratic values, impulses, and practices of a civil society by either dismissing them or reordering them to service the imperatives of the market. Educators need a critical language to address and resist these challenges. But they also need to join with other groups outside of the spheres of public and higher education in order to create broad national and international social movements that share a willingness to defend education as a common good and to creatively engage in a broader struggle to continually renew and energize democratic public life. The quality of educational reform can, in part, be gauged by the caliber of public discourse concerning the role that education plays in furthering the imperatives of public awareness, independent media, social justice, and a participatory democracy.

By defining pedagogy as a moral and political exercise, education can highlight the performative character of schooling and civic pedagogy as a practice that moves beyond simple matters of critique and understanding. Pedagogy is not simply about competency or teaching young people the great books, established knowledge, predefined skills and values; it is also about the possibility of interpretation as an act of intervention in the world. Such a pedagogy should challenge common sense and take on the task, as the poet Robert Hass once put it, "to refresh the idea of justice going dead in us all the time."[34] Within this perspective, critical pedagogy foregrounds the diverse conditions under which authority, knowledge, values, and subject positions are produced and interact within unequal relations of power. Pedagogy in this view also stresses the labor conditions necessary for teacher autonomy, cooperation, decent working conditions, and the labor practices and pedagogical relations necessary to give teachers and students the capacity to restage power in productive ways—ways that point to self-development, self-determination, and social agency.

Making Pedagogy Meaningful in Order to Make It Critical and Transformative

Any analysis of critical pedagogy needs to address the importance that consciousness, meaning, and emotion play in the formation of individual identity and social agency. Any viable approach to critical pedagogy suggests taking seriously those maps of meaning, affective investments, and sedimented desires that enable students to connect their own lives and everyday experiences with what they learn. Pedagogy in this sense becomes more than a mere transfer of received knowledge, an inscription of a unified and static identity, or a rigid methodology; it presupposes that students are moved by their passions and are motivated, in part, by the identifications, range of experiences, and commitments they bring to the learning process. In part, this suggests connecting what is taught in classrooms with the cultural capital and inner worlds that young people inhabit.

For instance, schools often have little to say about the ever-evolving influence of mobile technologies, and how social media and the lives of young people impact each other. Hence, questions concerning both the emancipatory and manipulative aspects of these media are often ignored, and students find themselves bored in classrooms in which antiquated modes operate. Or they find themselves using new technologies with no understanding of how deeply connected such technology is to matters of corporate power, ideology, and commercialism. The issue here is not a call for teachers to simply become familiar with the new digital technologies, however crucial, but to address how they are being used as a form of cultural politics and pedagogical practice in regard to citizenship, spectatorship, community, desires, values, activism, and apathy. At stake here is the larger question of how these technologies enhance or shut down the meaning and sustainability of democracy.

Understanding the influence of Internet and mobile media is a political issue and not merely a technological one. Sherry Turkle is right in arguing that the place of technology can only be addressed if you have a set of values from which you are working.[35] This is particularly important given the increase of surveillance in the United States and Canada, and the growing acceptance of invasiveness on the part of a generation that is now hooked on the ever-evolving offerings of corporate products, offerings that at the time of this writing include Twitter, Instagram, and Facebook.

The "events" that shape young people's lives are increasingly mediated experiences in which some are viewed as more valuable than others, especially around matters of race, sexual orientation, residency status, and class. Low-income white students, impoverished immigrants, and people of color are often defined through experiences that are viewed as deficits. In this instance, different styles of speech, clothing, and body language can be used as weapons to punish certain students. How else to explain the high rate of Black students in the U.S. and indigenous students in Canada who are punished, suspended, and expelled from their schools because they violate dress codes or engage in what can be considered minor rule violations?

An increasing range of mediated experiences that are marketed to students and youth, such as video games, sell oppressive modes of behavior that are isolating, self-defeating, and brutally violent. We also see too many students influenced by the empty values of malls, corporate entertainment, and commercial fashion. Clearly, such influences must be critically engaged and understood within a range of broader forces that subject students to a narrow range of values, identities, and social relations. Such experiences should be both questioned and, where possible, unlearned. This suggests a pedagogical approach in which such experiences are interrogated through what Roger Simon and Deborah Britzman call troubling or difficult knowledge. For instance, it is sometimes difficult for students to take a critical look at Disney culture as a manifestation of demeaning stereotypes that indoctrinate impressionable young minds into a narrow range of commercial notions of beauty, heterosexuality, gender, and race. Crucial here is developing pedagogical practices that not only interrogate how knowledge, identifications, and subject positions are produced, unfolded, and remembered, but also how such systems of knowledge can be unlearned, particularly when they come to be dominated by stifling forms of cultural, economic, political and social power.

Conclusion

America is at war with itself, and pedagogy has an essential role to play in fighting back creatively and nonviolently. The challenges we face are immense, as the civil rights, resources, community spaces, and political processes required to struggle are under direct and relentless assault. The very notions of the social and the public are being reconstructed under circumstances in which public forums for serious debate, including public education, are being eroded—all of which help consolidate authoritarian modes of governance, a warfare state, and a predatory economy by and for the interests of the wealthiest few.

Under constant pressure from political gentrification, teaching and learning are increasingly evicted from the discourse of democracy and civic culture. Under the influence of self-interested financial forces and war, we now witness the open rise of authoritarianism and intolerance. This rise is marked by the steady takeover of public and higher education by a corporate logic that numbs both the mind and heart, reinforces repressive modes of learning that promote winning at all costs, emphasizes obedience to hierarchy and authority, and undermines the hard work of learning how to be thoughtful, critical, and attentive to the power relations that shape everyday life and the larger world. As learning is increasingly marketed as a product, depoliticized, and reduced to instructing young people how to be reliable debt holders, any viable notions of the social, public values, citizenship, democracy, and the common good are foreclosed, forgotten, and written over.

The tasks before us are many, and central to them all is the defense of public spheres capable of producing thoughtful citizens, critically engaged communities, and an ethically and socially responsible society. Such spheres include not only public schools, but libraries, non-commercial media, public radio, the arts, and non-commercial public spaces such as plazas and parks where people can connect, protest, organize, advance plans, and form networks, movements, and countercultures.

The greatest threat to young people does not come from lowered standards, the absence of privatized choice schemes, or the lack of rigid testing measures. On the contrary, it comes from societies that refuse to invest in their children, that permit millions of families to vanish into poverty, that reduce creative learning to mind-deadening testing programs, that promote policies that eliminate crucial health care and public services, and that define masculinity through the degrading celebration of gun culture, extreme sports, and the spectacles of violence that permeate corporate-controlled media products. Students are not at risk because of the absence of market incentives in the schools; they are at risk because education is being stripped of public funding and public values, infiltrated by corporate interests, and devalued as a public good. Children and young adults are under siege in both public and higher education because far too many of these institutions have become breeding grounds for commercialism, segregation by class and race, social intolerance, sexism, homophobia, consumerism, surveillance, and the increased presence of armed authorities, all of which is spurred on by the right-wing discourse of pundits, politicians, educators, and a supine mainstream media.

Critical pedagogy, when linked to the ongoing project of democratization, provides opportunities for educators and other cultural workers to redefine and transform the connections between language, desire, meaning, everyday life, and material relations as part of a broader social movement to reclaim the possibility of democracy not as an end, but as a process toward greater levels of freedom and emancipation. Critical pedagogy is dangerous to many because it provides the conditions for students to develop the intellectual and ethical capacity to question authority, hold power accountable, and advance a sense of social responsibility that challenges the very legitimacy of an economic system programmed to benefit the already rich no matter the consequences to climate, water, air, kids, families, or the future. Authoritarian societies cultivate what John Steppling calls "landscapes of paranoia" whose function is to peddle violence, racism, and consumerism while dishing out punitive practices for the poor and expanding "racial and ethnic hierarchies."[36] Central to contesting the ideological and affective spaces of authoritarianism is the development of counter-commercial spheres and critical formative cultures that can challenge and eliminate human suffering, provide social provisions, dismantle the war machine, take apart the commanding institutions of capital, and protect the environment. This is both a political and an eminently pedagogical task, one that demands both a new language and a new understanding of politics itself.

Hence, one of the most serious challenges facing teachers, artists, journalists, writers, and other cultural workers is the task of developing a discourse of both critique and possibility. This means developing languages and pedagogical practices that connect reading the word with reading the world, and doing so in ways that enhance the capacities of young people as critical agents and engaged citizens. In taking up this project, educators and others should attempt to create the conditions that give students the opportunity to become autonomous actors who have the knowledge and courage to struggle in order to make cynicism unconvincing and hope practical.

Educated hope is not a call to overlook the difficult conditions that shape both schools and the larger social order. On the contrary, it is the precondition for providing those languages and values that point the way to achieving and sustaining a more democratic and just world. As Judith Butler has argued, there is more hope in the world when we can question commonly held assumptions and believe that what we know is directly related to our ability to help change the world around us, though it is far from the only condition necessary for such change.[37]

Democracy should be a way of thinking about education, one that thrives on connecting equity to excellence, learning to ethics, and agency to the imperatives of social responsibility and the public good.[38] We may live in dark times, but the future is still open. The time has come to develop a common language in which civic values, social responsibility, and the institutions that support them become central to invigorating and fortifying a new era of social imagination, a renewed sense of possibility and agency, and an impassioned international social movement capable of winning local battles. We live in a volatile political moment. America is in the grip of an authoritarian culture in which ignorance and the inability to think independently prevail. As Hannah Arendt once said, thinking itself has become dangerous, and as she noted in her seminal essay, "The Crisis of Education:"

> Education is the point at which we decide whether we love the world enough to assume responsibility for it, and by the same token save it from that ruin which except for renewal, except for the coming of the new and the young, would be inevitable.[39]

America stands at the endpoint of a long series of attacks on democracy, and the choice faced by many Americans today points to the divide between those who are and are not willing to commit to democracy. Debates over whether Trump is a fascist are a tactical diversion, because the real issue is what it will take to prevent the United States from sliding further into a distinctive form of authoritarianism.

The willingness of contemporary politicians and pundits to use totalitarian themes echoes alarmingly fascist elements of the past. This willingness also prefigures new projections of power and the emergence of a distinctive mode of authoritarianism that threatens to further foreclose venues for social justice and civil rights. The need for resistance has become urgent. The struggle is not over specific institutions such as higher education or so-called democratic procedures such as elections, but over what it means to get to the root of the problems facing the United States and to draw more people into subversive actions modeled after historical struggles from the days of the underground railroad to contemporary movements for economic, social, and environmental justice.

Yet, such struggles will only succeed if more progressives embrace an expansive understanding of politics, not fixating singularly on elections or any other issue but rather emphasizing the connections among diverse social movements. An expansive understanding such as this links the calls for a living wage and environmental justice to calls for access to quality health care and the elimination of the conditions fostering assaults by the state against people of color, immigrants, workers, and women. The movement against mass incarceration and capital punishment cannot be separated from movements for racial justice, full employment, free quality health care, and housing. In fact, Black Liberation struggles have strongly embraced this mode of politics by connecting police violence to poverty, under-resourced schools to the collapse of the welfare state, deportations to forms of racialized terrorism, and the death penalty to an analysis of the legacies of slavery. Such an analysis also suggests the merging of labor unions and social movements, and the development of progressive cultural operations such as alternative media, think tanks, and social services for those marginalized by race, class, and ethnicity. These alternative institutions must also embrace those who are angry at existing political parties and casino capitalism but who lack a critical frame of reference for understanding the conditions of their anger.

What is imperative in rethinking the space of the political is the need to reach across specific identities and stop mobilizing exclusively around single-issue movements, in order to "perceive and refocus their struggles as part of a larger movement for social transformation."[40] Our political agenda must merge the pedagogical and the political by employing a language and mode of analysis that resonates with people's needs while making social change a crucial element of the public imagination. At the same time, any politics that is going to take real change seriously must be highly critical of any reformist efforts that do not include both a change of consciousness and structural changes.

If progressives are to join in the fight against authoritarianism in the United States, we all need to connect issues, bring together diverse social movements, and produce long-term organizations that can provide a view of the future that does not simply mimic the present. This requires connecting private issues to broader structural and systemic problems both at home and abroad. This is where matters of translation become crucial in developing broader ideological struggles and in fashioning a more comprehensive notion of politics.

Struggles that take place in particular contexts must also be connected to similar efforts at home and abroad. For instance, police violence in places like Ferguson can be connected to the rise of ongoing criminalization of a wide range of everyday behaviors and the rise of the punishing state. Gun violence can be connected to the ongoing militarization of society itself. Moreover, such issues in the United States can be connected to those in other authoritarian societies that are following a comparable script of widespread repression. For instance, it is crucial to think about what racialized police violence in the United States has in common with violence waged by authoritarian states such as Egypt against Muslim protesters. This allows us to understand various social problems globally, so as to make it easier to develop political formations that connect such diverse social justice struggles across national borders. It also helps us to understand, name, and make visible the diverse authoritarian policies and practices that point to the parameters of a totalitarian society.

There has never been a more pressing time to rethink the meaning of politics, justice, struggle, collective action, and the development of new political parties and social movements. The ongoing violence against Black youth, the impending ecological crisis, the use of prisons to warehouse people who represent social problems, and the ongoing war on women's reproductive rights, among other crises, demand a new language for developing modes of creative long-term resistance, a wider understanding of politics, and a new urgency to create modes of collective struggles rooted in more enduring and unified political formations. The American public needs a new discourse to resuscitate historical memories and methods of resistance to address the connections between the escalating destabilization of the Earth's biosphere, impoverishment, inequality, police violence, mass incarceration, corporate crime, and the poisoning of low-income communities.

Not only are social movements from below needed, there is also a need to merge diverse single-issue movements that range from calls for racial justice to calls for economic fairness. Of course, there are significant examples of this in the Black Lives Matter movement and the ongoing strikes by workers for a living wage.[41] But these are only the beginning of what is needed to contest the ideology and supporting apparatuses of neoliberal capitalism.

The call for broader social movements and a more comprehensive understanding of politics is necessary in order to connect the dots between, for instance, police brutality and mass incarceration, on the one hand, and the diverse crises producing massive poverty, the destruction of the welfare state, and the assaults on the environment, workers, young people, and women. As Peter Bohmer observes, the call for a meaningful living wage and full employment cannot be separated from demands for "access to quality education, affordable and quality housing and medical care, for quality child care, for reproductive rights and for clean air, drinkable water," and an end to the pillaging of the environment by the ultra-rich and mega-corporations.[42] He rightly argues:

> Connecting issues and social movements and organizations to each other has the potential to build a powerful movement of movements that is stronger than any of its individual parts. This means educating ourselves and in our groups about these issues and their causes and their interconnection.[43]

In this instance, making the political more pedagogical becomes central to any viable notion of politics. That is, if the ideals and practices of democratic governance are not to be lost, we all need to continue producing the critical formative cultures capable of building new social, collective, and political institutions that can both fight against the impending authoritarianism in the United States and imagine a society in which democracy is viewed no longer as a remnant of the past but rather as an ideal that is worthy of continuous struggle. It is also crucial for such struggles to cross national boundaries in order to develop global alliances.

At the root of this notion of developing a comprehensive view of politics is the need for educating ourselves by developing a critical formative culture along with corresponding institutions that promote a form of permanent criticism against all elements of oppression and unaccountable power. One important task of emancipation is to fight the dominant culture industry by developing alternative public spheres and educational institutions capable of nourishing critical thought and action. The time has come for educators, artists, workers, young people, and others to push forward a new form of politics in which public values, trust, and compassion trump neoliberalism's celebration of self-interest, the ruthless accumulation of capital, the survival-of-the-fittest ethos, and the financialization and market-driven corruption of the political system. Political responsibility is more than a challenge—it is the projection of a possibility in which new modes of identification and agents must be enabled that can sustain new organizations and transnational anti-capitalist movements. Democracy must be written back into the script of everyday life, and doing so demands overcoming the current crisis of memory, agency, and politics by collectively struggling for a new form of politics in which matters of justice, equity, and inclusion define what is possible.

Such struggles demand an increasingly broad-based commitment to a new kind of activism. As Robin D. G. Kelley has recently noted, there is a need for more pedagogical, cultural, and social spaces that allow us to think and act together, to take risks and to get to the roots of the conditions that are submerging the United States into a new form of authoritarianism wrapped in the flag, the dollar sign, and the cross.[44] Kelley is right in calling for a politics that places justice at its core, one that takes seriously what it means to be an individual and social agent while engaging in collective struggles. We don't need tepid calls for repairing the system; instead, we need to invent a new system from the ashes of one that is terminally broken. We don't need calls for moral uplift or personal responsibility. We need calls for economic, political, gender, and racial justice. Such a politics must be rooted in particular demands, be open to direct action, and take seriously strategies designed to both educate a wider public and mobilize them to seize power.[45]

The left needs a new political conversation that encompasses memories of freedom and resistance. Such a dialogue would build on the militancy of the labor strikes of the 1930s, the civil rights movements of the 1950s, and the struggle for participatory democracy by the New Left in the 1960s. At the same time, there is need to reclaim the radical imagination and to infuse it with a spirited battle for an independent politics that regards a radical democracy as part of a never-ending struggle.

None of this can happen unless progressives understand education as a political and moral practice crucial to creating new forms of agency, mobilizing a desire for change, and providing a language that underwrites the capacity to think, speak, and act so as to challenge the sexist, racist, economic, and political grammars of suffering produced by the new authoritarianism.

The Left needs a language of critique that enables people to ask questions that appear unspeakable within the existing vocabularies of oppression. We also need a language of hope that is firmly aware of the ideological and structural obstacles that are undermining democracy. We need a language that reframes our activist politics as creative acts that respond to the promises and possibilities of a radical democracy.

Movements require time to mature and come to fruition. They necessitate educated agents able to connect conditions of structural oppression to the cultural apparatuses that legitimize, persuade, and shape individual and collective attitudes. Under such conditions, radical ideas can be connected to action once diverse groups recognize the need to take control of the political, economic, and cultural circumstances that shape their world views, exploit their labor, control their communities, appropriate their resources, and undermine their dignity and lives. Raising consciousness alone will not change authoritarian societies, but it can provide the foundation for making oppression visible and for developing from below what Etienne Balibar calls "practices of resistance and solidarity."[46] We need not only a radical critique of capitalism, racism, and other forms of oppression, but a formative critical culture and politics that inspires, energizes, and provides elements of a transformative radical education in the service of a broad-based democratic liberation movement.

ENDNOTES

CHAPTER 1

1. See, for instance, Mabel Berezin, *Making the Fascist Self: The Political Culture of Interwar Italy* (Ithaca, NY: Cornell University Press, 1997).

2. See, for instance, Emilio Gentile, "Fascistese: The Religious Dimensions of Political Language in Fascist Italy," Willibald Steinmetz, ed. *Political Languages in the Age of Extremes* (Oxford University Press, 2011), pp. 69-82.

3. See, for example, Victor Klemperer, *The Language of the Third Reich*, translated by Martin Brady (New York: Bloomsbury, reprinted 2006).

4. Hannah Arendt, *The Origins of Totalitarianism* (New York: Houghton Mifflin Harcourt, 2001). Sheldon S. Wolin, *Democracy Incorporated: Managed Democracy and the Specter of Inverted Totalitarianism* (Princeton University Press, 2008).

5. Marie Luise Knott, *Unlearning With Hannah Arendt*, translated by David Dollenmayer (New York: Other Press, 2011, 2013), p 17.

6. I have taken this term from Zygmunt Bauman, *Living on Borrowed Time: Conversations with Citlali Rovirosa-Madrazo* (Cambridge, UK: Polity Press, 2010), p. 132.

7. See Bill Dixon's insightful commentary on Arendt's use of "sand storm" as a metaphor for analyzing the protean elements of totalitarianism. Bill Dixon, "Totalitarianism and the Sand Storm," Hannah Arendt Center, February 3, 2014. www.hannaharendtcenter.org/?p=12466

8. The following three paragraphs draw from previous work in Henry A. Giroux, "Barack Obama and the Resurgent Specter of Authoritarianism," *JAC* 3:4 (2011), pp. 415-440.

9. Paul Bigioni, "The Real Threat of Fascism," *CommonDreams.org* (September 30, 2005). www.commondreams.org/views05/0930-25.htm

10. Robert O' Paxton, *The Anatomy of Fascism* (New York: Knopf, 2004), p. 202.

11. Umberto Eco, "Eternal Fascism: Fourteen Ways of Looking at a Blackshirt," *New York Review of Books*, February 2010, pp. 12-15.

12. Amy Goodman, "Father of Fascism Studies: Donald Trump Shows Alarming Willingness to Use Fascist Terms & Styles," *Democracy Now*, March 15, 2016. www.democracynow.org/2016/3/15/father_of_fascism_studies_donald_trump

13. Alfred Ng, " 'Heil Donald Trump': Neo-Nazis, white supremacists show support for billionaire's policy to ban all Muslims from U.S.," *Daily News* (December 8, 2015). www.nydailynews.com/news/politics/heil-donald-trump-racists-support-donald-trump-policy-article-1.2459327

14. David Theo Goldberg, "Mission Accomplished: Militarizing Social Logic," in *Enrique Jezik: Obstruct, destroy, conceal*, ed. Cuauhtémoc Medina (Mexico: Universidad Nacional Autónoma de México, 2011), pp. 183-198. Goldberg also develops this theme in great detail in David Theo Goldberg, *The Racial State* (Malden, MA: Blackwell Books, 2002).

15. Ibid., Goldberg, "Mission Accomplished," pp. 184-185.

16. Andrew J. Bacevich, *The New American Militarism* (Oxford University Press, 2005); Melvin Goodman, "American Militarism: Costs and Consequences," *Truthout* (March 5, 2013). http://www.truth-out.org/progressivepicks/item/14926-american-militarism-costs-and-consequences

17. See, for example, Michelle Alexander, T*he New Jim Crow: Mass Incarceration in the Age of Colorblindness* (New York: The New Press, 2010); Matt Taibbi, *The Divide: American Injustice in the Age of the Wealth Gap* (New York: Spiegel & Grau, 2014).

18. Mark Koba, "U.S. Military Spending Dwarfs Rest of World," *NBC News* (February 24, 2014). www.nbcnews.com/storyline/military-spending-cuts/u-s-military-spending-dwarfs-rest-world-n37461\. The best source on the cost of war and militarization in the United States can be found at Brown University's Watson Institute for International and Public Affairs. See: http://watson.brown.edu/costsofwar/costs

19. There is a long scholarly history of American militarism and far too many sources to mention. Some of the more exemplary include: Tom Engelhardt, *Shadow Government: Surveillance, Secret Wars, and a Global Security State in a Single Superpower World* (Chicago: Haymarket, 2014); Andrew Bacevich, *The New American Militarism*,

updated edition (Oxford University Press, 2013); Melvin Goodman, *National Insecurity: The cost of American Militarism* (San Francisco: City Lights Books, 2013); Chalmers Johnson, *The Sorrows of Empire: Militarism, Secrecy, and the End of the Republic* (New York: Metropolitan Books, 2004).

20. David Vine, "The United States Probably Has More Foreign Military Bases Than Any Other People, Nation, or Empire in History," *The Nation*, September 14, 2015. www.thenation.com/article/the-united-states-probably-has-more-foreign-military-bases-than-any-other-people-nation-or-empire-in-history/

21. Ibid.

22. See, for instance, Nick Turse, *Tomorrow's Battlefield: U.S. Proxy Wars and Secret Ops in Africa* (Chicago: Haymarket Books, 2015).

23. Andrew Bacevich, "After Iraq, War Is US," *Reader Supported News* (December 20, 2011). http://readersupportednews.org/opinion2/424-national-security/9007-after-iraq-war-is-us

24. Tom Engelhardt, "Tomgram: Engelhardt, Washington's Militarized Mindset," *TomDispatch* (July 5, 2012). www.tomdispatch.com/blog/175564/

25. Michael Schwalbe, "Micro Militarism," *CounterPunch* (November 26, 2012). www.counterpunch.org/2012/11/26/mico-militarism/

26. Chris Hedges, "Kneeling in Fenway Park to the Gods of War," *Truthdig* (July 8, 2014). www.truthdig.com/report/item/kneeling_in_fenway_park_to_the_gods_of_war_20140707

27. Sarah Lazare, "Patriotism at a Price: US Military Paid NFL Teams to 'Honor' Soldiers at Games," *CommonDreams* (May 8, 2015). www.commondreams.org/news/2015/05/08/patriotism-price-us-military-paid-nfl-teams-honor-soldiers-games

28. Norman Pollack, "Price Tag for International Villainy," *CounterPunch* (February 4, 20015). www.counterpunch.org/2015/02/04/price-tag-for-international-villainy/

29. Carl Boggs and Tom Pollard, *The Hollywood War Machine* (Boulder, CO: Paradigm, 2011).

30. David Sirota, "The Pentagon's strengthening grip on Hollywood," *Salon* (August 29, 2015). www.salon.com/2011/08/29/sirota_military_movies/

31. Robert Koehler, "Armed Insecurity," *CounterPunch* (July 24, 2015). www.counterpunch.org/2015/07/24/armed-insecurity/

32. AFTA petition, "Chris Christie: Apologize for Threatening Teachers," *AFT A Union of Professionals* (August 15, 2015). https://actionnetwork.org/petitions/chris-christie-apologize-for-threatening-teachers

33. Matt Taibbi, "Inside the GOP Clown Car," *Rolling Stone* (August 12, 2015). www.rollingstone.com/politics/news/inside-the-gop-clown-car-20150812

34. Emily Atkin, "Huckabee Supports Denying Abortion to 10-Year-Old Rape Victim," *Think Progress* (August 16, 2015). http://thinkprogress.org/election/2015/08/16/3692100/huckabee-paraguay-rape-abortion/

35. Emily Atkin, "Trump: I Would Intentionally Kill Families to Defeat ISIS," *ThinkProgress* (December 15, 2015). http://thinkprogress.org/politics/2015/12/15/3732671/trump-isis-kill-family-members/

36. John Dean, "Trump Is the Authoritarian Ruler Republicans—and Some Dems—Have Been Waiting For," *Alternet* (August 13, 2015). www.alternet.org/election-2016/trump-authoritarian-ruler-republicans-and-some-dems-have-been-waiting

37. Conor Lynch, "Donald Trump is an actual fascist: What his surging popularity says about the GOP base," *Salon* (July 25, 2015). www.salon.com/2015/07/25/donald_trump_is_an_actual_fascist_what_his_surging_popularity_says_about_the_gop_base/

38. Jeffrey A. Tucker, "Is Donald Trump A Fascist?," *Newsweek* (July 17, 2015). www.newsweek.com/donald-trump-fascist-354690

39. Ibid.

40. Murtaza Hussain, "Welsely Clark Calls for Internment Camps for 'Radicalized Americans.' " *The Intercept* (July 20, 2015). https://firstlook.org/theintercept/2015/07/20/chattanooga-wesley-clark-calls-internment-camps-disloyal-americans/

41. Bill Dixon, "Totalitarianism and the Sand Storm," Hannah Arendt Center (February 3, 2014). www.hannaharendtcenter.org/?p=12466

42. Hannah Arendt, "Ideology and Terror: A Novel Form of Government," *The Origins of Totalitarianism* (New York: Houghton

Mifflin Harcourt, 2001), p. 468.

CHAPTER 2

1. As is well known, a number of studies repudiate Trump's remarks. For example, see: Esther Yu-Hsi Lee, "An Undocumented Immigrant Killed an American. That Doesn't Prove All Immigrants Are Criminals," *ThinkProgress* (July 7, 2015) http://thinkprogress.org/immigration/2015/07/07/3677443/san-francisco-killing-woman-immigrant/; Esther Yu-Hsi Lee, "Native-Born Americans More Likely to Commit Crimes Than Immigrants, Study Finds," *ThinkProgress* (October 20, 2013) http://thinkprogress.org/immigration/2013/10/20/2807051/native-born-commit-crime/; Steve Chapman, "Trump and the Myth of Immigrant Crime," *TownHall* (July 5, 2015) http://townhall.com/columnists/stevechapman/2015/07/05/trump-and-the-myth-of-immigrant-crime-n2020695/page/full

2. Ginger Gibson, "Donald Trump Immigration Statements Draw Criticism, Praise," *International Business Times* (July 5, 2015). www.ibtimes.com/donald-trump-immigration-statements-draw-criticism-praise-1996126

3. CBS News, "Santorum on Trump: 'A unique individual,' " CBS News (July 5, 2015). www.cbsnews.com/videos/santorum-on-trump-a-unique-individual/

4. For a summary of the comments by Republican Party leaders in response to Trump's incendiary remarks, see Esther Yu-Hsi Lee, "What Republican Leaders Have to Say About Donald Trump," *ThinkProgress* (July 6, 2015). http://thinkprogress.org/immigration/2015/07/06/3676622/donald-trump-republicans-stance/

5. Jonathan Chait, "Why are Conservatives Defending Donald Trump?" *New York Magazine* (July 2, 2015). http://nymag.com/daily/intelligencer/2015/07/why-are-conservatives-defending-donald-trump.html

6. Cited in David Roediger, *Toward the Abolition of Whiteness* (London: Verso Press, 1994), p. 8.

7. Stephanie McCrummen, "Rick Perry family's hunting camp still known to many by old racially charged name," *Washington Post* (October 1, 2011). https://www.washingtonpost.com/national/rick-perry-familys-hunting-camp-still-known-to-many-by-old-racially-

charged-name/2011/10/01/gIQAOhY5DL_story.html

8. Chauncey Devega, "The GOP's secret 'n-word' politics: What their latest Obama outrage is really about—In the Age of Obama, conservatives continue their tradition of racial slurring—without actually saying the word," *Salon* (June 24, 2015). www.salon.com/2015/06/24/the_gop_is_still_the_party_of_the_n_word/

9. Bob Herbert, "The Scourge Persists," *New York Times* (September 19, 3009). www.nytimes.com/2009/09/19/opinion/19herbert.html?_r=0

10. Robert Kagan, "Trump is the GOP's Frankenstein monster. Now he's strong enough to destroy the party," *Washington Post* (February 25, 2016). https://www.washingtonpost.com/opinions/trump-is-the-gops-frankenstein-monster-now-hes-strong-enough-to-destroy-the-party/2016/02/25/3e443f28-dbc1-11e5-925f-1d10062cc82d_story.html

11. Eugene Robinson, "Trump: A Farce to Be Reckoned With," *Truthdig* (July 3, 2015). www.truthdig.com/report/item/trump_a_farce_to_be_reckoned_with_20150703; Juan Cole, "For Donald Trump, Forgetting to Use Racial Code Words Was an Expensive Mistake," *Informed Comment* (July 3, 2015). www.juancole.com/2015/07/comments-expensive-mouthing.html

12. Don Hazen, "Hey Pundits and the Media, Wake Up! Trump's Appeal Is Not Rational¾His Formula Is Based on Fear," *AlterNet*, (February 28, 2016). www.alternet.org/election-2016/hey-pundits-and-media-wake-trumps-appeal-not-rational-his-formula-based-fear

13. Mike Lofgren, "Blowback: Donald Trump Is the Price We Pay for the 'War on Terror,' " *Truthout* (March 1, 2016). www.truth-out.org/news/item/35030-blowback-donald-trump-is-the-price-we-pay-for-the-war-on-terror

14. Timothy Egan, "The Beast Is Us," *New York Times* (March 4, 2016). www.nytimes.com/2016/03/04/opinion/campaign-stops/the-beast-is-us.html

15. Paul Krugman, "Clash of Republican Con Artist," *New York Times* (March 4, 2016). www.nytimes.com/2016/03/04/opinion/clash-of-republican-con-artists.html?smprod=nytcore-ipad&smid=nytcore-ipad-share

16. Tom Engelhardt, "Don't Blame It All on Donald Trump,"

TomDispatch.com (March 27, 2016). www.tomdispatch.com/blog/176120/

17. Frank Rich, "If Only Arizona Were the Real Problem," *New York Times* (May 2, 2010). www.nytimes.com/2010/05/02/opinion/02rich.html

18. Chris Hedges, "The Radical Christian Right and the War on Government," *Truthdig* (October 6, 2013). www.truthdig.com/report/item/the_radical_christian_right_and_the_war_on_government_20131006

19. See, for instance, Tom Engelhardt, "Entering Uncharted Territory in Washington: Are We in a New American World," *Tomdispatch.com* (March 27, 2016). www.tomdispatch.com/blog/176120/. Also see Rev. Dr. William J. Barber II, "It's Not About Trump—Our Political Culture Is Corrupt," *Alternet* (March 15, 2016). www.alternet.org/election-2016/its-not-about-trump-our-political-culture-corrupt

20. Gina Kolatanov, "Death Rates Rising for Middle-Aged White Americans, Study Finds," *New York Times* (November 2, 2015). www.nytimes.com/2015/11/03/health/death-rates-rising-for-middle-aged-white-americans-study-finds.html?_r=0

21. Op. cit., Don Hazen, "Hey Pundits and the Media, Wake Up!"

22. Frank Rich, "There Was No Republican Establishment After All," *New York Magazine* (March 20, 2016). http://nymag.com/daily/intelligencer/2016/03/frank-rich-trump-didnt-hijack-gop.html#

23. Op. cit., Robert Kagan, "Trump is the GOP's Frankenstein monster."

24. Robert Jensen, "Florida's Fear of History: New Law Undermines Critical Thinking," *Common Dreams.org* (July 17, 2006). www.commondreams.org/views06/0717-22.htm

25. Noam Chomsky, "An Ignorant Public Is the Real Kind of Security Our Govt. Is After," *AlterNet* (March 3, 2014). www.alternet.org/chomsky-staggering-differences-between-how-people-and-powerful-define-security

26. Jacoby cited in Judith Shapiro, "Staying Smart in Dumbed-Down Times," *Inside Higher Ed* (June 13, 2008). http://insidehighered.com/views/2008/06/13/shapiro

27. Karl Grossman, "On Trump the Con Man," *CounterPunch* (March 1, 2016). www.counterpunch.org/2016/03/01/on-trump-the-con-man/

28. Sean Illing, "Donald Trump is a fraud: Report confirms the billionaire's presidential bid is a long and calculated con job," *Salon* (February 1, 2016). www.salon.com/2016/02/01/donald_trump_is_a_fraud_report_confirms_the_billionaires_presidential_bid_is_a_long_and_calculated_con_job/

29. Ibid.

30. Neal Gabler, "How the Media Enabled Donald Trump by Destroying Politics First," *Moyers & Company* (March 4, 2016). http://billmoyers.com/story/how-the-media-enabled-donald-trump-by-destroying-politics-first/

31. Ibid.

32. Op. cit., Sean Illing, "Donald Trump is a fraud."

33. Andrew Bacevich, "Don't Cry for Me, America," *Tom Dispatch* (March 1, 2016). www.tomdispatch.com/blog/176109

34. Liam Stack, "Trump's Remarks on Pigs' Blood Elicit Challenge From Sister of Chapel Hill Victim," *New York Times* (February 22, 2016). http://nyti.ms/1TvgEnb

35. Maxwell Tani, "Presidential candidate Martin O'Malley: Donald Trump is a 'fascist demagogue,' " *Business Insider* (December 7, 2015). www.businessinsider.com/donald-trump-muslim-ban-omalley-2015-12

36. See "Tom Brokaw Reflects on Trump's 'Dangerous Proposal' to Ban Muslims," *NBC Nightly News* (December 8, 2015). www.nbcnews.com/nightly-news/video/tom-brokaw-reflects-on-trump-s-dangerous-proposal-to-ban-muslims-582434371851

37. Sarah Parnass, "New Kasich ad: If Trump becomes president, 'you better hope there's someone left to help you,' " *Washington Post* (November 24, 2015). https://www.washingtonpost.com/news/post-politics/wp/2015/11/24/the-ad-in-which-john-kasichs-campaign-seems-to-compare-donald-trump-to-hitler/

38. Judd Legum, "Ben Carson Says Muslims Should Be Disqualified From Presidency," *Think Progress* (September 20, 2015). http://thinkprogress.org/politics/2015/09/20/3703527/ben-carson-says-there-should-be-a-religious-litmus-test-for-presidential-candidates/

39. Candace Smith, "Jeb Bush Says US Should Allow Syrian Refugees Who Can Prove They're Christian," *NBC News* (November 17, 2015). http://abcnews.go.com/Politics/jeb-bush-us-syrian-refugees-prove-christian/story?id=35263074

40. Kay Steiger, "Rubio Trumps Trump: Shut Down Any Place Muslims Gather To Be 'Inspired'—Not Just Mosques," *Think Progress* (November 20, 2015). http://thinkprogress.org/politics/2015/11/20/3724509/rubio-trump-shut-down-mosques/

41. I have taken these examples from CAP Action War Room, "It's Not Just Trump," *The Progress Report* (December 11, 2015). ***

42. Moustafa Bayoumi, "It's not just Trump—the US is gripped by anti-Muslim hysteria," *The Guardian* (December 14, 2015). www.theguardian.com/commentisfree/2015/dec/14/anti-islam-hysteria-united-states-donald-trump-obama

43. Michel E. Miller, "Donald Trump on a protester: 'I'd like to punch him in the face,' " *Washington Post*, (February 23, 2016). https://www.washingtonpost.com/news/morning-mix/wp/2016/02/23/donald-trump-on-protester-id-like-to-punch-him-in-the-face/

44. John Kiriakou, "Donald Trump and the Legacy of Joe McCarthy," *Reader Supported News* (November 15, 2015). http://readersupportednews.org/opinion2/277-75/33687-focus-donald-trump-and-the-legacy-of-joe-mccarthy

45. Ross Douthat, "Is Donald Trump a Fascist?," *New York Times* (December 3, 2015). www.nytimes.com/2015/12/03/opinion/campaign-stops/is-donald-trump-a-fascist.html?mwrsm=Email&_r=0

46. Victor Wallis, "The Trump Phenomenon," *Monthly Review* (November 25, 2015). http://mrzine.monthlyreview.org/2015/wallis251115.html

47. Chas Danner, "Black Lives Matter Protester Tackled, Beaten by Crowd at Trump Rally in Alabama [Updated]," *New York Magazine*, (November 22, 2015). http://nymag.com/daily/intelligencer/2015/11/protester-tackled-by-crowd-at-trump-rally.html

48. Zaid Jilani, "Donald Trump Won't Rule Out Special ID Cards For Muslim Americans," *AlterNet* (November 19, 2015). www.alternet.org/donald-trump-wont-rule-out-special-id-cards-muslim-americans

49. Patrick Healy and Maggie Haberman, "95,000 Words, Many of Them Ominous, from Donald Trump's Tongue," *New York Times* (December 5, 2015). www.nytimes.com/2015/12/06/us/politics/95000-words-many-of-them-ominous-from-donald-trumps-tongue.html?smprod=nytcore-ipad&smid=nytcore-ipad-share&_r=1

50. Greg Richter, "Trump: I Hate the Press, But 'I'd Never Kill Them,' " Newsmax.com (December 21, 2016). www.newsmax.com/Headline/trump-hates-journalists-wouldnt/2015/12/21/id/706735/#ixzz410fYiHwY

51. Trump's comments can be viewed on YouTube at https://www.youtube.com/watch?v=d32577Hom08

52. Jenna Johnson, " 'Torture Works,' and Waterboarding Doesn't Go Far Enough, Trump Says," *Boston Globe* (February 17, 2015). https://www.bostonglobe.com/news/world/2016/02/17/torture-works-and-waterboarding-doesn-far-enough-trump-says/uz8uWHo7BZ83cm5Tm53oxM/story.html

53. The Senate intelligence report can be found at https://www.amnestyusa.org/pdfs/sscistudy1.pdf

54. Heather Digby Parton, "The Unprecedented Nightmare of Donald Trump: He's Actually a Fascist," *AlterNet*, (November 25, 2015). www.alternet.org/news-amp-politics/unprecedented-nightmare-donald-trump-hes-actually-fascist. It is interesting to note that John Kasich released an ad connecting Donald Trump directly to the Nazis. Hopefully, the corporate media will wake up and do the same thing. See Truebluemountaineer, "Kasich's new Trump ad goes full on Godwin and it's a doozy," *Daily Kos* (November 24, 2015). www.dailykos.com/stories/2015/11/24/1454059/-Kasich-s-new-Trump-ad-goes-full-Godwin-and-it-s-a-doozy?detail=email

55. See, for instance, Robert O. Paxton, *The Anatomy of Fascism* (New York: Vintage, 2005); also see the informative article by Richard Steigmann-Gall, "One Expert Says, Yes, Donald Trump Is a Fascist. And It's Not Just Trump," *Tikkun* (January 5, 2016). www.tikkun.org/nextgen/one-expert-says-yes-donald-trump-is-a-fascist-and-its-not-just-trump-2

56. See, especially, Hannah Arendt, *The Origins of Totalitarianism* (New York: Houghton Mifflin Harcourt, 2001).

57. Mark Summer, "This is fascism, and we should say it clearly

. . . while we can," *Daily Kos* (November 29, 2015). www.dailykos.com/stories/2015/11/29/1453681/-This-is-fascism-and-we-should-say-it-clearly-while-we-can?detail=email

58. Personal correspondence with David L. Clark. November 30, 2015

59. Sheldon Wolin, "Inverted Totalitarianism," *The Nation* (May 1, 2003). www.thenation.com/article/inverted-totalitarianism

60. Matthew MacWilliams, "The best predictor of Trump support isn't income, education, or age. It's authoritarianism," *Vox* (February 23, 2016). www.vox.com/2016/2/23/11099644/trump-support-authoritarianism

61. See: Amanda Taub, "The rise of American authoritarianism," *Vox* (March 1, 2016) www.vox.com/2016/3/1/11127424/trump-authoritarianism

62. Ibid.

CHAPTER 3

1. Marie Luise Knott, *Unlearning With Hannah Arendt*, trans. David Dollenmayer (New York: Other Press, 2011, 2013), p. 47.

2. Of course, the alternative media, including *Truthout*, *Truthdig*, *CounterPunch*, *Salon*, *TomDispatch.com*, and *Democracy Now!*, have exhibited an enormous amount of journalistic integrity in situating Trump's demagoguery in a historical context. See, for instance, Amy Goodman, "Father of Fascism Studies: Donald Trump Shows Alarming Willingness to Use Fascist Terms & Styles," *Democracy Now!* (March 15, 2016). www.democracynow.org/2016/3/15/father_of_fascism_studies_donald_trump; Amy Goodman, "Is Donald Trump a Fascist? Part 2 of Interview with Robert Paxton, Father of Fascism Studies," *Democracy Now!* (March 15, 2016); Chris Hedges, "The Revenge of the Lower Class and the Rise of American Fascism," *Truthdig* (March 2, 2016). www.truthdig.com/report/item/the_revenge_of_the_lower_classes_and_the_rise_of_american_fascism_20160302; David Neiwert, "Donald Trump May Not Be a Fascist, But He Is Leading Us Merrily Down that Path," *Huffington Post* (March 3, 2016). www.huffingtonpost.com/david-neiwert/trump-may-not-be-a-fascist-but_b_8973768.html

3. Chip Berlet, "Corporate Press Fails to Trump Big-

otry," *Fair.org* (September 17, 2015). http://fair.org/home/corporate-press-fails-to-trump-bigotry/

4. Ibid.

5. Adele M. Stan, "A Nation of Sociopaths? What the Trump Phenomenon Says About America," *The American Prospect* (September 9, 2015). http://prospect.org/article/nation-sociopaths-what-trump-phenomenon-says-about-america

6. See: Brad Evans and Henry A. Giroux, *Disposable Futures: the Seduction of Violence in the Age of the Spectacle* (San Francisco: City Lights Books, 2016). See also, Zygmunt Bauman, *Liquid Times: Living in an Age of Uncertainty* (London: Polity, 2006).

7. Steve Weissman, "Bashing Blacks, Latinos, Jews, and Muslims: Never Again!," *Reader Supported News* (September 2011). http://readersupportednews.org/opinion2/277-75/32150-focus-bashing-blacks-latinos-jews-and-muslims-never-again

8. See, for example, Randy Blazak, "Donald Trump Is the New Face of White Supremacy," *CounterPunch* (August 28, 2015). www.counterpunch.org/2015/08/28/donald-trump-is-the-new-face-of-white-supremacy/

9. Daniel Chaitin, "WATCH: Trump supporter yells 'Go back to Africa' to black woman," *Washington Examiner* (March 12, 2016). www.washingtonexaminer.com/watch-trump-supporter-yells-go-back-to-africa-to-black-woman/article/2585671

10. Glenn Greenwald, "Jorge Ramos Commits Journalism, Gets Immediately Attacked by Journalists," *The Intercept* (August 27, 2015). https://theintercept.com/2015/08/26/jorge-ramos-commits-journalism-gets-immediately-attacked-journalists/

11. Glenn Greenwald, "The Rise of Trump Shows the Danger and Sham of Compelled Journalistic 'Neutrality,' " *The Intercept* (March 14, 2016). https://theintercept.com/2016/03/14/the-rise-of-trump-shows-the-danger-and-sham-of-compelled-journalistic-neutrality/

12. Timothy Egan, "The Beast Is Us," *New York Times* (March 4, 2016). www.nytimes.com/2016/03/04/opinion/campaign-stops/the-beast-is-us.html

13. Robert Reich, "The American Fascist," *RobertReich.org* (March

8, 2016). http://robertreich.org/post/140705539195

14. Ibid.

15. Mike Lofgren, "Blowback: Donald Trump Is the Price We Pay for the 'War on Terror,' " *Truthout* (March 1, 2016). www.truth-out.org/news/item/35030-blowback-donald-trump-is-the-price-we-pay-for-the-war-on-terror?tmpl=component&print=1

16. Ibid.

17. Rick Perlstein, "Down with the Flag, Up with Trump!," *Washington Spectator* (July 15, 2015). http://washingtonspectator.org/down-with-the-flag-up-with-trump/

18. Peggy Noonan, "What Voters See in Donald Trump," *The Wall Street Journal* (July 31, 2015). www.wsj.com/articles/what-voters-see-in-donald-trump-1438301641

19. Thomas Frank, "Millions of ordinary Americans support Donald Trump. Here's why," *The Guardian* (March 8, 2016). www.theguardian.com/commentisfree/2016/mar/07/donald-trump-why-americans-support

20. Ellen Willis, "Escape from Freedom," *Situations* 1:2 (2006), pp. 5-20.

21. See: Amanda Taub, "The rise of American authoritarianism," *Vox* (March 1, 2016) www.vox.com/2016/3/1/11127424/trump-authoritarianism

22. Ibid.

23. Ibid.

24. John B. Judis, "This election could be the birth of a Trump-Sanders constituency," *Vox* (January 30, 2016). www.vox.com/2016/1/30/10869974/trump-sanders-economic-history

25. Arthur Goldhammer, "Trump-L'Oeil," *The American Prospect* (March 10, 2016). http://prospect.org/article/trump-l%E2%80%99oeil#.VuFgQBO7djg.facebook

26. Fritz Stern, "Historian Fritz Stern warns we are facing a dangerous period of social anxiety," *History News Network* (January 30, 2016). http://historynewsnetwork.org/article/161868

27. Roger Berkowitz, "Politics of the Deal," *Amor Mundi* (March 13-16, 2016). www.hannaharendtcenter.org/?cat=930

28. For an interesting analysis of this issue, see Bob Dreyfus, "It Can't Happen Here . . . Can it? Trump's Storm Troopers and

the Possibility of American Fascism," Tomdispatch (March 13, 2016). www.tomdispatch.com/post/176114/tomgram%3A_bob_dreyfuss%2C_will_the_donald_rally_the_militias_and_the_right-to-carry_movement/#more

29. Op. cit., Roger Berkowitz, "Politics of the Deal."

30. See, especially, Tony Judt and Timothy Snyder, "*Thinking the Twentieth Century* (New York: Penguin Group, 2012), pp. 322-325.

31. For an extensive critique of postracial ideology and policies, see David Theo Goldberg, *Are We All Postracial Yet?* (London: Polity, 2015), p. 30.

32. Ellen Willis made this argument flawlessly in her critique of the work of Thomas Frank. See: Ellen Willis, "Escape from Freedom," *Situations* 1:2 (2006), pp. 5-20.

33. David Neiwert, "Donald Trump May Not Be a Fascist, But He Is Leading Us Merrily Down that path," *Huffington Post* (March 3, 2016). www.huffingtonpost.com/david-neiwert/trump-may-not-be-a-fascist-but_b_8973768.html

34. Pierre Bourdieu, *Acts of Resistance* (New York: Free Press, 1998), p. 92.

35. Don Lee and Kurtis Lee, "Trump details immigration plan, including mass deportation, and backs ground troops in Iraq," *LA Times* (August 16, 2015). www.latimes.com/nation/la-na-trump-interview-20150817-story.html

36. Matt Taibbi, "Donald Trump Just Stopped Being Funny," *Rolling Stone* (August 21, 2015). www.rollingstone.com/politics/news/donald-trump-just-stopped-being-funny-20150821

37. Jenna Johnson and Mary Jordan, "Trump on rally protester: 'Maybe he should have been roughed up,' " *Washington Post* (November 22, 2015). https://www.washingtonpost.com/news/post-politics/wp/2015/11/22/black-activist-punched-at-donald-trump-rally-in-birmingham/

38. Dara Lind, "Protester gets punched at Trump rally. Trump: 'Maybe he deserved to get roughed up,' " *Vox: Policy and Politics* (November 22, 2015). www.vox.com/2015/11/22/9778330/trump-protester-rally-violent

39. Cited in Dylan Stableford, "Trump Protester Sucker-Punched at Rally in North Carolina," Yahoo.com (March 10, 2016). https://

www.yahoo.com/politics/trump-protester-sucker-punched-at-rally-172427733.html. Justin Wm. Moyer, Jenny Starrs, and Sarah Larimer, "Trump supporter charged after sucker-punching protester at North Carolina rally," *Washington Post* (March 11, 2016). https://www.washingtonpost.com/news/morning-mix/wp/2016/03/10/trump-protester-sucker-punched-at-north-carolina-rally-videos-show/

40. Ibid.

41. Jamelle Bouie, "The Violence of Donald Trump," *Slate* (February 23, 2016). www.slate.com/articles/news_and_politics/politics/2016/02/the_violence_of_donald_trump_in_las_vegas.html

42. Mark Torrence, "Donald Trump: Will 'Look Into' Paying Legals Fees for Sucker-Punching Supporter," *Patch.com* (March 13, 2016). http://patch.com/us/across-america/donald-trump-keeping-promise-will-look-paying-sucker-puncher-0

43. Zygmunt Bauman and Carlo Bordoni, *State of Crisis* (London: Polity Press, 2014), p. 15.

44. Zygmunt Bauman and Leonidas Donskis, *Moral Blindness: The Loss of Sensitivity in Liquid Modernity* (Cambridge, UK: Polity Press, 2013), p. 84.

45. Mark J. Osiel, *Mass Atrocity, Ordinary Evil, and Hannah Arendt: Criminal Consciousness in Argentina's Dirty War* (Yale UP, 2001), p. 86.

46. Hannah Arendt, *The Origins of Totalitarianism* (New York: Harcourt Brace Jovanovich, 1973), p. 189.

47. Elisabeth Young-Bruehl, *Why Arendt Matters* (New York: Integrated Publishing Solutions, 2006), p. 38.

48. Eugene Robinson, "The GOP Will Be Forever Changed," *Truthdig* (December 28, 2015). www.truthdig.com/report/item/the_gop_will_be_changed_forever_20151228

49. Sheldon S. Wolin, *Democracy Incorporated: Managed Democracy and the Specter of Inverted Totalitarianism* (Princeton University Press, 2008).

50. Hannah Arendt, *Hannah Arendt: The Last Interview and Other Conversations* (Brooklyn, NY: Melville House Publishing, 2013)

51. Glenn Greenwald, *No Place to Hide* (New York: Metropolitan, 2014).

52. Charles Lewis, *935 Lies: The Future of Truth and the Decline of*

America's Moral Integrity (New York: Public Affairs, 2014).

53. Susan Jacoby, *The Age of American Unreason* (New York: Pantheon, 2008); Robert N. Proctor and Londa Schiebinger, eds. *Agnotology: the Making and Unmaking of Ignorance* (Stanford University Press, 2008). The classic text here is Richard Hofstadter, *Anti-Intellectualism in American Life* (New York: Knopf, 1963).

54. Op. cit., Hannah Arendt, *Hannah Arendt: The Last Interview*, p. 31.

55. Jonathan Crary, *24/7: Late Capitalism and the Ends of Sleep* (Brooklyn, NY: Verso, 2013), p. 5.

56. Christian Marazzi, *The Violence of Financial Capitalism* (New York: Semiotext(e) 2011), p. 96.

57. Doreen Massey, "Vocabularies of the economy," *Soundings* (2013) http://lwbooks.co.uk/journals/soundings/pdfs/Vocabularies%20of%20the%20economy.pdf

58. Erin Ramlo in a final paper for my class, titled "Avoiding the Void: Mapping Addiction and Neoliberal Subjectivity," May 2016.

59. Zygmunt Bauman and Leonidas Donskis, *Moral Blindness: The Loss of Sensitivity in Liquid Modernity* (Cambridge, UK: Polity Press, 2013), p. 7.

60. Paul Rosenberg, "Destroying the government," *Al Jazeera* (October 7, 2013). www.aljazeera.com/indepth/opinion/2013/10/destroying-government-2013103123810419741.html

61. Noam Chomsky and Edward Herman, *Manufacturing Consent: The Political Economy of the Mass Media* (New York: Pantheon, 2002); Susan Jacoby, *The Age of American Unreason* (New York: Pantheon, 2008); and Richard Hofstadter, *Anti-Intellectualism in American Life* (New York: Knopf, 1963).

62. Michael Tomasky, "Trump," *New York Review of Books* (September 24, 2015). www.nybooks.com/articles/archives/2015/sep/24/trump/

63. See, for instance, Cornelius Castoriadis, "The Destinies of Totalitarianism," *Salmagundi* No. 60 (Spring-Summer, 1983), www.jstor.org/stable/40547754

64. Hannah Arendt, *Eichmann in Jerusalem: A Report on the Banality of Evil* (New York: Penguin, 2006).

65. Tanya Golash-Boza, "Trump's Wall: Pandering to Fear and

Nativism," *CounterPunch* (September 8, 3015). www.counterpunch.org/2015/09/08/trumps-wall-pandering-to-fear-and-nativism/

66. Chris Hedges, "The War on Language," *Truth-Dig* (September 28, 2009). www.truthdig.com/report/item/20090928_the_war_on_language/

67. Mark Slouka, "A Quibble," *Harper's Magazine* (February 2009). www.harpers.org/archive/2009/02/0082362

68. Ryan Sartor, "Trump on Protesters: 'So Bad for Our Country, You Have No Idea,' " *Patch.com* (March 11, 2016). http://patch.com/us/across-america/trump-protesters-so-bad-our-country-you-have-no-idea

69. Op. cit., Bauman and Bordoni, *State of Crisis*, p. 13.

70. President Eisenhower delivered "The Chance for Peace" address before the American Society of Newspaper Editors on April 16, 1953. See www.eisenhower.archives.gov/all_about_ike/speeches/chance_for_peace.pdf

71. Ibid.

72. Deirdre Fulton, "Divisive Election Bad for America but 'Damn Good' for Corporate Media," *Common Dreams* (March 1, 2016). http://goo.gl/ETzJZH

73. Matt Taibbi, "How America Made Donald Trump Unstoppable," *Rolling Stone* (February 24, 2016). http://rol.st/1oAKCKU

74. Walter Benjamin, "The Work of Art in the Age of Mechanical Reproduction," in *Illuminations: Essays and Reflections*, translated by Harry Zohn, edited by Hannah Arendt (New York: Schocken Books, 1968). Originally published in Germany in 1955.

75. Jerome Kohn, "Totalitarianism: The Inversion of Politics," The Hannah Arendt Papers at the Library of Congress Essays and Lectures; "*On the Nature of Totalitarianism: An Essay in Understanding*" (Series: Speeches and Writings File, 1923-1975, n.d.) http://memory.loc.gov/ammem/arendthtml/essayb1.html

76. James Baldwin, "A Talk to Teachers," 1963 (delivered in a speech first on October 16, 1963, as "The Negro Child—His Self-Image" and originally published in the *Saturday Review* [December 21, 1963], then reprinted in *The Price of the Ticket, Collected Non-Fiction 1948-1985* [New York: Saint Martins Press, 1985]).

CHAPTER 4

1. Nina Howe, ed. *A Voice Still Heard: Selected Essays of Irving Howe* (Yale University Press, 2014), p. 139.

2. I have taken this term from Zygmunt Bauman and Carlo Bordoni, *State of Crisis* (London: Polity Press, 2014), p. 121

3. Wendy Brown, *Undoing the Demos: Neoliberalism's Stealth Revolution*, (Brooklyn: Zone Books, 2015), pp. 9, 17.

4. Kristi Tanner, "All Flint's children must be treated as exposed to lead," *Detroit Free Press* (January 16, 2016). www.freep.com/story/opinion/contributors/raw-data/2016/01/16/map-8657-flints-youngest-children-exposed-lead/78818888/

5. Ben Klayman in Detroit and Susan Heave, "Two officials charged in Flint water crisis plead not guilty," Reuters (April 21, 2016). www.reuters.com/article/us-michigan-water-idUSKCN0XH1U1

6. Leonard N. Fleming, "Jesse Jackson: Flint has 'wounded' Snyder," *Detroit News* (January 19, 2016). www.detroitnews.com/story/news/politics/2016/01/19/jesse-jackson-flint-wounded-snyder/79036760/

7. Andrew Bacevich, "Don't Cry for Me, America," *Tom Dispatch*, (March 1, 2016). www.tomdispatch.com/blog/176109/

8. Mark LeVine, "Why Charlie Hebdo attack is not about Islam," *Al Jazeera* (January 10, 2015). www.aljazeera.com/indepth/opinion/2015/01/charlie-hebdo-islam-cartoon-terr-20151106726681265.html

9. The landscape of domestic terrorism and various movements that respond to it both in the U.S. and abroad can be found in a number of books by Angela Y. Davis. See, most recently, *Freedom Is a Constant Struggle: Ferguson, Palestine, and the Foundations of a Movement* (Chicago: Haymarket, 2016).

10. On the failure of charter schools in the aftermath of the hurricane, see Colleen Kimmett, "10 Years After Katrina, New Orleans' All-Charter School System Has Proven a Failure," *In These Times* (August 28, 2015). http://inthesetimes.com/article/18352/10-years-after-katrina-new-orleans-all-charter-district-has-proven-a-failur

11. Kenneth J. Saltman, *Capitalizing on Disaster: Taking and Breaking Public Schools* (New York: Routledge, 2007).

12. Editors, "Democracy, Disposability, and the Flint Water Crisis," *Third Coast Conspiracy* (January 18, 2016). https://thirdcoastconspiracy.wordpress.com/2016/01/18/democracy-disposability-and-the-flint-water-crisis/

13. Dorian Bon, "Flint Refuses to Be Poisoned," *Socialist Worker* (January 14, 2016). http://socialistworker.org/2016/01/14/flint-refuses-to-be-poisoned

14. Amy Goodman, "Thirsty for Democracy: The Poisoning of an American City: Special Report on Flint's Water Crisis," *Democracy Now!* (February 25, 2016). www.democracynow.org/2016/2/17/thirsty_for_democracy_the_poisoning_of

15. Jacob Lederman, "Flint's Water Crisis Is No Accident. It's the Result of Years of Devastating Free-Market Reforms," *In These Times* (January 2, 2016). http://inthesetimes.com/article/18794/flint-water-crisis-neoliberalism-free-market-reforms-rick-snyder

16. Michael Moore, "10 Things They Won't Tell You About the Flint Water Tragedy. But I Will," *Reader Supported News* (January 30, 2016). http://readersupportednews.org/opinion2/277-75/34902-10-things-they-wont-tell-you-about-the-flint-water-tragedy-but-i-will

17. Amy Goodman, "Privatization on Steroids: Emergency Manager Who Switched Flint Water Resigned from Detroit Schools," *Democracy Now!* (February 03, 2016) www.democracynow.org/2016/2/3/privatization_on_steroids_emergency_manager_who

18. Julie Bosman, "Crumbling, Destitute Schools Threaten Detroit's Recovery," *New York Times* (January 20, 2016), p. A24.

19. Bruce Lesnick, "Flint: A Tale of Two Cities," *CounterPunch* (February 11, 2016). www.counterpunch.org/2016/02/11/flint-a-tale-of-two-cities/

20. Nika Knight, "Flint Hearing Reveals Disgraced Officials as 'Unremorseful, Unrepentant,' " *Commondreams* (March 15, 2016). http://commondreams.org/news/2016/03/15/flint-hearing-reveals-disgraced-officials-unremorseful-unrepentant

21. Op. cit., Michael Moore, "10 Things They Won't Tell You."

22. Op. cit., Amy Goodman, "Thirsty for Democracy."

23. Daniel Dale, "Michigan city lead-poisoned by water government said was safe," *Toronto Star* (January 15, 2016). www.thestar.com/news/world/2016/01/15/michigan-city-lead-poisoned-by-water-

government-said-was-safe.html?referrer=

24. Ibid.

25. Editorial, "Events that Led to Flint's Water Crisis," *New York Times* (January 1, 2016). www.nytimes.com/interactive/2016/01/21/us/flint-lead-water-timeline.html?_r=0

26. Op. cit., Amy Goodman, "Thirsty for Democracy."

27. David Rosner and Gerald Markowitz, "Rosner and Markowitz, Welcome to the United States of Flint," *Tom Dispatch* (February 9, 2016). www.tomdispatch.com/blog/176101/tomgram%3A_rosner_and_markowitz,_welcome_to_the_united_states_of_flint/

28. See: CDC, "What Do Parents Need to Know to Protect Their Children?," Centers for Disease Control and Prevention website (February 2016). www.cdc.gov/nceh/lead/acclpp/blood_lead_levels.htm

29. Marian Wright Edelman, "Tick, Tock, Tick Tock: Flint's Disposable Poor Children," *Huffington Post* (March 18, 2016). www.huffingtonpost.com/marian-wright-edelman/tick-tock-tick-tock-flint_b_9501676.html

30. This term comes from Teju Cole, "Unmournable Bodies," *The New Yorker* (January 8, 2015). www.newyorker.com/culture/cultural-comment/unmournable-bodies

31. Op. cit., Nika Knight, "Flint Hearing Reveals Disgraced Officials as 'Unremorseful, Unrepentant.' "

32. Bryce Covert, "Rick Snyder Testified Before Congress on the Flint Crisis. It Didn't Go So Well," *Think Progress* (March 17, 2016). http://thinkprogress.org/health/2016/03/17/3761413/flint-congressional-hearing-day-two/

33. Op. cit., Marian Wright Edelman, "Tick, Tock, Tick Tock."

34. Cited in Nika Knight, "Flint Hearing Reveals Disgraced Officials as 'Unremorseful, Unrepentant,' " op. cit.

35. Matt Latimer, "Republicans Ignore a Poisoned City," *New York Times* (January 21, 2016). www.nytimes.com/2016/01/21/opinion/republicans-ignore-a-poisoned-city.html?_r=0

36. Steve Kolowich , "The Water Next Time: Professor Who Helped Expose Crisis in Flint Says Public Science Is Broken," *Chronicle of Higher Education* (February 2, 2015). http://chronicle.com/article/The-Water-Next-Time-Professor/235136

37. Op. cit., Nika Knight, "Flint Hearing Reveals Disgraced Officials as 'Unremorseful, Unrepentant.' "

38. Jesse Jackson, "Flint's Water Crisis and the GOP's Class War," *CounterPunch* (January 27, 2016). www.counterpunch.org/2016/01/27/flints-water-crisis-and-the-gops-class-war/

39. Julie Bosman, Monica Davey, and Mitch Smith, "As Water Problems Grew, Officials Belittled Complaints From Flint," *New York Time* (January 20, 2016). www.nytimes.com/2016/01/21/us/flint-michigan-lead-water-crisis.html

40. Ibid.

41. Dorian Bon, "Flint Refuses to Be Poisoned," *Socialist Worker* (January 14, 2016). http://socialistworker.org/2016/01/14/flint-refuses-to-be-poisoned

42. The term "catastrophe of indifference" was coined by London-based U.S. psychoanalyst Dr. Stephen Groz and cited in Zygmunt Bauman and Leonidas Donskis, *Moral Blindness: The Loss of Sensitivity in Liquid Modernity* (London: Polity, 2013), p.120.

43. Cited in William Robinson, "In the Wake of Ayotzinapa, Adonde va México?" *Truthout* (December 8, 2014). Online; http://truth-out.org/opinion/item/27862-in-the-wake-of-ayotzinapa-adonde-va-mexico

44. Op cit., Wendy Brown, *Undoing the Demos*, p. 39.

45. Editors, "Democracy, Disposability, and the Flint Water Crisis," *Third Coast Conspiracy* (January 18, 2016). https://thirdcoastconspiracy.wordpress.com/2016/01/18/democracy-disposability-and-the-flint-water-crisis/

46. Ibid.

47. Zygmunt Bauman, *Identity: Conversations with Benedetto Vecchi* (London: Polity Press, 2004), p. 40.

48. Op. cit., Bosman, Davey, and Smith, "As Water Problems Grew, Officials Belittled Complaints."

49. Op. cit., Rosner and Markowitz, "Rosner and Markowitz, Welcome to the United States of Flint."

50. Op. cit., Dorian Bon, "Flint Refuses to Be Poisoned."

51. Sonali Kolhatkar, "Flint's Water Crisis Is a Warning to Us All," *TruthDig* (January 27, 2016). www.truthdig.com/report/item/flints_water_crisis_is_a_warning_to_us_all_20160127

52. Ibid.

53. Susan J. Douglas, "Without Black Lives Matter, Would Flint's Water Crisis Have Made Headlines?" *In These Times* (February 10, 2016). http://inthesetimes.com/article/18843/without-black-lives-matter-would-flints-water-crisis-have-made-headlines

54. Nicholas Kristof, "America Is Flint," *New York Times* (February 6, 2016). www.nytimes.com/2016/02/07/opinion/sunday/america-is-flint.html?ref=opinion&_r=0

55. Alison Young and Mark Nichols, "Beyond Flint: Excessive lead levels found in almost 2,000 water systems across all 50 states," *USA Today* (March 17, 2016). www.13newsnow.com/news/health/excessive-lead-levels-found-in-almost-2000-water-systems-across-all-50-states/86689719

56. David Rosner and Gerald Markowitz do a terrific job of charting some of this history. See "Rosner and Markowitz, Welcome to the United States of Flint," op. cit.

57. Ibid.

58. A typical example of these positions can be found in David J. Krajicek, "7 Toxic Assaults on Communities of Color Besides Flint: The Dirty Racial Politics of Pollution," *Alternet* (January 23, 2016) www.alternet.org/environment/7-toxic-assaults-communities-color-besides-flint-dirty-racial-politics-pollution; and Nicholas Kristof, "Are you a Toxic Waste Disposal Site?," *New York Times* (February 13, 2016) www.nytimes.com/2016/02/14/opinion/sunday/are-you-a-toxic-waste-disposal-site.html?_r=0. On the crisis regarding the related issue of the politics of deregulation ignoring the nation's infrastructures, see Elizabeth Drew, "A Country Breaking Down," *New York Review of Books* (February 25, 2016). www.nybooks.com/articles/2016/02/25/infrastructure-country-breaking-down/

59. J. Anthony A. Jones, "Population Growth, Terrorism, Climate Change, or Commercialization?" in J. A. A. Jones, T. Vardanian, C. Hakopian, eds. *Threats to Global Water Security* (New York: Springer, 2009), p. 9.

60. Frank Joyce, "The Big Lesson from Flint: Resistance Is NOT Futile," *Alternet* (February 25, 2016). http://web.alternet.org/news-amp-politics/big-lesson-flint-resistance-not-futile

61. Rev. Dr. William J. Barber, "The Misdiagnosis of Terror-

ism," *The Nation* (February 9, 2016). www.thenation.com/article/the-misdiagnosis-of-terrorism/

62. João Biehl, *Vita: Life in a Zone of Social Abandonment* (Los Angeles: University of California Press, 2005), p. 20.

63. Ibid. pp. 10, 20.

64. David Harvey, *A Brief History of Neoliberalism* (Oxford University Press, 2005), pp. 159-60.

65. Paul Buchheit, "The Real Terrorists: The .01%," *Commondreams* (January 11, 2016). www.commondreams.org/views/2016/01/11/real-terrorists-01?utm_campaign=shareaholic&utm_medium=printfriendly&utm_source=tool

66. Ibid.

67. Chris Hedges, "Flint's Crisis Is About More Than Water," *Truthdig* (February 7, 2016). www.truthdig.com/report/item/flints_crisis_is_about_more_than_water_20160207

68. Doreen Massey, "Vocabularies of the economy," *Soundings* (2013)

http://lwbooks.co.uk/journals/soundings/pdfs/Vocabularies%20of%20the%20economy.pdf

69. Jean Comaroff and John L. Comaroff, "Millennial Capitalism: First Thoughts on a Second Coming," *Public Culture* 12(2), p. 322.

70. Zygmunt Bauman, *The Individualized Society* (London: Polity, 2001), p. 55.

71. Henry A. Giroux, *The Violence of Organized Forgetting: Thinking Beyond America's Disimagination Machines* (San Francisco: City Lights, 2014).

72. Op. cit., Wendy Brown, *Undoing the Demos*, p. 213.

73. Alicia Garza, "A Herstory of the #BlackLivesMatter Movement," *The Feminist Wire* (October 7, 2014) www.thefeministwire.com/2014/10/blacklivesmatter-2/; Keeanga-Yamahtta Taylor, "The rise of the #BlackLivesMatter movement," *Socialist Worker.org* (January 13, 2015) http://socialistworker.org/2015/01/13/the-rise-of-blacklivesmatter; Elizabeth Day, "#BlackLivesMatter: the birth of a new civil rights movement," *The Guardian* (July 19, 2015) www.theguardian.com/world/2015/jul/19/blacklivesmatter-birth-civil-rights-movement

CHAPTER 5

1. Steve Martinot, "Police Torture and the Real Militarization of Society," *CounterPunch* (November 11, 2015). www.counterpunch.org/2015/11/11/police-torture-and-the-real-militarization-of-society/

2. Sharon LaFraniere, Sarah Cohen, Richard A. Oppel Jr., "How Often Do Mass Shootings Occur? On Average, Every Day, Records Show," *New York Times* (December 2, 2015). http://nyti.ms/1XAepDo

3. As Nicholas Kristof points out: "It's not just occasional mass shootings like the one at an Oregon college . . . but a continuous deluge of gun deaths, an average of 92 every day in America. Since 1970, more Americans have died from guns than died in all U.S. wars going back to the American Revolution. . . . If that doesn't make you flinch, consider this: In America, more preschoolers are shot dead each year (82 in 2013) than police officers are in the line of duty (27 in 2013), according to figures from the Centers for Disease Control and Prevention and the FBI." See: Nicholas Kristof, "A New Way to Tackle Gun Deaths," *New York Times* (October 3, 2015). www.nytimes.com/2015/10/04/opinion/sunday/nicholas-kristof-a-new-way-to-tackle-gun-deaths.html?smid=tw-nytopinion&smtyp=cur&_r=0

4. Jack Healy, Julie Bosman, Alan Blinder, and Julie Turkewitz, "One Week in April, Four Toddlers Shot and Killed Themselves," *New York Times* (May 5, 2016). www.nytimes.com/2016/05/06/us/guns-children-deaths.html?emc=edit_na_20160505&nlid=15581699&ref=cta

5. Cited in Marian Wright Edelman, "Why are Children Less Valuable than Guns in America? It Is Time to Protect Children," *Children's Defense Fund* (December 18, 2015). http://cdf.childrensdefense.org/site/MessageViewer?dlv_id=45728&em_id=45049.0

6. Manny Fernandez, "Texas Lawmakers Pass a Bill Allowing Guns at Colleges," *New York Times* (June 3, 2015). www.nytimes.com/2015/06/03/us/texas-lawmakers-approve-bill-allowing-guns-on-campus.html?_r=0

7. See, for instance, Robert M. Pallitto , ed., *Torture and State Violence in the United States: A Short Documentary History* (Baltimore:

Johns Hopkins University, 2011) and Howard Zinn, *A People's History of the United States* (New York: Harper Perennial Modern Classics, 2010).

8. Russell Jacoby, *Bloodlust: On the Roots of Violence from Cain and Abel to the Present* (New York: Free Press, 2014).

9. Amy Goodman, "Terrorism Is Part of Our History: Angela Davis on '63 Church Bombing, Growing Up in 'Bombingham,' " *Democracy Now!* (September 16, 2013). www.democracynow.org/2013/9/16/terrorism_is_part_of_our_history

10. Angela Y. Davis, *Angela Davis: An Autobiography*, (New York: International Publishers Co., 2013). Originally published in 1974.

11. Op. cit., Martinot, "Police Torture and the Real Militarization of Society."

12. Adele Stan, "Trump Has His Finger on the Pulse of America's Bloodlust and We're All a Little Guilty," *AlterNet* (March 17, 2016). www.alternet.org/election-2016/trump-has-his-finger-pulse-americas-bloodlust-and-were-all-little-guilty

13. Ibid.

14. Ibid.

15. Michael Cohen, "Why does America lose its head over 'terror' but ignore its daily gun deaths," *The Guardian* (April 21, 2013). www.theguardian.com/commentisfree/2013/apr/21/boston-marathon-bombs-us-gun-law

16. Op. cit., Manny Fernandez, "Texas Lawmakers Pass a Bill Allowing Guns at Colleges."

17. Gabriel Kolko, "The Pentagon Pathology," *CounterPunch* (August 10-12, 2012). www.counterpunch.org/2012/08/10/the-pentagon-pathology/

18. João Biehl, *Vita: Life in a Zone of Social Abandonment* (Los Angeles: University of California Press, 2005), p. 10.

19. Marian Wright Edelman, *Protect Children Not Guns 2013* (Washington, D.C.: Children's Defense Fund, 2012). www.childrensdefense.org/library/data/protect-children-not-guns-2012.html

20. Carl Boggs, "The Great 'Mental Illness' Hoax: Rampage Killings and the Gun Culture," *CounterPunch* (October 23, 2015). www.counterpunch.org/2015/10/23/

the-great-mental-illness-hoax-rampage-killings-and-the-gun-culture/

21. Amy Wolf, "Mental illness is the wrong scapegoat after mass shootings," *Vanderbilt University Research News* (December 11, 2014). http://news.vanderbilt.edu/2014/12/mental-illness-wrong-scapegoat-shootings/. See also, Carl Boggs, op. cit.

22. Gabrielle Giffords, "A Senate in the Gun Lobby's Grip," *New York Times* (April 17, 2013). www.nytimes.com/2013/04/18/opinion/a-senate-in-the-gun-lobbys-grip.html

23. Adam Gopnik, "The Second Amendment Is a Gun-Control Amendment," *The New Yorker* (October 4, 2015). http://readersupportednews.org/opinion2/277-75/32756-focus-the-second-amendment-is-a-gun-control-amendment

24. Rich Broderick, "Our very own settler problem: America's Culture-of-Gun-Deaths," *Twin Cities Daily Planet* (January 13, 2013). www.tcdailyplanet.net/blog/rich-broderick/our-very-own-settler-problem-america-s-culture-death

25. Jenna Berbeo, "Guns R Us: The Stats Behind America's Firearms Industry," *Truthdig* (October 2, 2015). www.truthdig.com/eartotheground/item/guns_r_us_the_stats_behind_americas_firearm_industry_20151002

26. Editorial, "Statistics on the Dangers of Gun Use for Self-Defense," *Law Center to Prevent Gun Violence* (May 11, 2015). http://smartgunlaws.org/category/gun-studies-statistics/gun-violence-statistics/

27. Bob Herbert, "A Culture Soaked in Blood," *New York Times* (April 25, 2011). www.nytimes.com/2009/04/25/opinion/25herbert.html?scp=1&sq=Bob%20Herbert,%20%E2%80%9CA%20Culture%20Soaked%20in%20Blood&st=Search

28. Kate Murphy and Jordan Rubio, "At least 28,000 children and teens were killed by guns over an 11-year-period," *News21* (August 16, 2014). http://gunwars.news21.com/2014/at-least-28000-children-and-teens-were-killed-by-guns-over-an-11-year-period/

29. Mike McIntire, "Selling a New Generation on Guns," *New York Times* (January 26, 2013). www.nytimes.com/2013/01/27/us/selling-a-new-generation-on-guns.html

30. Nissim Mannathukkaren, "Tele-Jingoism and the Tyranny of Hashtags," *The Wire* (March 7, 2016). http://thewire.in/2016/03/07/

tele-jingoism-and-the-tyranny-of-hashtags-24076/

31. A.O. Scott, Manohla Dargis, Alessandra Stanley, and Chris Suellentrop, "Big Bang Theories: Violence on Screen," *New York Times* (February 28, 2013). www.nytimes.com/interactive/2013/03/03/arts/critics-on-violence-in-media.html

32. Etienne Balibar, *We, the People of Europe? Reflections on Transnational Citizenship* (Princeton University Press, 2004), p. 128.

33. Zygmunt Bauman and Carlo Bordoni, *State of Crisis* (London: Polity, 2014), pp. 121-122.

34. Ibid., p. 122.

35. Brad Evans and Henry A. Giroux, *Disposable Futures: The Seduction of Violence in the Age of the Spectacle* (San Francisco: City Lights Books, 2015).

36. Paula Mejia, "Trump wants to bring back waterboarding, establish a database for Syrian refugees," *Newsweek* (November 22, 2015). www.newsweek.com/trump-wants-bring-back-waterboarding-establish-database-syrian-refugees-397100

37. Andrew Ross Sorkin, "Wall Street, Invested in Firearms, Is Unlikely to Push for Reform," *New York Times* (December 17, 2012). http://dealbook.nytimes.com/2012/12/17/wall-street-invested-in-firearms-is-unlikely-to-push-for-reform/

38. Sam Becker, "10 Countries That Export the Most Weapons," *The Cheat Sheet* (May 19, 2015). www.cheatsheet.com/business/the-worlds-10-largest-arms-exporters.html/?a=viewall

39. Jenna Johnson, " 'Torture works' and waterboarding doesn't go far enough," *Boston Globe* (February 17, 2016). https://www.bostonglobe.com/news/world/2016/02/17/torture-works-and-waterboarding-doesn-far-enough-trump-says/uz8uWHo7BZ83cm5Tm53oxM/story.html

40. Andrew Bacevich, "Don't Cry for Me, America," *Tom Dispatch* (March 1, 2016). www.tomdispatch.com/blog/176109/

41. Bernardine Dohrn, "Watch Out for Fake Gun Control Reforms," *Truthout* (January 16, 2013). http://truth-out.org/news/item/13937

42. Zhiwa Woodbury, "The American Disease of Mass Killing," *Tikkun* (October 23, 2015). www.tikkun.org/tikkundaily/2015/10/23/the-american-disease-of-mass-killing/

43. John Pilger, "The Revolutionary Act of Telling the Truth," *johnpilger.com* (October 1, 2015). http://johnpilger.com/articles/the-revolutionary-act-of-telling-the-truth

44. Fritz Stern, "Historian Fritz Stern warns we are facing a dangerous period of social anxiety," *History News Network* (January 30, 2016). http://historynewsnetwork.org/article/161868

45. Ibid.

46. Cited in C. J. Polychroniou, "Noam Chomsky: '2016 Elections Puts US at Risk of Utter Disaster,' " *Truthout* (March 9, 2016). www.truth-out.org/news/item/35138-noam-chomsky-2016-election-puts-us-at-risk-of-utter-disaster

47. Teju Cole, "Unmournable Bodies," *The New Yorker* (January 8, 2015). www.newyorker.com/culture/cultural-comment/unmournable-bodies

48. "Hugh Hewitt Questions Ben Carson If He Was Ruthless Enough to Kill Thousands of Innocent Kids in War," *Democracy Now!* (December 16, 2015). www.democracynow.org/2015/12/16/ben_carson_i_am_ok_with

49. Citation in C. J. Polychroniou, "Noam Chomsky: '2016 Elections,' " op. cit.

CHAPTER 6

1. Stephen A. Crockett Jr. "Sandra Bland Drove to Texas to Start a New Job, so How Did She End Up Dead in Jail?," *The Root* (July 16, 2015). www.theroot.com/articles/news/2015/07/sandra_bland_drove_to_texas_to_start_a_new_job_so_how_did_she_end_up_dead.html. See also, Amy Goodman and Juan González, "*Truthout*'s Maya Schenwar and Former Prisoner Jason Hernandez Speak Out on Prisons and Policing," *Democracy Now!* (July 17, 2015). www.truth-out.org/news/item/31939-former-el-reno-prison-inmate-freed-by-obama-speaks-out

2. Tom Dart, "Sandra Bland dashcam video shows officer threatened: 'I will light you up,' " *The Guardian* (July 22, 2015). www.theguardian.com/us-news/2015/jul/21/sandra-bland-dashcam-video-arrest-released

3. Terri Langford, "Officials Say Bland Should Not Have Been Arrested," *Texas Tribune* (July 21, 2015). https://www.texastribune.

org/2015/07/21/waller-county-press-conference/; and Sam Sanders, "Dashcam Video of Sandra Bland's Arrest Released," *NPR* (July 21, 2015). www.npr.org/sections/thetwo-way/2015/07/21/425105015/dashcam-video-of-sandra-blands-arrest-released

4. Charles Blow raises a number of questions about the video and the legality of the arrest. See Charles Blow, "Questions about the Sandra Bland case," *New York Times* (July 22, 2015). www.nytimes.com/2015/07/23/opinion/charles-m-blow-some-questions-about-the-sandra-bland-case.html?action=click&pgtype=Homepage&module=opinion-c-col-left-region&region=opinion-c-col-left-region&WT.nav=opinion-c-col-left-region. See also, Ben Norton, "Dashcam Video of Violent Arrest of Sandra Bland Was Edited. Major discrepancies in the video indicate it was tampered with—but why?," *Salon* (July 21, 2015). www.alternet.org/dashcam-video-violent-arrest-sandra-bland-was-edited

5. Aviva Shen, "Woman Dies in Jail after Being Roughed Up During Traffic Stop. Police Say It Was Suicide," *ThinkProgress* (June 16, 2015). http://thinkprogress.org/justice/2015/07/16/3681278/sandra-bland-video/

6. Op. cit., Stephen A. Crockett Jr. "Sandra Bland Drove to Texas."

7. Op. cit., Tom Dart, "Sandra Bland dashcam video."

8. Jamie Stengle and Jason Keyser, "Family Says Woman Found Dead at Texas Jail Would Not Kill Herself; Authorities Investigating," *U.S. News and World Report* (July 16, 2015). www.usnews.com/news/us/articles/2015/07/16/texas-probing-death-in-jail-of-woman-with-chicago-ties

9. Ibid.

10. Shaun King, "Texas sheriff involved in the death of Sandra Bland fired from previous post for racism," *Daily Kos* (July 16, 2015). www.dailykos.com/story/2015/07/16/1402770/-Texas-Sheriff-involved-in-the-death-of-Sandra-Bland-fired-from-previous-post-for-racism#

11. Amy Goodman, "Sandra Bland Laid to Rest; First Black Judge in Waller County Demands Sheriff Resign over Her Death," *Democracy Now!* (July 28, 2015), http://readersupportednews.org/news-section2/318-66/31522-sandra-bland-laid-to-rest-first-black-judge-

in-waller-county-demands-sheriff-resign-over-her-death

12. Op. cit., Aviva Shen, "Woman Dies in Jail."

13. On the issue of state violence, see Brad Evans and Henry A. Giroux, *Disposable Futures: The Seduction of Violence in the Age of Spectacle* (San Francisco: City Lights Books, 2015).

14. Personal correspondence, July 22, 2015.

15. Daily Mail Reporter, " 'These kids don't expect to lead a full life.' Fears for Chicago teens as fatal shootings in city outnumber US troops killed in Afghanistan," *Dailymail.co.UK* (June 19, 2012). www.dailymail.co.uk/news/article-2161690/Chicago-crime-More-people-shot-dead-Chicago-killed-duty-Afghanistan.html

16. Christine Hauser, "Chicago Teenager in Video Against Gun Violence Is Shot and Wounded," *New York Times* (March 28, 2016). http://nyti.ms/22I4LkG

17. Douglas A. Blackmon, *Slavery by Another Name: The Re-Enslavement of Black Americans from the Civil War to World War II* (New York: Anchor Books, 2008).

18. CAP Action War Room, "Say Her Name: Sandra Bland," *The Progress Report* (July 22, 015). http://thinkprogress.org/progress-report/say-her-name-sandra-bland/

19. See Michelle Alexander, "Michelle Alexander on 'Getting Out of Your Lane,' " *War Times* (Aug 28, 2013). www.war-times.org/michelle-alexander-getting-out-your-lane

20. William C. Anderson, "From Lynching Photos to Michael Brown's Body: Commodifying Black Death," *Truthout* (January 16, 2015. www.truth-out.org/news/item/28580-from-lynching-photos-to-michael-brown-s-body-commodifying-black-death

21. Allen Feldman, "On the Actuarial Gaze: From 9/11 to Abu Ghraib," *Cultural Studies* 19, no. 2 (March 2005), p. 203.

22. Marina Warner, "Disembodied Eyes, or the Culture of Apocalypse," *Open Democracy* (April 18, 2005), pp. 1-2, available online at www.OpenDemocracy.net.

23. On domestic terrorism, see the important work of Ruth Gilmore, *Golden Gulag: Prisons, Surplus, Crisis, and Opposition in Globalizing California* (Oakland: University of California Press, 2009).

24. Sharon LaFraniere, Sarah Cohen, Richard A. Oppel Jr., "How Often Do Mass Shootings Occur? On Average, Every Day,

Records Show," *New York Times* (December 2, 2015). http://nyti.ms/1XAepDo

25. Ibid.

26. David A. Graham, " 'Insult to Homicide': Cleveland Sues Tamir Rice's Family for Ambulance Fees: The city has filed a suit demanding $500 in payment for emergency treatment for the boy after a police officer fatally shot him," *The Atlantic* (February 11, 2016) www.theatlantic.com/national/archive/2016/02/cleveland-tamir-rice-bill/462354/; Jason Stanley, "The War on Thugs," *The Chronicle of Higher Education* (June 10, 2015). http://chronicle.com/article/The-War-on-Thugs/230787

27. Oliver Laughland, "Tamir Rice 'directly and proximately' responsible for own police shooting death, says city," *The Guardian* (March 1, 2015). www.theguardian.com/us-news/2015/mar/01/tamir-rice-directly-proximately-responsible-police-shooting-death-city

28. Marian Wright Edelman, "Ten Rules to Help Black Boys Survive," *Childrendefense.org* (July 24, 2015). www.childrensdefense.org/newsroom/child-watch-columns/child-watch-documents/ten-rules-to-help-black-boys-survive.html#comment

29. Jennifer Gonnerman, "Kalief Browder, 1993-2015," *The New Yorker* (June 7, 2015). www.newyorker.com/news/news-desk/kalief-browder-1993-2015

30. Robin D. G. Kelley, "Why We Won't Wait," *CounterPunch* (November 25, 2014).
www.counterpunch.org/2014/11/25/75039/

31. Taylor Kate Brown, "The cases where US police have faced killing charges," *BBC News* (April 8, 2015). www.bbc.com/news/world-us-canada-30339943

32. Sheryl Gay Stolberg and Jess Bidgood, "Mistrial Declared in Case of Officer Charged in Freddie Gray's Death," *New York Times* (December 16, 2015). www.nytimes.com/2015/12/17/us/freddie-gray-baltimore-police-trial.html?_r=0; Dana Ford and Ed Payne, "Grand jury decides against indictments in Sandra Bland case," *CNN* (December 22, 2015). www.cnn.com/2015/12/21/us/sandra-bland-no-indictments

33. Editorial Board, "Cleveland's Terrible Stain," *New York Times*

(December 29, 2015). www.nytimes.com/2015/12/30/opinion/clevelands-terrible-stain.html?emc=edit_ty_20151230&nl=opinion&nlid=51563793&_r=0

34. Ibid.

35. Mitch Smith, "Cleveland Officer Will Not Face Charges in Tamir Rice Shooting Death," *New York Times* (December 28, 2015). www.nytimes.com/2015/12/29/us/tamir-rice-police-shootiing-cleveland.html?emc=edit_na_20151228&nlid=15581699&ref=cta&_r=0

36. Arianna Skibell, "We are fighting for our lives: The little-known youth movement rising against police brutality," *Salon* (February 25, 2015). www.salon.com/2015/02/25/we_are_fighting_for_our_lives%E2%80%9D_the_little_known_youth_movement_rising_against_police_brutality/; Danielle Allen and Cathy Cohen, "The New Civil Rights Movement Doesn't Need an MLK," *The Washington Post* (April 10, 2015). www.washingtonpost.com/opinions/the-new-civil-rights-movement/2015/04/10/e43d2caa-d8bb-11e4-ba28-f2a685dc7f89_story.html

37. Amy Goodman, "Michelle Alexander: Ferguson Shows Why Criminal Justice System of 'Racial Control' Should be Undone," *Democracy Now!* (March 4, 2015). www.democracynow.org/2015/3/4/michelle_alexander_ferguson_shows_why_criminal

38. Jody Sokolower, "Schools and the New Jim Crow: An Interview with Michelle Alexander," *Truthout* (June 4, 2013). www.truth-out.org/news/item/16756-schools-and-the-new-jim-crow-an-interview-with-michelle-alexander

CHAPTER 7

1. Peter Bouckart cited in Amy Goodman, "Brussels Is Under High Security Alert, But Will Europe Address Muslims in 'Marginalized Ghettos'?" *Democracy Now!* (November 23, 2015). www.democracynow.org/2015/11/23/brussels_is_under_high_security_alert?utm_source=Democracy+Now%21&utm_campaign=c2b5bd06c5-Daily_Digest&utm_medium=email&utm_term=0_fa2346a853-c2b5bd06c5-190213053

2. Ian Buruma, "How fear became the politician's weapon of choice," *The Globe and Mail* (December 7, 2015). www.theglobeandmail.com/globe-debate/

how-fear-became-the-politicians-weapon-of-choice/article27614782/

3. Judith Butler, "Letter from Paris, Saturday 14th November," *Verso Books Newsletter* (November 16, 2015). www.versobooks.com/blogs/2337-mourning-becomes-the-law-judith-butler-from-paris

4. Noam Chomsky, *Because We Say So* (San Francisco: City Lights Books, Open Media Series, 2015), p. 22.

5. See George Packer's description of the alienation faced by Muslim youth in France. George Packer, "The Other France," *The New Yorker* (August 31, 2015). www.newyorker.com/magazine/2015/08/31/the-other-france

6. Op cit., Ian Buruma, "How fear became the politician's weapon of choice."

7. Heiner Flassbeck, "The Attacks in Paris and Our Responsibility to Work Toward an Open and Tolerant Society," *CounterPunch* (November 19, 2015). www.counterpunch.org/2015/11/19/the-attacks-in-paris-and-our-responsibility-to-work-toward-an-open-and-tolerant-society/

8. Abdelkader Benali, "From Teenage Angst to Jihad," *New York Times* (January 13, 2015). www.nytimes.com/2015/01/14/opinion/the-anger-of-europes-young-marginalized-muslims.html?_r=0

9. Op. cit., Heiner Flassbeck, "The Attacks in Paris and Our Responsibility."

10 John Pilger, "From Pol Pot to ISIS: The Blood Never Dried," *CounterPunch* (November 17, 2015). www.counterpunch.org/2015/11/17/from-pol-pot-to-isis-the-blood-never-dried/

11. Ibid.

12. On the dangers of the surveillance state, see: James Bamford, *The Shadow Factory: The NSA from 9/11 to the Eavesdropping on America* (New York: Anchor Books, 2009); Zygmunt Bauman and David Lyon, *Liquid Surveillance: A Conversation* (Cambridge, UK: Polity Press, 2013); Heidi Boghosian, *Spying on Democracy: Government Surveillance, Corporate Power, and Public Resistance* (San Francisco: City Lights Books, Open Media Series, 2013).

13. Henry A. Giroux, *The Violence of Organized Forgetting* (San Francisco: City Lights Books, Open Media Series, 2014).

14. Mary Kaldor, "Why Another 'War on Terror' Won't Work," *The Nation* (November 17, 2015). www.thenation.com/article/

why-another-war-on-terror-wont-work/

15. Brett Weinstein, "Let's Not Get It Wrong This Time: The Terrorists Won After 9/11 Because We Chose to Invade Iraq, Shred Our Constitution," *Common Dreams* (November 16, 2015). www.commondreams.org/views/2015/11/16/lets-not-get-it-wrong-time-terrorists-won-after-911-because-we-chose-invade-iraq

16. Op cit., Mary Kaldor, "Why Another 'War on Terror' Won't Work."

17. Peter Van Buren, "Paris: You Don't Want to Read This," *Common Dreams*, (November 15, 2015). www.commondreams.org/views/2015/11/15/paris-you-dont-want-read

18. Sheldon Richman, "How to Respond to the Paris Attacks," *CounterPunch* (November 17, 2015). www.counterpunch.org/2015/11/17/76841/

19. Tiffany Ap, "Al-Shabaab recruit video with Trump excerpt: U.S. is racist, anti-Muslim," *CNN* (January 3, 2016). www.cnn.com/2016/01/02/middleeast/al-shabaab-video-trump/

20. Dr. Gideon Polya, "Paris Atrocity Context: 27 Million Muslim Avoidable Deaths from Imposed Deprivation in 20 Countries Violated by US Alliance Since 9-11," *Countercurrents* (November 22, 2015). www.countercurrents.org/polya221115A.htm

21. Tony Judt with Timothy Snyder, *Thinking the Twentieth Century* (New York: Penguin Press, 2012), p. 277.

22. John Pilger, "From Pol Pot to ISIS: The Blood Never Dried," *CounterPunch* (November 17, 2015). www.counterpunch.org/2015/11/17/from-pol-pot-to-isis-the-blood-never-dried/

23. Chris Floyd, "The Age of Despair: Reaping the Whirlwind of Western Support for Extremist Violence," *CounterPunch* (November 13, 2015). www.counterpunch.org/2015/11/13/against-moral-imposters-mourning-the-dead-as-a-part-of-the-world/

24. Joseph G. Ramsey, "Against Moral Imposters: Mourning the Dead as a Part of the World," *CounterPunch* (November 13, 2015). www.counterpunch.org/2015/11/13/against-moral-imposters-mourning-the-dead-as-a-part-of-the-world/

25. Deirdre Fulton, "Hysterical Corporate Media Fueling War Fervor, Xenophobia in 24/7 Cycle," *Common Dreams* (November 18, 2015). www.commondreams.org/news/2015/11/18/

hysterical-corporate-media-fueling-war-fervor-xenophobia-247-cycle

26. Rabbi Michael Lerner, "Paris: A World that Has Lost Its Ethical Direction & Spiritual Foundation and a Media that Cheerleads for Fear and Militarism," *Tikkun* (November 15, 2015). www.tikkun.org/nextgen/25711

27. Ben C. Solomon, Taige Jensen, Stefania Rousselle and Leslye Davis, "A Terror Attack, Then Far Right Moves In," *New York Times* (March 31, 2016). http://nyti.ms/22R9b8J

28. Editorial, "Mass Surveillance Isn't the Answer to Fighting Terrorism," *New York Times* (November 17, 2015). www.nytimes.com/2015/11/18/opinion/mass-surveillance-isnt-the-answer-to-fighting-terrorism.html

29. For a list of some of Brennan's lies, see Trevor Timm, "CIA director John Brennan lied to you and to the Senate. Fire him," *The Guardian* (July 31, 2014). www.theguardian.com/commentisfree/2014/jul/31/cia-director-john-brennan-lied-senate

30. Op. cit., Editorial, "Mass Surveillance Isn't the Answer."

31. William C. Anderson, "Security Culture and Xenophobia in the Wake of Terror: What We Have to Lose," *Truthout* (November 29, 2015). www.truth-out.org/news/item/33812-security-culture-and-xenophobia-in-the-wake-of-terror-what-we-have-to-lose

32. Bruce Schneier, "Paris Terrorists Used Double ROT-13 Encryption," *Schneier on Security* (November 2015). https://www.schneier.com/blog/archives/2015/11/paris_terrorist.html; see also, Dan Froomkin, "Signs Point to Unencrypted Communications Between Terror Suspects," *The Intercept* (November 18, 2015). https://theintercept.com/2015/11/18/signs-point-to-unencrypted-communications-between-terror-suspects/

33. Marina Jimenez, "France urged by hard-right party to annihilate Islamic radicals," *The Star* (November 15, 2015). https://www.thestar.com/news/world/2015/11/15/france-urged-to-annihilate-islamic-radicals.html

34. Amanda Terkel and Jessica Schulberg, "Donald Trump's Islamophobia Is Bad, But His Rivals Aren't Much Better," *Huffington Post* (December 8, 2015). www.huffingtonpost.com/entry/donald-trump-islamophobia_5666eee9e4b08e945ff0d656?2ajj1yvi=

35. David A. Fahrenthold and Jose A. DelReal, " 'Rabid' dogs and

closing mosques: Anti-Islam rhetoric grows in GOP," *Washington Post* (November 19, 2015). https://www.washingtonpost.com/politics/rabid-dogs-and-muslim-id-cards-anti-islam-rhetoric-grows-in-gop/2015/11/19/1cdf9f04-8ee5-11e5-baf4-bdf37355da0c_story.html

36. Op. cit., Marina Jimenez, "France urged by hard-right party to annihilate Islamic radicals."

37. Kay Steiger, "Rubio Trumps Trump: Shut Down Any Place Muslims Gather to Be 'Inspired'—Not Just Mosques," *Think Progress* (November 20, 2015). http://thinkprogress.org/politics/2015/11/20/3724509/rubio-trump-shut-down-mosques/

38. Regarding Carson's bizzare comments on a number of issues, see Jeb Lund, "What the Hell Is Going On With Ben Carson?," *Rolling Stone* (November 20, 2015). www.rollingstone.com/politics/news/what-the-hell-is-going-on-with-ben-carson-20151120#ixzz3sT5sm4SO

39. Esther Yu-Hsi Lee, "State Lawmaker Supports Putting Muslim Refugees in 'Segregated' Camps," *Think Progress* (November 20, 2015). http://thinkprogress.org/immigration/2015/11/20/3724419/rhode-island-elaine-morgan/

40. Op. cit., Amy Goodman, "Brussels Is Under High Security Alert."

41. Bernard-Henri Lévy, "Thinking the unthinkable: This is war," *The Globe and Mail* (November 16, 2015). www.theglobeandmail.com/globe-debate/thinking-the-unthinkable-this-is-war/article27284617/

42. Niall Ferguson, "Paris and the fall of Rome," *Boston Globe* (November 16, 2015). https://www.bostonglobe.com/opinion/2015/11/16/paris-and-fall-rome/ErlRjkQMGXhvDarTIxXpdK/story.html

43. See: Brad Evans and Henry A. Giroux, *Disposable Futures: The Seduction of Violence in the Age of the Spectacle* (San Francisco: City Lights Books, 2016).

44. Zygmunt Bauman, *This Is Not a Diary* (Cambridge, UK: Polity Press, 2012), p. 64.

45. Robert Fisk, "Isis: In a borderless world, the days when we could fight foreign wars and be safe at home may be long gone,"

The Independent (November 19, 2015). www.independent.co.uk/news/world/middle-east/isis-in-a-borderless-world-the-days-when-we-could-fight-foreign-wars-and-be-safe-at-home-may-be-long-a6741146.html

46. James Risen, *Pay Any Price: Greed, Power and Endless War* (New York: Houghton Mifflin, 2014). Risen exemplifies what it means to be an engaged, critical, and fearless public intellectual.

47. Leo Lowenthal, *False Prophets: Studies in Authoritarianism* (New Brunswick, NJ: Transaction Books, 1987), p. 182.

48. Walter Benjamin, "Critique of Violence" in *Reflections: Essays, Aphorisms, Autobiographical Writings*, ed. Peter Demetz (Shocken Books: New York, 1986), pp. 277-300

49. Stanley Aronowitz, "Introduction," in Paulo Freire, *Pedagogy of Freedom* (Boulder, CO: Rowman and Littlefield, 1998), p. 7.

50. Op. cit., Rabbi Michael Lerner, "Paris: A World that Has Lost Its Ethical Direction."

CHAPTER 8

1. See, for example, Wendy Brown, *Undoing the Demos: Neoliberalism's Stealth Revolution* (New York: Zone Books, 2015); David Harvey, *The New Imperialism* (Oxford University Press, 2003); David Harvey, *A Brief History of Neoliberalism* (Oxford University Press, 2005); Wendy Brown, *Edgework* (Princeton University Press, 2005); Henry A. Giroux, *Against the Terror of Neoliberalism* (Boulder, CO: Paradigm Publishers, 2008); Manfred B. Steger and Ravi K. Roy, *Neoliberalism: A Very Short Introduction* (Oxford University Press, 2010).

2. Bill Dixon, "Totalitarianism and the Sand Storm," Hannah Arendt Center (February 3, 2014). www.hannaharendtcenter.org/?p=12466

3. Michael Yates, *The Great Inequality* (New York: Routledge, 2016). On the separation of power and politics, see Zygmunt Bauman and Carlo Bordoni, *State of Crisis* (London: Polity Press, 2014).

4. See Brad Evans and Henry A. Giroux, *Disposable Futures: The Seduction of Violence in the Age of the Spectacle* (San Francisco: City Lights, 2015).

5. Hannah Arendt, *The Origins of Totalitarianism* (New York:

Houghton Mifflin Harcourt, 2001).

6. Paul Krugman, "Privilege, Pathology and Power," *New York Times* (January 1, 2016). www.nytimes.com/2016/01/01/opinion/privilege-pathology-and-power.html?_r=0. See also: Maia Szalavitz, "Wealthy Selfies: How Being Rich Increases Narcissism," *Time* (August 20, 2013). http://healthland.time.com/2013/08/20/wealthy-selfies-how-being-rich-increases-narcissism/; and Chris Hedges, "The Pathology of the Rich," *Real News*, (December 5, 2013). http://therealnews.com/t2/index.php?option=com_content&task=view&id=31&Itemid=74&jumival=11150

7. Wendy Brown, "Neoliberalized Knowledge," *History of the Present: A Journal of Critical History*, (Vol. 1, No. 1, 2011), pp. 118-119.

8. Terry Eagleton, "Reappraisals: What is the worth of social democracy?" *Harper's* (October 2010), p. 78. www.harpers.org/archive/2010/10/0083150

9. Alex Honneth, *Pathologies of Reason* (Columbia University Press, 2009), p. 188.

10. Cited in Maria Popova, "James Baldwin on the Creative Process and the Artist's Responsibility to Society," *BrainPickings* (August 20, 2014). www.brainpickings.org/2014/08/20/james-baldwin-the-creative-process/

11. See, for instance, Evgeny Morozov, "The Rise of Data and the Death of Politics," *The Guardian* (July 20, 2014). www.theguardian.com/technology/2014/jul/20/rise-of-data-death-of-politics-evgeny-morozov-algorithmic-regulation

12. Personal correspondence with David Clark.

13. Gary Olson and Lynn Worsham, "Staging the Politics of Difference: Homi Bhabha's Critical Literacy," *Journal of Advanced Composition*, 1999, pp. 3-35.

14. For examples of this tradition, see Maria Nikolakaki, ed., *Critical Pedagogy in the Dark Ages: Challenges and Possibilities* (New York: Peter Lang, 2012); and Henry A. Giroux, *On Critical Pedagogy* (New York: Continuum, 2011).

15. Paulo Freire, *Pedagogy of Freedom* (Lanham: Rowman & Littlefield, 1999), p. 89.

16. Ibid., pp. 94-95.

17. Roger Simon, "Empowerment as a Pedagogy of Possibility,"

Language Arts 64:4 (April 1987), p. 372.

18. Henry A. Giroux, *Education and the Crisis of Public Values*, 2nd edition (New York: Peter Lang, 2015).

19. Cornelius Castoriadis, "Institutions and Autonomy," in Peter Osborne, ed., *A Critical Sense* (New York: Routledge, 1996), p. 8.

20. Raymond Williams, *Communications* (New York: Barnes and Noble, 1967), p. 15.

21. Pierre Bourdieu and Gunter Grass, "The 'Progressive' Restoration: A Franco-German Dialogue," *New Left Review* 14 (March-April, 2002), p. 2.

22. Vicki Abeles, "Is the Drive for Success Making Our Children Sick?" *New York Times* (January 2, 2016). www.nytimes.com/2016/01/03/opinion/sunday/is-the-drive-for-success-making-our-children-sick.html?partner=rssnyt&emc=rss&_r=0

23. Rachel Donadio, "The Failing State of Greece," *New York Times* (February 26, 2012). www.nytimes.com/2012/02/26/sunday-review/the-failing-state-of-greece.html?_r=0

24. Maya Schenwar, Joe Macaré and Alana Yu-lan Price, eds., foreword by Alicia Garza, *Who Do You Serve, Who Do You Protect?: Police Violence and Resistance in the United States* (Chicago: Haymarket, 2016).

25. Greig de Peuter, "Universities, Intellectuals and Multitudes: An Interview with Stuart Hall," in Mark Cote, Richard J. F. Day, and Greig de Peuter, eds., *Utopian Pedagogy: Radical Experiments Against Neoliberal Globalization* (University of Toronto Press, 2007), pp. 113-114.

26. Ibid., p. 117.

27. Tony Judt with Timothy Snyder, *Thinking the Twentieth Century* (New York: Penguin Press, 2012), p. 286.

28. Ibid., pp. 286, 296.

29. Noam Chomsky, "The Death of American Universities," *Reader Supported News* (March 30, 2015). http://readersupportednews.org/opinion2/277-75/29348-the-death-of-american-universities

30. This idea is central to the work of Paulo Freire, especially his books *Pedagogy of the Oppressed* and *Pedagogy of Freedom*.

31. Jean Comaroff and John L. Comaroff, "Millennial Capitalism: First Thoughts on a Second Coming," *Public Culture* 12, no. 2 (Duke

University Press, 2000), pp. 305-306.

32. For a brilliant discussion of the ethics and politics of deconstruction, see Thomas Keenan, *Fables of Responsibility: Aberrations and Predicaments in Ethics and Politics* (Stanford University Press, 1997), p. 2.

33. Terry Eagleton, *The Idea of Culture* (Malden, MA: Basil Blackwell, 2000), p. 22.

34. Robert Hass cited in Sarah Pollock, "Robert Hass," *Mother Jones* (March/April, 1992). http://www.motherjones.com/media/1997/03/robert-hass.

35. Sherry Turkle, *Reclaiming Conversation: The Power of Talk in a Digital Age* (New York: Penguin, 2015).

36. John Steppling, "Landscape of Paranoia," *John Steppling: The Practice of Writing* (May 26, 2014). http://john-steppling.com/landscape-of-paranoia/

37. Cited in Gary Olson and Lynn Worsham, "Changing the Subject: Judith Butler's Politics of Radical Resignification," *JAC* 20:4 (2000), p. 765.

38. Henry A. Giroux, *Education and the Crisis of Public Values*, 2nd edition (New York: Peter Lang, 2015); see also: Stanley Aronowitz, *Against Schooling: For an Education that Matters* (Boulder, CO: Paradigm, 2008).

39. Hannah Arendt, "The Crisis of Education," in *Between Past and Future* (New York: Penguin Books, 1993), p. 196.

40. Situations Manifesto, *Left Turn: An Open Letter to U.S. Radicals* (New York: The Fifteenth Street Manifesto Group, March 2008), p. 1

41. Alicia Garza, "A Herstory of the #BlackLivesMatter Movement," *The Feminist Wire* (October 7, 2014) www.thefeministwire.com/2014/10/blacklivesmatter-2/; Keeanga-Yamahtta Taylor, "The rise of the #BlackLivesMatter movement," *Socialist Worker.org* (January 13, 2015) http://socialistworker.org/2015/01/13/the-rise-of-blacklivesmatter; and Elizabeth Day, "#BlackLivesMatter: the birth of a new civil rights movement," *The Guardian* (July 19, 2015). www.theguardian.com/world/2015/jul/19/blacklivesmatter-birth-civil-rights-movement

42. Peter Bohmer, "Connecting $15 an Hour Move-

ment to Other Social Movements," *CounterPunch* (September 28, 2015). www.counterpunch.org/2015/09/28/connecting-15-an-hour-movement-to-other-social-movements/

43. Ibid.

44. Robin D. G. Kelley, "Black Study, Black Struggle," *Boston Review* (March 7, 2016). https://bostonreview.net/forum/robin-d-g-kelley-black-study-black-struggle

45. Chris Hedges, "Tariq Ali: The Time Is Right for a Palace Revolution," *Truthdig* (March 1, 2015). www.truthdig.com/report/item/tariq_ali_the_time_is_right_for_a_palace_revolution_20150301. See also: Gene Sharp, *From Dictatorship to Democracy: A Conceptual Framework for Liberation* (New York: Free Press, 2012).

46. Clement Petitjean, "Étienne Balibar: War, racism and nationalism," *Verso Book Blog* (November 17, 2015). www.versobooks.com/blogs/1559-etienne-balibar-war-racism-and-nationalism

INDEX